CAPTAIN IN THE CAULDRON

John Smit with Mike Greenaway

Captain in the Cauldron
First published 2009
© John Smit, Mike Greenaway, and Highbury Safika Media (Pty) Ltd
2004 03/1056/03, Highbury Safika Media, 21st floor, Metlife Centre,
7 Coen Steytler Avenue, Foreshore, 8001, Cape Town, South Africa

Editor: Simon Borchardt
Designer: Kirsty Reid
Copy Editors: Philippa Byron, Nick van Rensburg
Proofreader: Mark Etheridge
Statistician: Kobus Smit
Index: Linda Retief
Repro Artists: Karin Livni, Donnevan van der Watt, Janette Wright,
Adri van der Watt
Cover Photo: Rory Ross/HSM Images
Inside Front Cover Photo: Greg Cox
Other Photos: Smit collection, Gallo Images, Getty Images, Anne Laing
Marketing Manager: Kara Ross
Printer: CTP Book Printers

ISO 12647 compliant

CONTENTS

DEDICATION

I dedicate this book to my darling wife Roxy, who's been with me through every moment since we left school.

When most people reflect on my life they will speak of World Cup and Tri-Nations titles, but when I sit on my rocking chair as an old man and look back at my greatest accomplishments I will thank the Lord for my soulmate and the two miracles she gave me, Emma-Joan and Tyron.

Roxy, the rugby chapter of our lives is coming to an end, and I will be eternally grateful to you for holding my hand through the good and bad times. You are the one who inspired me throughout and you are my greatest hero, best friend and, to top it all off, my wife.

I hope I can hold your hand in the next chapter of our lives like you have held mine in this one.

I love you, baby.

ACKNOWLEDGEMENT

Mike Greenaway and I go way back. He was reporting on rugby in this country and predominantly for the Sharks when I made my debut in 1997. He has seen my every move on the field of play since then and became a friend long before I considered writing a book. There really couldn't have been a better man for the job and his patience with me throughout our many interviews at Mama Luciana's in Greyville, Durban, was incredible.

Mike, I really want to thank you for this wonderful book that you have created with me – it's been so much fun and a lot of that has been because of your approach. It's much appreciated.

MESSAGE FROM JOHN SMIT

I deliberated for some time over whether or not to write a book but in the end I decided that because I have been so blessed in my life I should put it down in print. I wanted an opportunity to thank everyone who has played a role in my life and I hope the people who know me and my story will nod their heads and smile when they read this book. Hopefully my kids will also read this book one day and say, 'Wow, that sounds just like Dad!'

I also felt that having lived in the heart of the South African rugby beast for so long, I could provide supporters with an insight into the inner workings of the wonderful world of the Springboks.

I love rugby, I love this country and I love giving people hope. I have lived, and am still living, in a historic time for South Africa and have grown with the country from the birth of democracy in 1994, when I was just 16. I started my rugby career a year after the 1995 World Cup and this book illustrates the progression of this remarkable game since the dawn of the professional era in 1996.

I hope and pray that the next decade will be as fruitful for us as a country and a rugby nation.

Finally, this book doesn't signify imminent retirement. If my body holds out, my mind is willing to give 2010 and possibly 2011 a crack but as we say all too often in rugby, it's one game at a time, never mind one season at a time!

Nkosi Sikelel' iAfrika.

Smit had played 90 Tests for the Springboks by the end of the 2009 Tri-Nations – 64 of them as captain. He led the Boks to World Cup glory in 2007.

MESSAGE FROM MIKE GREENAWAY

When Mark Keohane, the chief operating officer of Highbury Safika Media, called and said 'Gringo [only Keo knows why he bestowed that nickname on me], Smitty wants you to write his book,' I was simultaneously flattered, honoured and a touch intimidated.

There's a massive responsibility attached to accurately capturing the facts and, most importantly, the spirit and ethos of quite probably the most distinguished career in South African rugby history.

By September 2009, John had played 90 Tests – 64 of them as captain – and each one of them could be a chapter on its own. Also, there was a 13-year career at the Sharks packed with trials, tribulations and triumphs to consider.

John didn't know where to start – nor did I – so we dived in at the deep end and began recording almost countless hours of interviews, much of which were done over lengthy lunch sessions at Mama Luciana's. It was quite a sight seeing the big fellow work his way though the menu while we chewed the cud, not to mention the pasta.

As we wove together the colourful tapestry of his life in rugby, the secret to his longevity soon emerged. Smitty has been so successful in a team environment because there's no pretension or ego about him. He's just a good bloke, plain and simple (his nickname is Barney, after the bar-fly from *The Simpsons*, who spends his days in Moe's Tavern).

Remarkably, it also became clear that after almost a decade-and-a-half in rugby, John has made no enemies. I never encountered one dissenting voice at the Sharks or the Springboks, which speaks volumes about his personality, given the infamous politics of South African rugby.

During the writing of this book, Smitty was leading the Springboks to a series win over the British & Irish Lions and then to the 2009 Tri-Nations title, necessitating some expanded chapters. The good news is that he isn't done with rugby just yet and we might well find this story having to be revised over the next couple of years as further victorious chapters are added. Here's hoping …

My sincere gratitude goes to my lovely wife Wendy for her patience during the long periods when my laptop became an extension of my arms, especially the nightmarish fortnight when swine flu struck down our three kids when I was on deadline.

Finally, a very big thank you to the ultra-conscientious Simon Borchardt, who edited this project superbly. Thanks also to copy editors Philippa Byron and Nick van Rensburg, designer Kirsty Reid, Rory Ross, who took the cover photo, as well as Kobus Smit, who compiled John's career statistics.

Greenaway is the group rugby correspondent for Independent Newspapers (he is based at The Mercury *in Durban) and a regular contributor to* SA Rugby *magazine.*

MESSAGE FROM OS DU RANDT

When Jake White recalled me to the Springbok squad in 2004 after a five-year absence, I told Cheetahs coach Naka Drotské that John Smit, who Jake had named as his captain, didn't really impress me. How wrong was I?

Over the next four years, I would play under a captain whose integrity could never be questioned. He would give every player the same time, respect and admiration as he would to his father. You could go to him with any problem and know he would keep it confidential.

John is a people person and knows exactly how to deal with each player, whether it's by being sympathetic, a bit firm or confronting him head on. He always embraces responsibility and overcomes every obstacle in his path.

I remember how much pressure John was under from 'Joe Public' early in Jake's tenure as Bok coach because so few people believed he should be in the side. But John believed in his own ability and went on to lead us to World Cup glory in 2007. However, he never believed he was more important than the team, and never made excuses when things went wrong.

John, you are a highly intelligent captain, an outstanding player and a loyal friend, which makes you tops in my world! What a privilege it was to scrum next to you, where a person's fighting spirit comes to the fore.

You have my respect and admiration and I'm grateful to Jake for giving me the opportunity to play alongside you.

You are a worthy and proud ambassador for the game of rugby and your country. I can only take my hat off to you and say 'encore!'

You are, and will always be, an idol to me.

Du Randt played 80 Tests for the Springboks and was part of the 1995 and 2007 World Cup-winning teams.

MESSAGE FROM VICTOR MATFIELD

What makes a captain and a rugby player successful? Is it everything that he's achieved in his career, or is it about the respect he's earned from team-mates and opponents? I believe most rugby players would say it's about respect and that's why I believe John Smit is so highly regarded today. In my 12 years of professional rugby, I've never encountered someone who has earned so much respect as player and captain from friend and foe alike.

To single out one outstanding aspect of John's captaincy in the six years that I've played under him is a very difficult task, as I can think of many.

He managed to keep Jake White calm before the 2007 World Cup, when the pressure on the Springbok coach was immense. John and Jake always had an amazing relationship and that's one of the reasons why they were so successful together. In saying that, though, they didn't always agree on everything. When John thought Jake was making a mistake, he went straight to the coach, they discussed the issue and settled on what was best for the team.

John also stood by Peter de Villiers when a lot of people wanted him to fail as Bok coach. I remember how, when I returned to South Africa to discuss my future, Peter told me that he knew – after only one meeting – that he couldn't take on this job without John. He has told me a number of times since then that bringing John back from France was the best decision he's ever made.

However, the one moment that stands out for me – which proves without doubt what a special leader John is – came during the 2008 Tri-Nations in Jo'burg. We had endured a disappointing season up to then after winning the World Cup and I had taken over the captaincy when John got injured in New Zealand. He came to me and asked me if he could address the team at the hotel before we left for Ellis Park.

I was very thankful for that, because we were under huge pressure after losing to the Wallabies in Durban the previous week. John then asked the team management to excuse themselves from the room. When it was only us players left, John got up. It was the most emotional I've ever seen him. He spoke about what the Bok jersey represents and what we had built up over the past four years, and that he felt some players were putting their own interests above those of the team. He said it like it was and how he saw it – his words made every single player think and I've never experienced a team room as quiet as it was on that day.

We went out later that afternoon and gave the Wallabies the biggest *pak slae* (hiding) ever. It underlined just how much John means to the team. Even though he wasn't on the field that day, he knew exactly what was needed to get every player to give his all for his country.

It's been an amazing seven years with John at the Boks. Yes, it has been tough at times, especially in those first few years, but we have great memories – from winning countless trophies to late nights around a campfire with Robbie Wessels. These are moments none of us will ever forget.

We are truly living our dream and hopefully Barney can become the first captain to lift the Webb Ellis Cup twice when we defend our title in 2011.

Matfield had played 89 Tests for the Springboks by the end of the 2009 Tri-Nations and was part of the 2007 World Cup-winning team.

MESSAGE FROM PERCY MONTGOMERY

A sporting legend, a hero, a father, a team-mate, a husband – John Smit is many things to many people.

John and I moved up through the ranks together, from provincial to Test level. During our years of playing rugby together, we've experienced amazing and difficult times, but through it all John has always shown the calibre of man he is – committed, passionate and always there with a smile or some wise advice.

I'm proud to have worn the green and gold with John, I'm proud to have called him my captain and my team-mate, but most of all, I'm proud to call him a true friend.

Montgomery played 102 Tests for the Springboks and was part of the 2007 World Cup-winning team.

1

SOMETHING SPECIAL

In the first week of my Springbok captaincy during a team meeting, our shrink Henning Gericke sat us down in a circle and put a Springbok jersey in the middle. I was asked to talk about what it meant to me, where I wanted to go with the jersey, what it had done for me, and what I thought I could do for it. Then it was the turn of the rest of the guys.

Third down the line was Os du Randt. He grabbed the jersey, bent his head and then remained quiet for some time. Nobody knew what was going on ... and then we realised this colossal man was crying. Os, the epitome of Springbok rugby, was overcome with emotion. In a choking voice he told us what it meant to him to touch the jersey again. His career was dead and buried until Jake White resurrected it in 2004. Os could barely talk, but his message was crystal clear, through the gripping emotion he showed in expressing his gratitude at being restored to his beloved Springboks.

That story will be remembered by all of us who were there for the rest of our lives. We were profoundly moved. At the beginning of Jake's tenure, the vast majority of our team were young bucks, and here was our father figure inadvertently teaching us the lesson of how fortunate we were to play for the Springboks – that when it's gone it's supremely missed and there's no coming back (unless you are Os, of course).

I needed no convincing. I love the jersey and I love the Springboks, even when it's not going well and I sense an air of uncertainty and doubt, which means I have to act to get the guys back on track.

Every time I've been presented with a Springbok jersey I've experienced the same heart-warming sensation, and each time it prompts the same private covenant I make with the green and gold.

I take the jersey and kiss the Springbok, whether it's on the Friday at the official team presentation or at half-time the next day when I have the option to pull on the dry 'second jersey' we are given.

I kiss that leaping Springbok because I've always known that circumstances can end a sporting career in an instant, and you have to treat every minute of an international career in the same valued way. I don't want to wake up on a Sunday morning and regret that I never kissed the last jersey I wore.

I make a promise to each jersey. I promise to do it justice to the best of my ability, and I tell myself that I can't just 'do a job' in it that day. This is a reaffirmation for me that each match could be my last, as well as an acknowledgement of the great players who have gone before and will come after me.

I understand that very well. The jersey belongs to no man. The incumbent is the custodian, and he never knows for how long, so he has to do it uncompromising justice.

In 2009 I mentioned to my wife Roxy that if the Springbok was taken away from me tomorrow, I'd still be a happy and grateful man, but I don't believe I could find anything else to do for a living that would give me as much pleasure.

The actual playing of the game is only one part of it – a big part, sure, because I love playing – but it has become so much more for me.

It's become about mentoring, for instance, and the pride I take in Bismarck du Plessis playing so well after having helped him from when he was a teenager, or the satisfaction of starting a Test with Chiliboy Ralepelle, a first for our alma mater, Pretoria Boys High.

There are so many special things I've been a party to over my nine-year journey with the Boks, and none of them can be remotely taken for granted or underappreciated.

It's been a phenomenal ride, from the very beginning when I was about to make my Test debut, against Canada in East London in 2000, and I'm not yet sure when it will end. I am contracted to the Sharks until the end of 2010 and will decide then whether or not to call time – if I'm still being selected, that is.

My first interaction with the Springboks was at a training camp in Plettenberg Bay in 2000, just a week or two after my 22nd birthday. I recall throwing the ball to Mark Andrews and thinking, 'This isn't really happening, there must have been a mistake. These guys are legends, so what the heck am I doing here?!'

I haven't forgotten the awe I felt then and occasionally I remind myself that many of the current players are going to be serious legends, and that I must never take them for granted – guys like Victor Matfield, Bakkies Botha, Fourie du Preez, Bryan Habana, Jean de Villiers and Schalk Burger. Sometimes I look at these guys lacing up their boots in the change room, and I afford myself an appreciative smile.

I think the key to my longevity and freshness is that I don't allow myself to get used to the Springboks. I make myself understand that every week is a story on its own, a unique chapter that could be the last in which I feature.

I've always wanted to be the best at what I do, but I've had a greater wish to be part of something special rather than to be the most special. So the Springbok environment is the perfect fit for my personality.

I really don't care if I'm not Man of the Match as long as my team wins – that's more special. I get more enjoyment deciding who's going to be the Springbok team's Man of the Match than being the man of the moment.

Sometimes a person's ego induces him to take things for granted, but I would like to think I have an ego that's not as prominent as most. I'm not the self-congratulatory type who pats himself on the back because he's 'arrived'.

It's also very difficult to accurately judge and criticise yourself and that's where you need a strong and sensible family infrastructure. I got that from my parents and then from Roxy. I have been further blessed with good friends and excellent schooling, so circumstance has been good to me.

When I was first selected for the Boks, it was the Bob Skinstad era, and my mother phoned and said, 'JoJo [my nickname], well done but I don't want to see you with your shirt off in the centrefold of *You* magazine. Leave that to the pop stars, you're an ambassador now.'

My mother once walked me off a tennis court after I had thrown a tantrum in a tournament. I'd done a John McEnroe and thrown my racket, which nearly hit my opponent on the other side. She strode onto the court and pulled me off without saying a word. She then sat me down and told me – calmly, but very sternly – if I ever behaved like that again, she wouldn't allow me to play sport.

I was 11 and that was a big moment for me because I lived for sport. I used to cry when Ivan Lendl lost at Wimbledon – that's how passionate I was about sport – so I was in tears every July!

That day on the tennis court I learnt what composure is about, and that you have to be in control of your emotions all the time. It was an invaluable lesson.

Roxy has exactly the same kind of influence on me. She's the first one to warn me not to get ahead of myself.

It's probably helped that throughout my life I've always been uncomfortable with praise. I try to deflect it. I find it difficult when people say things like, 'You've done so well at X, Y or Z', 'Well done for being head boy', 'Well done for this, well done for that'. I get embarrassed.

When I was 15, we were on holiday in Scottburgh and my dad took me to a sports shop to buy a swimming costume. While I was in the booth changing, I overheard him telling the assistant how well I was doing at sport, making the rugby 1st XV in Standard 8 (Grade 10), and so on. I was so embarrassed that I didn't want to come out!

I've always had an appreciation of the good things that have happened at the various stages of my life, without ever getting carried away. I've always tried to enjoy whatever I do, and most of the things I've achieved have been in a team environment.

After the Springboks had won the Test series against the British & Irish Lions in 2009, I was pleased to be able to say to myself, 'Heck, you changed so much of your life to be part of the Springboks again and to have an opportunity to play in the series, and it worked out.' That gave me a warm feeling of satisfaction. I had changed my whole plan for a career in France, and I had come back for a coach I had never met before, all to be a part of that Lions series.

It's like making a life-altering decision so that you can attempt to achieve a difficult goal, and you do it. I got a lot of joy out of that.

I've hated it when personal milestones have come around during my career, because I feel they detract from the team focus. I worry about them rather than enjoy them.

If I had to look back one day – as a middle-aged man, while having a beer with my son or sitting at a Christmas table – on the person I once was, I wouldn't like to see someone who took too much credit.

I've had good players around me for the majority of my career. Everything I've achieved in my career has been due to a collective effort, and in years to come, I would love to periodically get together with my old team-mates and talk about the good old days. I would love to read in a book about what the team achieved, but I would hate it to become about 'I did this and I did that', because really, I haven't done anything. I've been part of something very special.

2

RAINBOW NATION RUGBY

Before we get cracking on my life in rugby, I think it would be useful to give you a rough guide to the complex drama that is South African rugby politics. It can be a weighty topic so let's kick off on a lighter note.

At the 2007 World Cup, Springbok manager Zola Yeye was a political appointment, as was our muddling media officer Vusi Kama.

However, both found themselves in top positions in the Bok set-up, whereas our opposition had proven experts in these fields, and were often former internationals, men who could add value to the operation.

Zola was inoffensive by nature but not respected because of his inability to make a meaningful contribution – apart from simultaneously embarrassing and amusing us – as he comically did at an arrival function in Paris.

The hosts had assigned each team to a particular suburb in Paris where they would train and integrate themselves into the local community. It was a good idea, and to get the ball rolling, each squad attended a ceremony at the local town hall.

Zola was called up to introduce each Springbok and give him his World Cup cap in front of about 300 dignitaries. We were in our No 1s (formal wear with Bok blazer), mingling with the people, when the action started.

Zola called the guys up one by one as he saw them in the crowd, rather than reading their names off a squad list. The guys cottoned on to this and started hiding behind the pillars and each other just to apply a little pressure, but he handled it well enough and got through the majority of the players until he saw Francois Steyn, and called him up as Francois Pienaar!

This had the guys in stitches but it didn't end there. Our 'beloved' manager had left Wynand Olivier for last and went out in style: 'Ladies and gentlemen, last but not least, the great Wynand Claassen!'

We were still laughing when we boarded the team bus to return to the hotel, but were in absolute hysterics when Jaque Fourie shouted out: 'Is Zola Budd on board?!'

If you are thinking that I'm opposed to the quota system and transformation you are wrong. Yes, there are many things I don't like about the quota system. But I believe the end justifies the means and that the implementation of quotas accelerated some of the careers of the great players of colour we have playing for South Africa.

To understand this process one needs to understand the complexities involved in forgiveness and reconciliation, which is what has made South Africa the success story it has been since the abolishment of apartheid.

I understand that it's difficult to be sympathetic to the quota system when it's your position on the line, but if you look at the bigger picture we have seen the rise of wonderful players of colour. The culmination of this was seeing Bryan Habana being crowned the 2007 IRB (International Rugby Board) Player of the Year after we won the World Cup.

The downside of the quota system has been how it belittled the players of colour who were selected. They were often there on merit but had this quota cloud hanging over their heads, creating unfair doubt about their ability.

It's important to clarify that sport and politics in this country are inextricably linked and to deny that would be naive. We have come a long way as a nation since becoming a democracy in 1994, much of it due to the sound early piloting by Nelson Mandela. He's played a massive role in the history of not only South Africa, but Springbok rugby too – from stepping into the Bok change room before the 1995 World Cup final in his No 6 jersey, to becoming godfather to captain Francois Pienaar's child.

Madiba's influence didn't end with that Bok era. He gave our class of 2004-07 so much of himself throughout our four-year build-up to the World Cup, culminating in him travelling to Paris during the event to wish us well, in his elderly state. It gave me enormous pleasure to hand him my own No 2 jersey.

I vividly recall another spell of 'Madiba magic' at Ellis Park in 2005, 10 years after his 'debut' for the Springboks at the same venue. We were playing the Wallabies in a Mandela Plate match and urgently needed a win after we had lost to them in Sydney two weeks earlier.

Madiba wasn't well enough to walk out and greet us on the field but waited strategically in the middle of the tunnel for us to come back from our warm-up to chat to us. I don't remember what he said, because I was too busy looking at the shock on the faces of the Wallabies as they filed past us to get to their change room and saw this great man taking the time to motivate us for the game. Their eyes were the size of dinner plates and I knew from their stunned reaction that the Test was won.

Madiba has really had a huge impact on every Bok Test he's attended – both on us, his adopted children, and the unfortunate opposition.

But this journey of transformation will always encounter potholes along the way and, believe me, there are many. I can think back to 2004 when we had to prepare for the All Blacks in Jo'burg and the team had already been approved by Saru (South African Rugby Union) president Brian van Rooyen, with Fourie du Preez as the starting scrumhalf. However, on the Saturday morning of the Test, Jake White called me in and said he had been instructed to add more balance to the demographics of the team. He then had to call Fourie into his hotel room and tell him that he wanted to play a more attacking game against the All Blacks due to the good weather conditions, and was going to start with Bolla Conradie at No 9. The whole episode was disgraceful, and it was handled badly by the powers-that-be. Had Jake known earlier, he would never have been put in a position where he had to lie to a player, and this, in my opinion, led to the continual erosion of Jake and Fourie's relationship over the next couple of seasons.

You must be wondering who these 'powers' are, the 'they' that everyone refers to. I can't tell you exactly other than to put it like this: There are many people responsible for the administration of South African rugby, people from all walks of life – white and black.

I've always tried to decide on their motives by asking one question: Are they there to benefit South African rugby or themselves? Sadly the latter is often the answer, based on personal experiences.

Consider former Saru deputy president Mike Stofile, for instance. He certainly didn't support me in any way or form during my time as Springbok captain when Jake was coach, which was especially disappointing bearing in mind that to this day I haven't had one conversation with him. Stofile continually questioned Jake on why he persisted in picking me when there were many far superior hookers, in his opinion, such as Chiliboy Ralepelle, Gary Botha and his favourite, Schalk Brits.

He even told Jake during one of their several 'crisis' meetings that he thought our relationship was too close. To Jake's credit he never let this influence his opinion of me, which further aggravated Stofile, who then expressed his views on me in the media. It hardly filled me with confidence knowing that my employer felt this negativity towards me. It didn't take me long to get over it, though, because Stofile continued to do very strange things and thus lost credibility.

I remember, too, when I was called to a meeting in Jo'burg at the team hotel before going on our end-of-year tour to Ireland and England in 2006. Saru president Regan Hoskins, Stofile, Saru vice-president Koos Basson and SA Rugby chairman Mpumelelo Tshume were all in the boardroom.

I felt like I was being called into the headmaster's office after being caught smoking at school. The meeting related to an incident regarding a possible strike by the Boks in conjunction with Sarpa (South African Rugby Players Association), because SA Rugby (the professional arm of Saru) hadn't given the players contracts before our tour departure as previously agreed.

Sarpa CEO Piet Heymans was the go-between and in our talks we had discussed possible measures the players could take to show our strength. A strike was mentioned, but legally we couldn't go through with it due to previous deals struck with our union, so it wasn't an option.

But there must have been a prior telephonic discussion between Piet and Tshume where Piet had declared that we were going to strike and not get on the plane, which was absolute rubbish considering the players weren't even aware of the current situation (I was negotiating on their behalf). I'm sure Piet made this up to speed up the process of us being granted contracts, and this is why I was called into the headmaster's office to be asked who I thought I was to make threats to SA Rugby. I got the impression, from this group of men leading our game, that their authority, and not results, was their priority.

Of all the Saru presidents I've operated under, Brian gave me and the coach the most support rugby-wise. He never questioned our motives, he always asked what he could do for us and he was there during a critical time for South African rugby in 2004. Perhaps it's no coincidence that we won the Tri-Nations that year.

However, it's public knowledge that he did some irregular and questionable things on the administrative side, and in general his stint was seen as a bad time for South African rugby. For instance, it was Brian who changed the Saru constitution in order to give the president the power to change the Springbok team.

Regan, whom I regard as a friend, has been one of the longest-standing Saru presidents and has a World Cup title under his leadership. I find his manner easy to deal with. He's well spoken, has a good heart and comes from Kwa-Zulu-Natal, my home province. He's shown me great support throughout my tenure as Bok captain, for which I'm very grateful, but sadly he will be mostly remembered for one thing: picking Luke Watson behind Jake's back in 2007, even though the instruction came from Tshume.

This situation, which would never happen in any other country, was always going to end badly. To be fair, Luke was put in a difficult position and I'm pretty sure he didn't ask Tshume to select him, but as the situation unfolded, it worsened. There was an awkward feeling in our camp due to Luke's presence because we knew Jake hadn't picked him. That made it quite tough to achieve unity due to the very nature of team dynamics.

Jake and Luke were very professional about the situation forced upon them by Tshume and Regan and went about their business. To my knowledge, Tshume told Regan that Jake didn't have to pick Luke in his World Cup squad as long as he gave him a Test cap beforehand. The Samoa match at Ellis Park, which took place before the Tri-Nations, gave Jake that opportunity.

Luke did well until he got injured 10 minutes after half-time. The next issue was his initiation, which happens to every new cap after his first match in the green and gold. A group of our senior players went to Jake to ask how best we could handle a unique situation in that somebody else had picked the player and frankly no one was pleased about it. We discussed the pros and cons in Jake's room and he said Luke had to be handled like any other Bok. The decision was made, although not unanimously.

More often than not, a player is initiated the same night as the Test but there are occasions where, for logistical reasons, he's initiated the following week, which was to be the case with Luke. But then he left the squad and wasn't to return for some time, so the conspiracy theorists made a meal of his non-initiation. On his return to the squad, he was initiated just like any other Bok (more on that later).

I think it's important to clarify why our leaders sometimes don't do things for the greater good of South African rugby, and to do this I can only give you my opinion formed over my years of experience with the Springboks.

Important matters regarding our game are discussed in meetings and voted upon by the 14 presidents of our 14 provincial unions, and the majority vote stands. This may sound democratic but it's heavily flawed. The five major unions – the Blue Bulls, Free State Cheetahs, Golden Lions, Sharks and Western Province – have only one vote each and together count as five, which as an entity makes them a minority. The phrase 'the tail wagging the dog' immediately comes to mind. It's also interesting to note that not many of the unions outside the big five are profitable – in fact they run at a loss.

Let's take an example of what this all means. SA Rugby has to subsidise these unions in order for them to survive, which means less money for development, the running of our national teams and a number of other things. So, to make a decision to stop unnecessary spending, a vote must be taken, and there's no way a small-union president will vote in favour of downsizing as it means he will literally be voting himself out of a presidency. I can assure you it's way more complex than how I've explained it, but I think you get the picture.

My Springbok captaincy started with a baptism of fire in 2004, again due to player contracts, or the lack thereof. We had played Ireland (twice) and Wales at home and were set to meet the Pacific Islanders in Gosford, Australia, before our Tri-Nations fixtures against the All Blacks in Christchurch and the Wallabies in Perth.

During the build-up to that tour there was an obvious concern from the players that no one had contracts except for a select few who had signed lengthy contracts with former Bok coach Rudolf Straeuli. I happened to be one of these players, but as skipper of the side it fell to me to sort out all the contracts.

As a team, we held many undercover meetings to discuss the best way forward. We had, through Sarpa, voiced our concern to the hierarchy of SA Rugby, but to no avail – they quite liked the pay-as-you-go system, which looked OK at first but created a few issues.

Firstly, to play for your country is the greatest honour a player can aspire to. We spend our childhood dreaming about playing for the Boks. The complication is when you factor money into the equation. I think it's hard for some people to accept that we get paid to represent our country, as the diehards from the amateur era believe playing for your country is enough of an honour, but the reality is that we no longer have the time to play part-time and work during the day. The game has changed dramatically and now we have the privilege of playing this wonderful game as our primary line of work and source of income. Not a day goes by that I don't appreciate just how lucky I am.

Secondly, when playing for the Boks without a contract, you run the risk of injury without any real cover. This worries players because, while playing Test rugby is awesome, your bread and butter is the contract you have with your provincial union and a serious injury in the green and gold puts your only stable income at risk.

We also knew how much revenue SA Rugby was making and believed that a good portion of that should be allocated to the organisation's greatest assets, the players.

After being led down the garden path a number of times by our bosses, we decided that a statement had to be made to indicate how serious we were about getting contracts.

A number of the senior Boks came to my room to discuss options, and we settled on wearing white armbands against the Pacific Islanders, which we would keep secret until we ran onto the field.

We then had to take the idea to the rest of the Bok team, which was sensitive as we were a pretty young bunch of guys, myself included. Schalk Burger was 21, Jean de Villiers was 23 and the list goes on. I must say, we as the senior players did have to persuade a few of the younger guys, who were nervous of what their fathers, and the public for that matter, would think. We also knew we could potentially be sent home because of our actions and never play for South Africa again.

It was a terrifying experience for me as I was only 26 and in the middle of what was potentially the first strike action by a Springbok team. The emotions I felt were immense. Due to the sensitivity of the topic, I had no one to talk to other than Roxy, and I certainly couldn't speak to Jake about it because we as players didn't want to add to the already huge strain of being Bok coach.

I remember lying in bed one night, desperately praying that the whole episode would just blow over. I'd never pioneered a mass protest in my life and although I had captained many sides at Pretoria Boys High and had been head boy, this was the first time people who looked up to me were counting on me to be strong.

As strange as it may sound, I have never been comfortable with conflict, I always look to diffuse sticky situations and try to create harmony which makes me more comfortable. Roxy will attest to the fact that although in my older age I can get quite uptight about certain things, when she met me I was a very laid-back, easy-going bloke with no worries in the world. But a few years under constant scrutiny as Bok captain have changed that. It's certainly made me far more cautious in my approach to life.

I was extremely nervous about what had to be done, but I would get great satisfaction from successfully serving my team in a tough situation and in my first true test as a leader. An underlying factor for me was knowing that by standing up for the team, I could very well lose my contract with SA Rugby, but this didn't frighten me as much as I thought it would. I was more afraid that our stand together would not amount to anything, but boy was I wrong ...

I remember catching a taxi with AJ Venter on our day off to find a roll of white tape. We looked everywhere and eventually came across a hardware store that stocked the thickest roll of white tape I had ever seen. AJ was delighted and I cringed. I suggested we look for a thinner one and AJ replied: 'Smitty, if we want to make a statement, let's do it properly. I can always buy that big thick pink roll over there!' At that I threw the white roll into the basket and went to the till.

Logistics were sorted, now it was just a matter of getting our big statement out there on the Saturday without any of our coaches or management getting wind of it and, oh yes, we also had a game to win!

I didn't sleep too well that week. We were going to face a powerful Pacific Islanders side (made up of players from Fiji, Samoa and Tonga), and losing against them would be disastrous considering all that was going on. We knew we would be ripped apart for focusing on our pockets rather than the game, so the stakes were high.

I recall the atmosphere in the change room that Saturday as if it were yesterday. Everyone was extremely nervous, but the funniest thing was getting the white tape on. There just wasn't enough space in the room to do it secretly, the coaches wouldn't leave and the players were looking at each other wondering what to do next as kick-off was approaching.

I eventually walked up to Jake and said: 'This is a big one, give me some time alone with the boys just to get them worked up a little, then you can come in and deliver the final talk.'

It worked like a charm and Jake got all his management out of the room. We then scurried around like bunking schoolboys trying to get the white tape onto 22 arms.

I called the coaches back in when we had put our tracksuit tops on again to conceal the tape. As Jake finished and started leaving the room I walked over to him and handed him a folded-up letter I'd written earlier that morning, which explained what was happening. I thought he should be the first to know.

My team talk that day was simple enough. I mentioned that our actions were not only for our benefit, but also for those who would follow. We'd taken the responsibility upon ourselves and there was only one way to deliver – on the field. We won 38-24 and two weeks later we had contracts.

The laughable footnote to this saga was that once we had removed our tops to reveal the white armbands, Springbok manager Arthob Petersen realised what was happening and tried to counter our move. He went to the press box and said that we were honouring someone who had died that week in Bloemfontein. I was quick to inform everyone at the press conference about the true meaning of our white armbands, although at the same time we sent our condolences to the family of Thabo van Rooyen, the administrator who had passed away.

I think the responsibility I have as captain of the Boks is an amazing one, for many reasons. I often look at my overseas peers and wonder how they would cope with captaining our country. I get the feeling their toughest part of the week is deciding whether to go for poles or not on Saturday.

I shared a room with All Blacks captain Richie McCaw when we played for the Barbarians in 2008, and while lying in bed I fielded a call from a British media man on rugby and matters relating to life as a South African, which is pretty standard for me. After the call Richie said, 'Mate, I didn't mean to eavesdrop on your call but was that an interview?' and I said yes. He was surprised at the line of questioning, which incorporated apartheid, the quota system, whether there was a difference in captaining different cultures and races, and what my views were regarding the status of rugby transformation in South Africa.

I realised then just how different my role was to other international captains, but I wouldn't change it for the world. I've learnt so much about my country and how special it is by being involved with people from all walks of life, and I truly believe it's our diverse nature that makes us a country of survivors. We've come a long way, and we continue to progress and prosper with every year that unfolds.

3

BREAKING WITH TRADITION

The only name more common than John Smit in South Africa is John Smith. I suppose you could say that my Christian name and surname illustrate that I'm a genuine *soutie* – the crude but humorous nickname the Afrikaners have given us English-speaking South Africans, with a censored translation being that we have one foot in England, one in South Africa and an appendage dangling in the sea (thus the *sout* or salt).

The name Smit is of obvious Dutch heritage, going all the way back to the first settlers at the Cape in the 17th century. My dad's grandparents spoke Afrikaans but somewhere along the line we switched to English.

It's typical of the melting pot of cultures in South Africa that my Bok team-mate Juan Smith – who is from Bloem-fontein and is very Afrikaans – has the English surname, although he once explained in an interview that it came from the English soldier who had his way with Juan's great grandmother in the Boer War!

My mother is very English, though, as her maiden name – Valerie Ann Wetheral Graham – suggests.

My dad Basil is a mechanical engineer and he worked on mines all over the Rand in the Transvaal (now Gauteng) during my early years. We saw the bright lights of several *lekker* little one-horse – or should that be one-mine – towns, such as Mooinooi, Naboomspruit (now Mookgophong), Penge and Potgietersrus (now Mokopane) before spending a relatively lengthy period in Rustenburg.

I was a *laat lammetjie* (late arrival), and an unscheduled one at that. My mom sometimes teases my dad about how annoyed he was when she told him she was pregnant for the third time. He didn't know where he was going to get the ammo to pay for the new addition because he already had two monster sons chowing him out of house and home. So he wasn't overly charmed about the pregnancy, but from the day I popped out, my mom says he was completely taken by this beefy baby, and I became his blue-eyed boy.

During my childhood my older brothers called me 'the twins' because they reckoned I got double what they both got. I probably did get spoilt because I was mostly the only kid at home – Brian (who is eight years older than me) and David (six) were at boarding school when I was at primary school, and when I was at high school they were out in the big wide world.

We are a very close family. Roxy finds it incredible how I'm in my early 30s and I've played 90 Tests, yet after every match I still have to phone my mom and let her know that I'm OK and not hurt. She also lights candles for me whenever I play.

My mom was a school teacher, so she had time to drive me around to sports practices. I'm unashamedly a mommy's boy, and that's alright because I've learnt so many good values from that quality time I spent with her.

When I played rugby for Pretoria Boys High, my folks would drive an hour-and-a-half every Saturday to watch me. They wouldn't bother me before kick-off, but would sit in the same place up on a bank. When we ran out I would look to the right, check that they were there and feel at ease. There was one match when they weren't on the bank, and I couldn't get into the game until I saw them arrive 20 minutes late. They had been stuck in traffic.

I'm just as close to my dad, who has always given me unequivocal backing and unpressurised support. He never tried to teach me how to pass the ball or how to scrum, and if I wanted to play tennis or rugby, he would give me a tennis racket or a pair of rugby boots and tell me to look after them and enjoy myself.

My dad let me do what I wanted to do, and would provide praise and support. He was always in the background, and never shouted like a mad parent on the sidelines or pushed me in a certain direction.

So many parents can't help pushing their kids, especially in rugby, and it does more harm than good and is distasteful to witness.

In not being an overbearing parent, my dad taught me valuable life lessons by encouraging me to make my own decisions. He would guide me, so that I hopefully made the right decision, and by putting me in situations where I would have to make the decision myself, he was training me to be a leader. A good example was when I had to make a choice between rugby and tennis. He would ask me what my gut said or what sport I enjoyed the most. He wouldn't make the decision for me.

However, my dad would be the first to step in if I was in trouble. On our way back from our matric holiday, Roxy (my girlfriend at the time) and I rolled the car outside Plettenberg Bay. We weren't injured but my dad dropped everything and drove 1 200km to help us.

It's given me a great deal of pleasure to have made my parents proud, even though we are a family that's not too big on making ourselves out as big deals. After the second

Test against the British & Irish Lions at Loftus in 2009, I caught up with my dad that evening and noticed he was wearing my Bok jersey from my Test debut against Canada, which I'd given him. We had just won the series against the Lions and here was my dad in my first-ever Bok jersey. I felt quite a stir of emotion – a mixture of pride and love, I suppose.

Tennis was very much my first sporting love in primary school at Rustenburg Fields. Rugby didn't really grab me because I was convinced I was on the road to Wimbledon. I hadn't considered the possible limitations my body type would have on my game and couldn't get enough of the tennis court.

Inevitably, though, if you are a tubby kid in South Africa, you are going to be encouraged to play rugby, and that is what happened when I was 11. When they chose the teams, they lined up all the kids and separated the fat ones (welcome to the forwards) from the thin kids (who became the backs). I was immediately placed at tighthead prop (no surprise there).

When I arrived at Fields Primary from Boksburg – our family's previous location – I was put into the Standard 3B (Grade 5) class, which was for the 'average' pupils, with the boffins and nerds in Standard 3A.

The next year they moved me up to the A class, and who should I meet there but a pretty, freckly, confident little girl called Roxy Rech (the surname is Italian). I was 11, which is sort of the first time you start thinking about girls. They are more interesting, and not as 'yucky' as before.

We used to have these innocent primary school parties, but I'll never forget one party at my friend George's house, where there was no adult supervision, just an older brother. 'Georgie Porgie' always had the best parties, and when I say parties I mean music was played and when it stopped you sat down. It was reasonably silly but apt for our age at the time.

I'd never kissed a girl until I got to Rustenburg and in Standard 4 (Grade 6), Roxy became that girl. She was at one of George's parties where we played a kissing game called 'pass or fail'. I 'failed' so she had to kiss me. I'm surprised she didn't run a mile.

You don't really date at that stage of your life – you kind of have a girlfriend for a few weeks and there's drama and letters, and then you move on. But yes, she was the first girl I ever kissed and my first girlfriend.

We then went our separate ways – Roxy to Potchefstroom Girls High as a boarder and me to Pretoria Boys High. Our paths would cross again in matric, when we bumped into each other at a dinner party, but we'll pick up on the romance later ...

Fields Primary was the only English school in the area and we got *klapped* (badly beaten) at rugby every weekend by the Afrikaans schools. In Standard 5 (Grade 7) I went to Stellaland trials and was picked for the B team, which was almost unheard of for an English kid in that part of the world.

But what really set me on course for a career in rugby was my parents' decision to break with long-standing family tradition and send me to Pretoria Boys High.

Most of my family originated from Pietersburg (now Polokwane) in the dry, dusty far north of South Africa. My dad and his brothers had all gone to Capricorn High School in Pietersburg, as did my mom, which is where my parents met.

My brothers both played 1st XV rugby at Capricorn; Brian was head prefect and David a prefect. I recall their frustration with me when they were home for the holidays and wanted to teach me how to pass a rugby ball but couldn't get me off the tennis court.

They irritated me and I irritated them, and I think we only got on track as brothers when I started playing good rugby at high school and became more mature (I had been a brattish brother). Today we share a great family bond. One thing they did get through to me, though, was that I should support the Sharks, as they were big fans.

So the move to Pretoria Boys High was a new chapter for our family. My dad felt that with him moving around the country so much, it would be best for me to go to school in a central location.

Ironically, he was never transferred again, but I will never stop thanking him for sending me to Boys High, because the rugby culture there got me hooked on the sport.

As it is an English school and rugby isn't played at English primary schools in the area, most of the guys in Standard 6 (Grade 8) had never played the game before. Once again the coach lined us up and separated us according to body type, and once again I went straight to tighthead prop.

I was one of a few guys in my year who had actually played rugby, which was just as well because, being slightly older, I had to play in the U14A team where the majority of the guys were in Standard 7 (Grade 9). We had a good season and coaches Eddie Dory and Paul Anthony would have a big influence on my early career because they followed me through the age groups.

In 1994, in Standard 8 (Grade 10), I made the 1st XV, which I was chuffed about, seeing that most guys only make it in matric. My first game was against Jeppe Boys High who, funnily enough, were coached by Jake White. It was his last year of coaching Jeppe through their 'glory years', and I still remember missing out on *veldskool* (bush school) to play this game. I was asked by the school principal if I wanted to go to *veldskool* with the other Standard 8s or stay and play 1st XV rugby. It was an easy decision.

I was 15 when I played that first game and the Jeppe guy I scrummed against, Robbie de Santo, looked about 25. He had stubble coming out of his earlobes, not just his cheeks. We lost, but not badly, and it was quite an exciting occasion. I was just happy to have survived, although I had seen my rear end from many different angles. I remember waking up very stiff the next day and I had roasties on my face from Robbie's stubble. I joked afterwards that his kids had probably been there to watch him play, but I think he was 19 and doing a post-matric. It was quite an experience and things soon got better.

In Standard 9 (Grade 11) we had an excellent year. We had Brian Liebenberg, who would go on to play for France, at wing or fullback, and Darryl Eigner, who's been playing professionally in Italy for six or seven years, at flyhalf.

It was a very good team but we will always be remembered for one severe blot on our copy book: we lost 62-13 to arch-rivals Affies (Afrikaanse Hoër Seunskool), having been up 13-12 at half-time. That nightmare defeat lives with me to this day.

By this stage my tennis racket was starting to gather dust and in my daydreams Wimbledon was giving way to Ellis Park, Eden Park and Twickenham.

A big challenge for any guy who's keen on sport at Boys High is deciding what to play. In the summer you have to choose between water polo and cricket, and I never quite got that right. I played a few games of 1st XI cricket but was mainly in the 2nd XI because I was always juggling between water polo training and cricket practice.

I suppose the main reason that tennis took a back seat is because I realised that team sports were more my scene. And when I finally decided to take rugby seriously, things quickly turned for me. I played for Northern Transvaal (now the Blue Bulls) at the 1995 Craven Week when I was in Standard 9, and again in matric when I also made the SA Schools squad as the second-choice tighthead prop. Richard Kelly, who was the Maritzburg College and SA Schools captain, wore the No 3 jersey. He later got badly injured and was unable to further his career.

That year, my mate Dave Tubb's dad organised us tickets to the World Cup final between the Springboks and All

Blacks. His father fetched us, took us to Ellis Park, left us at the gate and we went and found our seats, right at the top of the grandstand, just left of centre. They were awesome tickets for a mind-boggling occasion. We were beside ourselves. We were supposed to be at our hostel watching the game on TV and there we were in this surreal vibe. It was one of the best days of my life.

I can't say that at that stage I made too much of a mental connection with Francois Pienaar holding up the Webb Ellis Cup after South Africa's 15-12 victory, but what I do recall vividly is how my homework cubicle, from Standard 6 onwards, was plastered with pictures of Springboks such as Francois and Os du Randt. Being a prop, Os was a huge hero to me. Two years later, I was invited to spend the week with the Springboks in Durban as part of the Elite programme that the then South African Rugby Football Union (Sarfu) was running for up-and-coming youngsters. I'd just turned 19 and I spent a week sitting around the table with Os and the other superstars. It was crazy. The pictures in my cubicle had come alive.

In my matric year, after the Craven Week in Stellenbosch, I was approached by scouts from the Natal Sharks. That was a wonderful development as I'd been supporting Natal from my first breath, because of my brothers' influence.

I'd been keen to stay in Pretoria and I'd been accepted into Tukkies (University of Pretoria) to study physiotherapy. But before I enrolled, my dad went to the Blue Bulls and said, 'My son has played SA Schools, he's from Pretoria, all his friends are here, they're going to varsity here. Is there something that you guys can put on the table in order for him to stay?' The very short and direct answer from the Bulls was, 'No'. They said they thought it was best that I took the offer from the Sharks, as they didn't have a place for me there.

Looking back, it was one of the best things they could have done for me. Moving to Durban was awesome, not only from a lifestyle and rugby perspective, but had I stayed in Pretoria

I would have had to deal with politics and it would have been tough trying to get somewhere as an English-speaking prop. With so many big props in that region, I could well have been lost in the herd, so to speak. Moving to Durban certainly enabled me to rise up a lot faster in the rugby circles and get recognised.

4
CUTTING MY SHARK TEETH

My dad bought my grandmother's car for me – an old box-shaped Mazda 323 – piled me into it with all my worldly possessions and gave me a pay-as-you-go cellphone. He escorted me all the way from Rustenburg to Pietermaritzburg, the capital city of KwaZulu-Natal, with me following him in convoy.

The Natal Rugby Union had recruited 12 players from the 1996 Craven Week and enrolled four of us – myself, Shaun Sowerby, Piet 'Spud' Myburgh and Jaco van der Westhuyzen – at the University of Pietermaritzburg.

My first contract with the Natal Sharks was understandably humble, and worked out to about R2 300 a month. When my dad dropped me off, he gave me a short pep talk along the lines of: 'You have a decent wage for an 18-year-old, now learn to budget. You have more than enough, so make it happen. Make sure you have enough money for food and petrol. Good luck, call me if you have a problem.' Then he was gone, and it was hello, big wide world.

He was trying to teach me a lesson, for sure, and having to stand on my own two feet a long way from home made me grow up a lot faster than if I had remained close to the comforts of home. My folks could have offered to subsidise certain things, such as the cellphone, but they didn't and I'm grateful for that in hindsight. Making me 'get on with it' was a valuable life lesson.

However, being accountable for my finances took me a while. I spent the money I earned in the first three months on a sound system for my car, so I didn't learn immediately. Eventually I realised I had to make a plan. I had to save money to buy credit for the phone; I had to buy chow, which was a substantial expense because I eat like a horse; and I had to save money for petrol, which was also a lot because we were driving the 80km from Maritzburg to Durban and back every day.

We got placed into a digs – 5 Poland Road in Maritzburg – with another two guys. It was chaos! We had a maid who cooked for us but we did our own shopping and with us all being growing lads, there wasn't a lot left in our budgets after groceries and petrol. Money was so tight that we would sometimes shoot the toll gate to save R2.50!

We were driving into Durban every day of the week except Sunday for training with the Natal U19s, U21s and the Wildebeest (the union's Vodacom Cup team, now known as the Sharks XV).

Driving in my gran's old car became quite an adventure. Its nickname, the Grizzly, came from the registration plate, GZY 155T (the T stood for Transvaal, that's how old the car was). It was pretty cramped in there with four beasts and after a while the front passenger seat had taken so much strain that we took it out, creating a little conference centre. I'd be in the driver's seat, Spuddy sat with his back to the cubby hole and his legs between Shaun's because the two of them were so tall, and Jaco sat behind me because he was the smallest.

In 1997, we were all 18 and playing for Natal U21 and the Wildebeest, so we were spending all our time in Durban.

Zero happened with our education. One of my few regrets is that I never got the chance to apply myself to my BCom degree (I was going to take the first year to decide whether to go into marketing or accounting). I spent seven months registered at varsity but in that time I went on SA U19, SA U21 and Natal U21 tours. I hadn't physically been at varsity.

I remember writing an accounting multiple-choice exam on the same day that Pretoria Boys High were playing Affies. The game was on TV and I didn't have a clue what was going on in the exam, so I just guessed the answers. I then walked out, found a pub, and watched the game.

In the end, I phoned my parents and said I was wasting someone's money by attending university (luckily it wasn't theirs, I think it was the varsity's). It really was a waste because I couldn't be studying in Maritzburg if I was spending all my time in Durban or on tour.

The four of us were in exactly the same boat, because we knew we had a chance to be professional rugby players. We decided to move to Durban and give rugby a full crack.

In the end, it worked out well for all of us. Spud is still playing rugby professionally in France and is the only one of the four who hasn't played senior international rugby. Shaun got a Test cap for the Springboks and is now one of the highest-profile players in France, and Jaco played 32 Tests for the Boks and is now making good money playing in Japan. So, looking back, we made the right decision.

When I was mulling it over, my parents said to me: 'Well, you're a grown man now, you need to make this decision on what you have in front of you. You've got an opportunity to study and an opportunity to be a rugby player.' So I thought, 'Well, I'm 18, it's gotta be rugger!'

We moved to Durban and stayed in a flat in Umgeni Park for about a year. During this time I became good friends with Butch James, Pieter Dixon and Trevor 'Bennie' Boynton (all of whom had attended Maritzburg College) and we moved into a digs together.

Butchie and I hit it off really well from the start and are still great friends to this day. His rise to fame is interesting because he had humble beginnings. He wasn't a regular in his school 1st XV and was a better cricketer than rugby player. He had no contract and was surviving on his match fees for the Wildebeest, so at R600 a game he made R2 400 a month if he played all the matches. That wasn't enough for his rent and food (and let's not forget that he can be a thirsty fellow), so he got a part-time job with a mate of his, Josef Solmes, who supplied flour to pizza places. It required him to load and deliver sacks of flour, so he would do this all day and then arrive at training looking like a white ghost. When he started to sweat at practice, the flour turned to dough, which was very funny.

My first year out of school proved to be an astonishing one. It actually started in December 1996 when I missed half of my matric holiday to go on tour to Wales with the Natal U21 side. When I returned, I moved to the University of Pietermaritzburg, then went on an SA U19 tour to Argentina, came back and won the U21 domestic competition (we beat Jake White's Golden Lions in the final).

While that U21 season was still on the go, Ian McIntosh, the legendary Natal coach, came over to a training session and called me aside.

'How much do you weigh?' he asked.

'I'm 111kg,' I replied.

'Do you think you're ready to play in the Currie Cup? Would you be scared?'

'Hell no, I won't be scared, sir!'

'Good, come train with us.'

The Sharks were short of players in the front row because Robbie Kempson had been suspended and Adrian Garvey was injured. Dave Morkel was called up to start at tighthead for the match against Western Province at Kings Park and I was the cover on the bench. When I got on, I was introduced to my backside by Springbok Garry Pagel.

I thought it was going to be a one-off appearance in the senior team, because they had temporarily been short of numbers, but when Robbie came back the next week, Mac dropped Dave straight out of the 22 and kept me on the bench for the game against the British & Irish Lions.

All of this was completely crazy for me. When I got on the field against the Lions, there were only a few minutes left but that was hardly the point. What a mind-boggling two weeks it had been – first my Sharks debut, then I was up against the famous red jerseys. I was in a dream world. I was 18, and a year earlier I had been in the middle of matric.

After that match, Lions tighthead prop Dai Young asked if I wanted to swap jerseys and I replied: 'Please understand, this is the first Natal jersey that I can keep [it was embroidered] and it's a very special thing, so for me to give it to you would be disrespectful to the Sharks. I'd love to swap but I can't.' He was a little taken aback and returned to their change room and obviously told the tale, because while I was getting changed, Mac told me there was a Lions player asking for me outside the change room.

It was Jason Leonard, who had been on the bench that day. He had a packet containing his Lions jersey that he had played in that afternoon and he said: 'I heard about your story, I know your jersey means a lot to you so I'd like you to have mine. I wish you all the best for your career.'

I couldn't believe it, he certainly didn't have to do that. I was brand new on the block, a complete unknown who might never have played another minute for the Sharks, and here was this England front-row legend – who would go on to win 119 Test caps – knocking on my door. I was flabbergasted at this generous gesture from a great player to a total nobody.

In 2000, when I started my first Test at hooker against England, at Twickenham, Leonard was in the front row.

After the match I put my Bok jersey into a plastic bag and approached him at the post-game reception. 'You might not remember me but I'd like to return a favour,' I said. 'Here's my jersey from today's game.'

We've been friends ever since. For me, it's a great rugby story. I just wish there was more of this camaraderie in the professional era.

At this time in 1997, the SA U21 trials were taking place in Pretoria and I was flown in for the latter stages. A lot of guys had already been eliminated from the trials and when I arrived at the Loftus B field they had progressed to playing the first of four chukkas (periods) of 20 minutes each with all the probable combinations. I wasn't under pressure to perform, as I was just happy to be there and saw it as a good opportunity. I was given two of the three chukkas that were left and scored two tries, which is probably not the criteria on which to select a prop, but it made an impression and I was picked. The captain was Bob Skinstad and there were future stars in Breyton Paulse, Grant Esterhuizen, Joggie Viljoen and Hottie Louw.

To summarise a scarcely believable first year out of school, I played for Natal U19, Natal U21, the Wildebeest, SA U19, SA U21 and earned three caps for the Sharks (two in the Currie Cup and one against the touring Lions).

In 1998 I was getting closer to the senior side and played a lot more Currie Cup games. I was the fourth-choice prop in the Sharks' Super 12 squad behind Ollie le Roux, Adrian and Robbie, and when none of those guys got injured, Mac had no cause to call on me. And that was alright. I was only 19 and just pleased to be in a squad of superstars coached by a legend.

My recollections of Mac are the same, I think, as those of any other player who spent time under him. He was passionate and very firm. When I was younger, I was quite fearful of him because he had a good rapport with the senior guys and he would play on that in how he treated the junior guys. He never ridiculed anyone, but he could certainly put you in your place.

At my first practice I dropped a pass, so he blew the whistle and yelled: 'Smit, is this your first practice? It could be your last, you prick.' The senior okes burst out laughing and I felt like an absolute twit. But Mac was never malicious. He's one of those guys who are just so passionate about the game.

I remember him sitting us down in 1997 after our captain's practice before the U21 domestic final against the Golden Lions. He explained that playing in a final is about dealing with pressure, and the only thing to worry about is doing the basics first. If things went badly, he added, we should concentrate even harder on the basics, and then the game would invariably turn for us. That stood out for me. I never forgot that advice, and still follow it.

Because of his passion, every player he has ever coached loves him. You won't meet a guy who would say anything negative about him.

Mac was highly competitive, he still is. He should be sitting at home with his pipe and slippers but he remains heavily involved in the game, whether it's working on new laws or selecting the Springboks. He's just an ultimate rugby man.

Mac didn't coach me for long – he retired after the 1999 season – so I was surprised when I got a call from him the following year ahead of my first Test cap. He said: 'With you I always felt that it was a question of when, not if. Well done, master.' That meant a lot to me. He had no need to call, but he did, and he had coached so many good players in his time.

5

LIVING THE DREAM

In 1998 – my first full-time year at the Natal Sharks – I had the feeling that the senior players were sussing me out to see if I had what it took after Jaco van der Westhuyzen had failed to make an impact at flyhalf in his first few games. He was the first of our little foursome to have been given a chance, so when I was the next one to come through, I was watched with reservation.

I think I proved myself at training and I wasn't the kind of guy who was going to make a big noise and be *windgat* (arrogant). I just did as much as I could without getting in anyone's way. I carried bags, moved cones – and said as little as possible.

I was star-struck at every Sharks practice session. There I was training with players I'd hung pictures of on my cubicle door, so it was amazing just to be there. They soon accepted me, probably because I was so willing and respectful.

Robbie Kempson helped me a lot technically as a prop. I think he saw a fellow English-speaker coming through and was happy to take me under his wing.

But I soon found myself involved in the team politics, because fellow front rankers Ollie le Roux and Chris Rossouw were in their prime, and in terms of political clout they were a formidable combination.

At that stage they were more than willing to help me because by the 1999 season I was the only tighthead at the union. They realised that they needed to make a plan and helped me a heck of a lot. I learnt plenty from Chris, who had played hooker for the Boks in the 1995 World Cup final, and from an established Bok in Ollie. But as soon as I moved to hooker the assistance dried up.

During the 2000 Super 12, Jake White – then a Sharks assistant coach – had a brainwave that I should move from tighthead prop to hooker. He felt I was being constrained at prop and that I could offer the team more as a hooker. He pointed out that the Springboks had no depth at hooker and that I would make the side a lot sooner if I changed. He was right – six months after playing my first game at hooker for the Sharks, I made my Test debut.

The scrummaging part of the transition wasn't a problem. It would have been a different story if I'd moved in the other direction – from hooker to prop. It helped that I knew from my experience as a prop what attacking hookers could do to make my life difficult.

The throwing in was the biggest and most nerve-wracking challenge. I was fortunate in that I had done a fair amount of throwing while helping my mate and Natal U21 hooker Pieter Dixon. I did the catching but watched his technique and threw the ball back to him the same way, so I had a bit of a head start in that department. I then spent hour after hour aiming the ball through a hoop and learning to vary and control the trajectory accurately.

I soon became public enemy No 1 among the Sharks' front-row fraternity. I remember a scrumming session in which I was being experimented with as hooker, and Ollie, Chris and Brent Moyle seemed to conspire against me (Brent unwittingly so). When they were the front-row unit they hit the machine ferociously and it surged backwards because they were giving everything. But when I came in with Ollie and Brent, and we crouched and they'd say 'engage', Brent and I would go forward but Ollie would hold back and there would be a noticeably lesser impact. This was Ollie's way of telling me that I needed to know my place.

Ollie and Chris became a poisonous collaboration against a number of younger guys, especially on the disastrous Super 12 tour of 2000 under Hugh Reece-Edwards.

One night on tour, Ollie and Chris paid a visit to myself and Craig Davidson's room and said, 'You guys must stop causing shit, you're causing a rift in the team.' We looked at them like they were a pair of Martians. We were the new kids on the block, content to park off in our room and play PlayStation. We certainly weren't out to ruffle any feathers, as we'd just got there. Those guys taught me a lot about what not to do in a team environment.

What made it difficult for me with Ollie, and later so disappointing, was that he had been one of my heroes. Ollie was a massive brand – people would scream his name – and it was hugely inspirational for me to be playing with him and Chris when I was at tighthead prop.

In my early days at the Sharks, Ollie was still manageable because the *ou manne* (old men), like Gary Teichmann, Mark Andrews, André Joubert, Henry Honiball and Steve Atherton were still there.

They were the big, big dogs and Ollie was deferential to them. There was still a chain of respect in the team because those guys had served their time and not even Ollie would challenge them.

During that period, Ollie was a guy you wanted to be around. He was friendly and helpful, a cool guy where you thought, 'If I'm going to be a professional rugby player I want to be like Ollie. He drives a Jeep, he's on TV, he's the epitome of cool.'

I think that because he didn't get along very well with the senior guys, when he saw a young guy come in he would pull him in as close as he could. It was company for him and it was somebody who would dig him.

The senior guys then left en masse and Ollie became the senior statesman, which wasn't good for his personality, unfortunately, because suddenly he was demanding respect rather than just playing rugby and earning it on the pitch. Before this, I'd have followed him over hot coals. These issues spilt over from the rugby context into my personal life.

Ollie was sponsored by a motor industry mover and shaker called Archie Sinclair, and with me being a car freak, I got drawn into Ollie's relationship with Archie.

The three of us ended up going into business together, and we started up the American Toy Store in Umhlanga Rocks near Durban. At the time I was warned against going into this business but I couldn't help myself. All I saw were the cars and I thought it would be the coolest thing ever. It actually went alright for a while but then my partners came in and said we should take it a step further and get a shared dealership.

We did, and a lot of dodgy things ensued. Archie was supposed to run everything but he was dealing with his other businesses and was never there. Nor was Ollie, but the two of them were drawing salaries.

That was also the year that Ollie was fighting the Sharks because they chose not to renew his contract on the grounds that he was unfit (more on that later).

To cut a long story short, the business went down. The bank wanted to foreclose and Ollie and I had to write big cheques to stop that from happening. We had to cover Archie's share, and he still hasn't repaid us. It took a lot of pain and suffering and a serious financial cost to get out of the situation.

But what a lesson it was. Nowadays, when younger guys want to rush into business ventures that they haven't really thought through, and with partners they don't know too much about, I share my experience with them.

When I was a teenage apprentice at the Sharks, I knew nothing of the ways of the world. I was being educated by the senior guys. If I wanted advice on tax I'd go to them, if I wanted to know what to do when buying a house, or who I should speak to about buying a car, I spoke to them.

It's where I learnt a lot of my life skills. Some guys gave me good advice and others gave me bad advice, and sadly I did listen to the latter, who perhaps weren't clever enough to provide good advice.

On the rugby field, there was inspiration everywhere. I wanted to be a Shark in the mould of senior players like Gary and Mark. They epitomised everything that I wanted to be. They set a good example on and off the field.

I revered Gary for how he captained the Sharks. I had captained a lot in my youth but Gary had unique attributes. As a leader he didn't feel the need to say too much and he didn't have to be in front of every camera. He just did his job and everyone respected him. He had a massive influence on the team without ever having to enforce it. He was just Gary. That's what I enjoyed most.

Much later in my career, when I started having the same kind of responsibility that Gary had as a leader, I recalled the kind of things he did and how valuable they were, the fact that he had the respect of everyone, and that people followed him because of the way he behaved on and off the field. I drew a lot from what I appreciated about Gary as a captain when I was finding my way in leadership.

Meanwhile, Mark was the most gifted player I'd ever seen. He was phenomenally talented and a wonderful team guy. We'd sit for hours after training, eating supper at Kings Park and listening to him tell war stories. He loved it and we lapped it up.

It amazes me that I played with those senior players for only two or three years, but I'm still in contact with most of them, and for me that's a wonderful thing. They still care deeply about the Sharks, which goes to show how passionate they are about the team and what type of people they are.

Those times were surreal. To think that at the age of 17 I'd had no thoughts of being a professional rugby player, but then at 18, 19 and 20 I was learning my trade from some of South Africa's greatest players.

Many of these guys were 1995 World Cup winners and, of course, they played a part in Natal being the so-called 'Team of the '90s' when the union won the Currie Cup four times.

I would attend training and have to pinch myself, it was unbelievable. During that time, each day was an amazing experience. I was playing more, and getting better contracts because my game was improving. I realised that I could make a good career out of rugby.

In 1999, Jake and I hooked up for the first time when I captained SA U21 in the Sanzar-UAR tournament (the forerunner to the U21 World Cup) in Argentina. He was our assistant coach under head coach Eric Sauls.

When I was in matric, Jake had approached my dad with an offer of a place for me at the Golden Lions academy he was overseeing, but the offer wasn't as good as the one at the Sharks, and in any case, I had my heart set on going to Durban and playing for that awesome team.

Our paths had crossed in '97 when our Natal U21 side beat Jake's Lions in the final. In the league game in Durban they thrashed us 30-12, but most people only remember the infamous free-for-all fight that involved substitutes and spectators joining from the sidelines. A few weeks later, we won the final at Newlands, 22-17.

Beating New Zealand 27-25 in the U21 final in Buenos Aires was an incredible achievement. Jake really did run the show there. He was just so organised. He brought to the U21 team what the Boks had been doing the year before, as he was a technical assistant under head coach Nick Mallett. Jake had analysis systems and video sessions that were new to that level of rugby. He gave the U21s the power to be a professional team within a short period. If you go through that New Zealand U21 team list and see how many of those players became All Blacks, you realise just what a strong outfit they were.

Even back in 1999, it was clear Jake had an excellent understanding of the game and a very good rapport with players. But to this day I say his greatest talent is his ability to choose a balanced rugby team. Selection is his greatest gift, and it started way back in those days.

Jake demands a lot from his players, and at U21 level he identified that I was a leader of the future, and certainly of that group. That was to my advantage because that's where I started learning how to lead professional players.

When I was breaking into rugby in 1997, '98 and '99, I was 19, 20, and 21 years old respectively – the prime party years. My mates were cutting loose and partying up a storm while I was having to limit my *jolling* to Saturday nights after games.

I was living the dream with rugby's rock stars. I was going out with the likes of André, Gary, Ollie and Robbie. These guys had enormous off-field presence wherever we went.

At the same time I was maintaining my long-distance relationship with Roxy, who was studying at Tukkies. Make no mistake, I didn't shy away from a party, but over the decade or so that we have been together I have kept on the straight and narrow, despite temptation.

People ask me about the women who are involved in rugby and I think it's important to talk about it because it's such a massive temptation for sportsmen and celebrities. It's an easy thing to fall into, and if you play rugby in this country for a decent team, it's always an issue. One thing I'm proud of is that while I used to enjoy the nightlife as much as the next guy and have the biggest *jol*, I kept it tidy.

Early on in my career, we'd get *koevertjies* (envelopes), as we used to call them, with R1 000 cash inside. We'd go out with our mates and spend it all on booze and have a huge party, and only wake up on Sunday afternoon, because that's generally what you do at that age.

I'm often asked about celebrity sex, drugs and rock 'n roll … It happens in rugby circles, for sure, for those who choose it.

Rugby players can lead a decadent life because all the ingredients are there – good money and celebrity status. The birds throw themselves at the majority of the players because they want to capture some of the limelight.

But of all the things that I did do wrong, the one thing I never fell prey to was 'loose' women. I started dating Roxy when I was 18 and we were married eight years later. During the time we were dating I made a conscious decision not to go down that route.

As a rugby player, whether you're an ugly tighthead or the good-looking try-scoring winger, you're going to get offers. Every high-profile rugby player in South Africa has to decide how he's going to handle it. Some guys, to their credit, stay single for the very reason that they don't want to be unfaithful and dishonest. Some guys try their best and they get it mostly right.

I must say, I've seen over time how the new generation is becoming better behaved than the old school, in that they stay single and so can't be accused of cheating. I suppose guys know that I'll hold it against them if they act dishonestly, so they either hide it from me or they don't do it. The point that I make to them is that it's a conscious decision, because it's just too easy as a rugby player in this country.

This leads into a topic I feel strongly about.

I believe the one thing that has helped me sustain longevity has been the ability to do regular reality checks to remind myself what an artificial place the world can be. I realised early on that stardom isn't the real world.

I was lucky because the two women in my life – my mother and my wife – didn't stand for bullshit and kept me sensible, but I also had a built-in defence mechanism which kept on telling me to take it all with a pinch of salt.

From the very beginning it registered with me that not everyone gets to go and blow R1 000 at a bar at the age of 19. I can only think that's because of how I was brought up. My dad would sit me down with a new tennis racket and say: 'This is what it cost. Look after it, enjoy it, but don't take it for granted.'

I've seen players getting so worked up about the public's opinion of them, and the truth is that for as long as you play rugby in South Africa – for the Springboks or one of the big provinces – people are going to watch everything you do. You can't want to be a rugby player at that level and not expect this to happen.

The press are very similar to the public in this regard. The two feed each other. The public get their opinions from what they read and what they see. I think rugby players' biggest battle with the media is the very human problem of finding it difficult to take criticism but easy to accept praise.

6

BULLETPROOF BOK

The new millennium could not have started on a worse note for the Sharks. Ian McIntosh had retired after the 32-9 loss to the Golden Lions in the 1999 Currie Cup final, along with Gary Teichmann, Henry Honiball and André Joubert. The 'Team of the '90s' was history and poor Hugh Reece-Edwards – the new head coach who had been Mac's long-serving assistant – was on a hiding to nothing with the imports he was given for the Super 12 (more on that later). It was a disaster, we came stone last and my eyes were opened as to how ugly rugby can get when a team falls apart.

But for me, the black clouds of the Super 12 gave way to glorious sunshine when Springbok coach Nick Mallett called me up for the mid-year Test against Canada in East London.

The squad announcement was made on TV and I watched it in a bed and breakfast opposite Loftus, which I found highly ironic as my career had been fast-tracked when the Bulls closed the door on me. I'd gone up to Pretoria to visit Roxy and brought our new puppy Bob with me, so the three of us sat there watching the telly with great excitement, and suddenly my name was on the screen. I remember feeling 10 feet tall, completely bulletproof, and very proud.

My Test debut was against low-key opposition, but being part of the Springboks for the first time was everything I had dreamt it would be.

My family, Roxy and close friends flew in for the occasion. All week I had been terrified of throwing the ball into the lineout, and Roxy told me I had talked in my sleep on the Friday night, going over the calls.

I came on as a blood replacement for Charl Marais for a short spell in the first half and returned to the field with about 10 minutes to go. The first thing I had to do was throw the ball in. In it went … straight into the hands of Phil Murphy, the Canada No 8. It wasn't the start I had hoped for in Test rugby but I guess it's how you finish that counts!

I came on six times that season as a substitute for Charl – against Canada, against Australia in the Mandela Plate Test and then in all four Tri-Nations games.

It was a difficult and tense time for the Boks because the knives were out for Nick. The game's administrators had their issues with him and we could sense they were looking for an excuse to get rid of him.

I was always a little wary of Nick because he was insanely competitive. I saw it for the first time at a pre-season training camp in Plettenberg Bay. We had a triathlon between four teams and he was manic in his efforts to win at all costs, driving his team on like a man possessed.

During our time in Australia, we stayed on a little island off the Gold Coast, Coran Cove. There was a tennis court, and Nick had heard that I was a keen tennis player, so he chose me as his partner. Heaven help me if I missed a serve or made a mistake. We simply had to clean everybody up 6-0, 6-0, 6-0. When Nick was competing he was crazy, and it was the most pressure I had ever felt in my life. But I enjoyed the fact that he was flipping knowledgeable and passionate.

It's hard for me to say whether his departure as Bok coach was the right or wrong thing for South African rugby, but those who played under him will tell you that he's a very good rugby coach. His results speak for themselves, and the Boks beat the All Blacks 46-40 at Ellis Park a week before he was sacked on trumped up charges of bringing the game into disrepute because of alleged comments about ticket prices.

I thought Nick was good for the Boks but I wonder if he felt the same thing about me, given my big blunder in what would be his last Test, the Tri-Nations match against the Wallabies in Durban in 2000.

I came on for the last four minutes at hooker, and the Aussies took a bloody tighthead off my first and only scrum. They sent the ball wide, set it up a few times, and Corné Krige was penalised at a ruck. Stirling Mortlock then kicked the injury-time penalty to give them a 19-18 win and their first Tri-Nations title.

I felt like an absolute idiot, although there was misfortune involved in that the ball hit a boot and bounced back on their side. It was a freak incident.

This was my first season at hooker. I was only 22 and very inexperienced. I felt guilty because if I'd just hooked that ball, we would have won that game and Nick might have won a reprieve.

I went up to Nick in the change room and apologised but he was beyond worrying about that. He was resigned to the fact that his time was up with the Boks. That change room was a very emotional place. Everybody knew he was gone, and for me, knowing how tense the situation was with him and Sarfu, losing that tighthead was a huge disappointment. I felt like I'd cost the guy his job when I could have given him a lifeline. It was a lesson about what Tests can come down to – just one scrum.

In that first season with the Springboks, I was mentored by legends of the game, just as I had been by the seniors at the Sharks.

André Venter was a guy who set an intimidating example. In the week before I wore the Bok No 2 jersey for the first time – the 37-33 win against Argentina in November 2000 – I shared a hotel room with him in Buenos Aires. I was terrified. I was still wet behind the ears and he was a highly respected senior Springbok. I was awestruck.

André made me train in the gym with him and nearly killed me. He was unbelievably strong.

At night when we'd go back to our room, he would have a can of Coke next to his bed with a Bible. I'd get into bed and the TV would be on, but at exactly 9pm he would tell me to switch it off and put the main light out. He would then read out aloud to me from the Bible. After the reading he would say a prayer, open his Coke, drink half of it, and fall asleep by 9:30pm. Every night was exactly the same.

I was a 22-year-old *soutie* living the dream in Durban and while I wouldn't say I was off the rails, it was quite a culture shock to interact with this colossus of a man, this Bok legend with such strong moral fibre. That's just how he lived his life.

I had experienced a taste of his discipline earlier that season at a team-building evening where the drinks were flowing. André wasn't a big drinker, but he would have the odd beer, and here I was, this *soutie* from Durban, with party boys Robbie Kempson and Robbie Fleck charging me up. We were going flat out when Venter pulled me aside.

'*Soutie, wat drink jy* [what are you drinking]?' he asked.

'Vodka, lime and lemonade,' I replied.

'*As jy rugby wil speel, drink jy net bier* [if you want to play rugby, you must only drink beer], no hard tack. OK?!'

I nodded respectfully and immediately switched to beer.

In Jake White's time as Springbok coach, André was the guest at our jersey presentation on two occasions, in 2004 and 2007.

The first occasion was hugely emotional. André had been struck down with a rare, debilitating muscle disease and arrived at our Bloemfontein hotel in a wheelchair. It was the most humbling experience of our careers because we all saw André as the lion, the ultimate Bok warrior, and none more so than Jake. For Jake, André epitomised everything good about a Bok: big, strong, skilful, honest, and hard-working, with the fearless, no-nonsense attitude of a true soldier.

That jersey presentation was the most emotional one I've ever attended. Jake, as usual, introduced the guest, but could barely get a word out, and the tears were flowing. He was struggling to contain his emotions, as were the players, because André was a hero who had trained harder than any Springbok before him and conquered everyone in front of him. I could see it was tough for Jake, but André just smiled at him every now and again and said, '*Moenie* [don't] worry *nie*, Jake.' It was incredibly moving.

I'm not surprised Jake got so choked up because he's one of the most passionate people about Springbok rugby I've ever met. He holds a high regard for the old-school values that have made the Boks such a force: tradition, honesty, loyalty, patriotism and hard work. André Venter epitomised all these qualities.

In late 2000, Harry Viljoen, a mega-wealthy businessman and former scrumhalf for Transvaal, succeeded Nick as Bok coach. Harry was like a breath of fresh air, and I still believe that he could have been very successful if he had hung in there and not taken the press so seriously.

Harry wanted to lift standards and shatter the Springboks' reputation of being the Neanderthals of world rugby.

One of the tricks to coaching the Boks is to create an environment that's superior to anything at provincial level. The player arriving at a Springbok camp should immediately think: 'Wow! OK, now I've got to up my game, these guys have got laptops, an eye coach, and a travelling gym … I had better pull finger.'

This was Harry's game and he encouraged a businesslike approach. For example, he didn't want players yelling out numbers in the team bus to show they were present. 'My directors don't scream "number" and act like schoolboys at board meetings,' he said.

Harry also believed the players should enjoy individuality in the way they dressed on tour. We became the snappiest dressers in rugby, and thought we were pretty cool in our chic leather jackets.

Unfortunately it didn't work out with Harry and after a year he quit abruptly. One of the problems was that the Boks were rebuilding after the Mallett era and Harry didn't have the type of players he needed for the attacking game he wanted to play. And when the press turned on him, he thought, 'I don't need this,' and went back to his businesses.

At the Sharks, Rudolf Straeuli took over from Reece in mid-2000 for the Currie Cup. He was just what the team needed after a period of chaos.

Poor old Reece. He had no chance. The last vestiges of the great Natal 'Team of the '90s' had just retired along with Mac, and in came a bunch of mercenaries recruited from the interior, who had no idea of the Natal rugby ethos or any interest in it.

What made it worse for Reece was that he was undermined by some of the older Sharks. Ollie le Roux and Chris Rossouw had a strong relationship as they played loosehead prop and hooker respectively, they were also in business together, and they wanted to control the team.

They ruthlessly overpowered Reece and then did a dirty on Wayne Fyvie by creating a rift in the team, with one faction against Wayne. This was treacherous because he was a son of Natal, a legend who put his body on the line in every match he played. Today he limps and the scars on his face are testimony to the total commitment he gave to the Sharks. They ousted him in a season.

When Ollie and Chris came into the room I was sharing with Craig Davidson on that horrible Super 12 tour of 2000 and admonished us for getting ahead of ourselves, they also said we must be careful because they were in charge, even though Wayne was captain, and if Craig was at scrumhalf, they were the guys he should pass to.

Rudolf restored discipline and swept out a lot of extra baggage from the squad. A new breed of talented Sharks came through in Shaun Sowerby, Trevor Halstead, Butch James, Stefan Terblanche, Warren Britz and Craig, and there were still senior players around like Ollie and Mark Andrews.

Butch and Trevor were at their blockbusting best and with them crashing over the advantage line our forwards were able to get into the game by providing support.

We pulled ourselves up from the Super 12 canvas to fight for the Currie Cup title that year, but lost the final 25-15 to Western Province in Durban, and the 'chokers' tag that would haunt us for years was born.

We had a simple yet effective game plan, and the following year it got us into the Super 12 final against the Brumbies in Canberra. We lost 36-6, but it was a remarkable turnaround after coming last in 2000.

I enjoyed playing under Rudolf. He was tough and he was hard work, and while he's never had too many fans, he was always good to me. He always backed me, big time. Some guys felt he was dishonest with them, but he was nothing but straight with me.

In 2001 we also got to the Currie Cup final, but lost 29-24 to Province at Newlands. I was Sharks captain that day after Mark Andrews' late withdrawal. It started well enough for me when I scored the first try, but I got knocked out just before half-time and had to remain in the change room for a few minutes after the break to gather my thoughts, and when I returned to the field, Province had scored two tries. Game over.

It was a good year, but I had now lost four consecutive finals – 1999 Currie Cup, 2000 Currie Cup, 2001 Super 12, 2001 Currie Cup – and was starting to take it personally.

7

TWO TEAMS IN TROUBLE

I wouldn't get to experience another final for some time, although the Sharks did make the decider of the 2003 Currie Cup – which was played without the World Cup Boks – where they got whipped 40-19 by the Blue Bulls at Loftus.

The feast was over for the Sharks and the famine had started in the very first month of the 2002 Super 12 when Rudolf Straeuli took the team on what would be his farewell tour. He was appointed as the new Bok coach midway through the trip, with Kevin Putt to take over at the Sharks when the squad returned to Durban. Sadly, in each tour game we got a major *klap* and while we didn't know it at the time, it kind of set the tone for Rudolf's tenure at the Boks.

We were in the Sharks' team room at the Coogee Beach Hotel in Sydney when CEO Brian van Zyl brought in Putty, who had been coaching in Ireland, to make the announcement to the players. Quite a few of us had played with Putty – including myself, Ollie le Roux and Mark Andrews – and everybody knew him as the scrumhalf general who had made the Natal 'Team of the '90s' tick. Rudolf was supposed to introduce Putty to the squad but before he could speak, Ollie shouted from the back, like he would have done when they were team-mates: 'Why don't you tell us about that time when you and [player X] staggered in at 3am!' Ollie wasn't trying to be derogatory – he just wanted to break the ice – but Putty was mortified and said sternly: 'That is *not* appropriate!' It was the most awkward introduction I've ever experienced – it went down like a lead balloon and was a reminder of the pitfalls there can be when a former player returns to coach his old team.

For that horror Super 12 tour we were mostly based at Wollongong, a depressing mining town in New South Wales, and travelled from there to our various matches. It was a shocker of a place.

Rudolf often had these misguided little plans to keep guys away from the bright lights, but they were so transparent to the players, and a mistake because it had a negative effect on morale.

As a player, Rudolf was a happy-go-lucky bloke – he was fun, a prankster, a character who built team spirit. But as a coach he seemed afraid that the players would behave like he had, so he was very conservative. There were curfews, guards at the door taking notes of times when people came in, etc.

This over-the-top discipline has the opposite effect, because it annoys players. They see they are being kept away from the enjoyable places and treated like kids, and if you start losing your matches, the situation is compounded because you are stuck in Dullsville. We'd lose a match on that tour (we actually lost all four) and the guys would drown their sorrows (not overly but you need a few pots after a defeat). Of course, Rudolf would find out and the next morning we'd get sorted out on the training field.

One Sunday morning, on a cricket field next to the hotel in Wollongong, Rudolf got stuck into us to such an extent that the locals out walking their dogs gathered to watch in

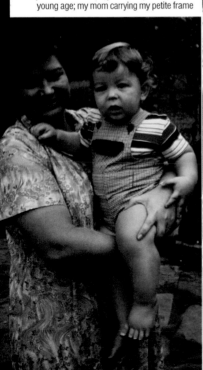

Clockwise from top left: Me as a baby; with Mina, my African mother; my love of toys started at a young age; my mom carrying my petite frame

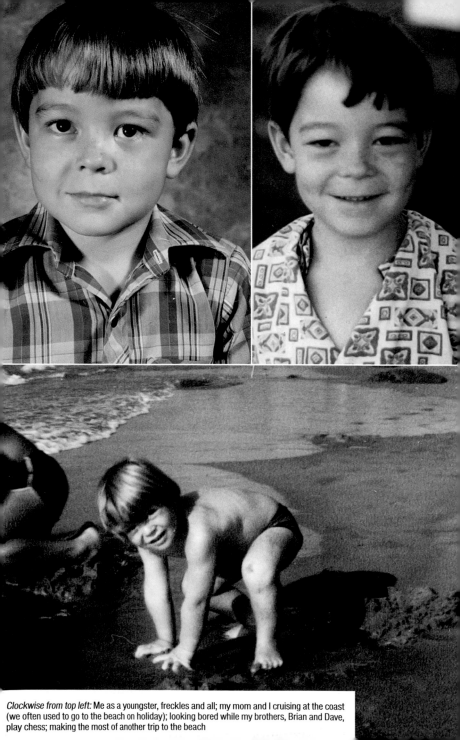

Clockwise from top left: Me as a youngster, freckles and all; my mom and I cruising at the coast (we often used to go to the beach on holiday); looking bored while my brothers, Brian and Dave, play chess; making the most of another trip to the beach

This page (clockwise from top): It's true, I have met Father Christmas; yes, our mommy did dress us; even by my eighth birthday I was crazy about cars, look at that cake!
Opposite page: A family meal with the Grahams (my mom's side of the family) – my aunt Les, her mom Granny Gwillim and my cousins Laurel and Mathew; in my Martin Primary and cubs uniforms

Clockwise from top left: The three Smit brothers with an '80s vibe going on; with our Uncle Kevin (he was a legendary guy who sadly passed away aged 24 in a car accident when I was in Standard 6); Fields Primary's U13A cricket team (I'm standing on the far right and my best mate Shane Chorley is sitting on the far right); My dad and I (wow, that's a serious *kuif!*)

FIELDS PRIMARY SCHOOL
CRICKET U/13A 1990

This page: Fields Primary's U13A rugby team (with Shane Chorley next to the coach, Tommy Malan); with my mom and Gran Graham before my first day at Pretoria Boys High
Opposite page: Wearing my Northern Transvaal Craven Week blazer; me in the famous candy stripe rugby jersey of Pretoria Boys High; holding a trophy that I won as a North West tennis player (at this stage my dream of playing at Wimbledon was still alive!)

FIELDS PRIMARY SCHOOL
RUGBY U/13 A   1990

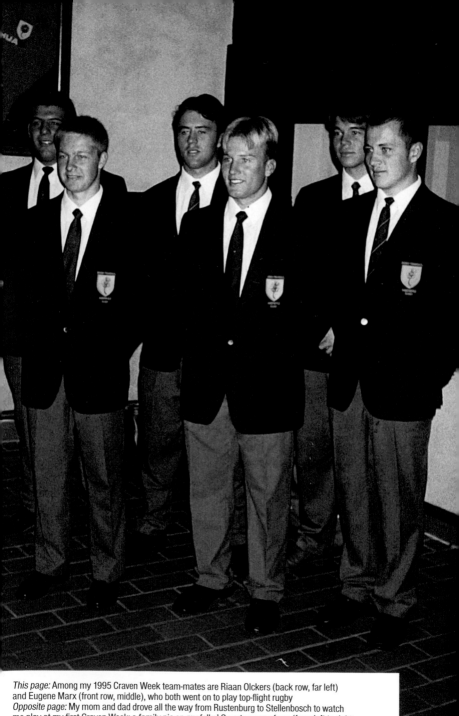

This page: Among my 1995 Craven Week team-mates are Riaan Olckers (back row, far left) and Eugene Marx (front row, middle), who both went on to play top-flight rugby
Opposite page: My mom and dad drove all the way from Rustenburg to Stellenbosch to watch me play at my first Craven Week; a family pic on my folks' Swartruggens farm (from left to right: Brian's wife, Danute; Brian; my mom; my neice Danian; my dad; Dave; Roxy and me)

This page (from top to bottom): My mistress, a 1965 Ford Mustang Coupe (Gav Vereges played a big role in her makeover); Christmas is always a massive thing in our family (from left to right: Dave; Liz, who's a family friend; Brian, me and Roxy; another family Christmas in Rustenburg *Opposite page (clockwise from top left):* My first boy, Bob (a legend); Roxy's first boy, Toby; me with all three of our dogs (the dark brown one is Daisy); Roxy and me in Bath

Opposite page: Roxy and me over the years
This page: The happy couple on our wedding
day at the Collisheen Estate in Ballito, 2004

My family is the most important thing in my life – here are a few of my favourite photos of Roxy, Emma and Tyron. I was at the birth of both of my kids (Emma, below right, and Tyron, bottom left corner). In the photo directly below I'm holding my neice, Danian

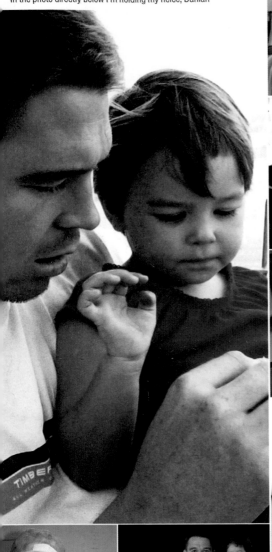

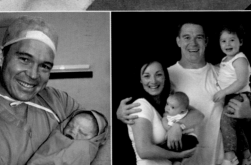

amazement. We did army-style exercises, loads of running, press-ups, etc. After the first two sets, Ricardo Loubscher went to Rudolf and said, 'My groin is tight and if I carry on it's going to snap.' Rudolf replied: 'No problem, go to [team manager] Piet Strydom's room, he has your ticket home.' A day later Ricky was back in South Africa, and I reckon there were quite a few blokes who envied him.

During this *opvok* (physical punishment), Rudolf was trying to toughen us up, to teach us to stick it out. Then he came to me and said he was done with the players, but he wanted me to go to them and recommend that we do a voluntary set to show that whatever the coach dished out to us, we had more in the tank. So I went back to the circle and said: 'Well done guys, but let's not end like this. Let's show Rudolf that we are tougher than he thinks, and do an extra set.' I can laugh now but I recall an anguished shout from AJ Venter: 'John, don't be a bloody hero!' We did it but it was ridiculous, and not the way to motivate a team after a loss. Rudolf always had the best intentions but was often misguided.

There were occasions, though, when the old Rudolf would come out, as was the case on the eve of the 2000 Super 12 final in Canberra. During that season, Butch James and I established a tradition of drinking a milkshake on the Friday night before a game. I thought I'd skip the milkshake before the final, but Butchie went ahead and ordered his through room service. A few minutes later, the doorbell rang, and when Butch opened the door, Rudolf was standing there with the milkshake on a tray and a big grin on his face (he had intercepted the waiter). Without missing a beat, Butch said, 'Smitty, your milkshake's here!' Rudolf came in and the three of us shot the breeze for ages.

Back in South Africa, my season soon went from bad to disastrous. Up until that Super 12 I couldn't have scripted a better start to my career. It had been a pleasure cruise but in sport there's inevitably an iceberg or two lurking beneath the surface, and mine came in the form of a collision with Juan Smith in our match against the Cats near the end of the Super 12.

I had passed the ball, was hit late and stupidly put my elbow out to break my fall because I had wrenched my shoulder on tour and was nursing an injury. I required surgery on my shoulder ligaments and missed the entire 2002 Test season.

The rehab was a mess although I believe the surgery hadn't been a success to start with. But then I stuffed it up good and proper about three months after the operation during a December holiday in the Transkei with Butchie, Shaun Sowerby, Deon Carstens, Eduard Coetzee and our partners. We were playing touch on the beach when I dived in the sand for the ball and landed awkwardly. Both pins popped out and there went the 2003 Super 12 campaign.

Rudolf instructed Bob Skinstad and me to join an elite rehabilitation group in Cape Town. We both had shoulder injuries yet were part of Rudolf's rather interesting plan to announce four potential captains for the Springboks' 2003 World Cup squad, along with Joost van der Westhuizen and Corné Krige.

I lived in a hotel for six weeks and underwent rehab and special training programmes every single day. I'd hate to know how much money was spent on Bob and me. It was all very flattering but it was also over the top as far as I was concerned, because at that stage there was no way I should have been in line to captain the Boks. I'd only just started captaining the Sharks and I was coming off a serious injury – my realistic objective was to get back on the field, play rugby and get to the World Cup.

Yet I had an inside lane. The coach wanted me to be there, and now he was saying I was one of four possible captains, and he had thrown it open to debate to try and encourage competitiveness between the four of us. It was unrealistic. For a start, the four guys he had chosen were never going to be able to work together.

Rudolf took us on a hunting trip during which he interviewed each of us separately and asked us who we thought should be Bok captain. But we all knew Corné was going to be in charge, and so he should have been. He was the incumbent and he wanted it. It was his time.

Rudolf asked each of us: 'Do you want to be captain?' Joost, Bob and obviously Corné all said yes.

Luckily I was last. I was sitting there thinking, 'The last thing on earth I want at this stage is to be captain. I just want to play rugby.' So I said: 'No, I shouldn't be captain. I don't command enough respect. Corné is the legitimate leader. I'd rather just help the captain and do whatever I can.'

I knew that there was no way I could successfully be the captain. At that stage, any guy other than Joost or Corné was going to struggle as captain. Joost had a major influence on the team simply through his reputation as a great player.

Bob would fall out of the equation, injuring himself again in a comeback game for UCT (University of Cape Town). I did get fit enough to be chosen for the Boks' World Cup squad but fittingly it was Corné who was appointed to lead us in Australia.

And the day the squad was announced to the public, we were put on a bus, and off we went into one of the most infamous chapters in South African rugby history (more on that later).

However, before that Bok squad announcement, we spent three weeks at the High Performance Centre in Pretoria. It was there that I first became aware of how much stuff goes on behind the scenes in the Bok camp and how the captain is intrinsically involved. Up until then my only concerns in life as a rugby player had been eating, training, sleeping, playing, and getting fit and strong. I hadn't really thought too much about things like quotas and transformation. It didn't concern me.

On the second day of the camp, we arrived at training to see a group of players, including Corné, running hills. We were told that there had been disobedience in the ranks and he had to run because he was the captain and should have kept control of the troops.

Geo Cronjé (who had been roomed with Quinton Davids, a coloured player) had changed rooms in order to be together with Fourie du Preez. It's not for me to get into the whole controversy about Geo reportedly not wanting to share with Quinton, because I really had no part in any of that.

By punishing the players I think Rudolf was trying to say that there was a big problem with a white guy not wanting to share a room with a black oke, for whatever reason, and he had to rescue the situation by turning it into an issue that focused on something else.

So it became an issue of who had swapped rooms without permission, because Rudolf had compiled the rooming list, and some players had done their own thing.

Rudolf asked the guys who had swapped rooms and Fourie, Geo, Quinton and Gcobani Bobo (who had originally been roomed with Fourie) put their hands up.

They flipping ran, and ran and ran. It was ugly.

8

KAMP STAALDRAAD

U sually, when a player joins the Bok camp, he's uplifted by an invigorating environment, but this was hardly the case when I joined the Boks in 2003. Guys felt like they were abandoning their home comforts for the survival of the fittest. It was scary. Results had been horrific (we had lost 52-16 to the All Blacks in Pretoria) and the vibe among the guys wasn't 'What can I do for the team?', but 'What can I do to survive in it because this is a World Cup year?'

The Bok camp was a dangerous and unhealthy place, there was no enjoyment, and the World Cup was always going to be a spectacular failure. There was no meaningful and constructive talk about what we could do to win it. There was a lot of hot air about sacrifice and fitness, but with no real conviction. Our campaign was doomed, backs-against-the-wall, let's-hope-for-the-best stuff, but in our hearts we knew we were irredeemably screwed.

I suppose, in Rudolf Straeuli's defence, with 2002 having been so bad results-wise, he felt he had to do something drastic, which brings us to that bus trip into the back of beyond straight after the squad announcement in Pretoria.

Kamp Staaldraad (Camp Barbed Wire) is a contentious issue. The first pictures of naked, distinctly unhappy Bok players broke in the international press on the day of the World Cup final between England and Australia. In terms of public perception, here were our international rivals strutting on the brightest stage in world rugby while the Neanderthal Boks were bumbling about like idiots.

How can I classify Staaldraad? My brothers went to the army, and when they asked me about Staaldraad I told them it sounded like their worst days of basic training. When I told them what we did, they said that kind of stuff had only happened in the more severe army camps. I understand that in the army there was never a fixation on making the troops exercise in their 'birthday suits', and it was terribly degrading for us when pictures and video clips of us naked were spread across the world's media.

I won't kid you, the camp was incredibly tough, so to get through it did give me a sense of achievement, even though the premise of it was skewed. We barely ate or slept, we did stupid things like carry poles and leopard crawl, and got drilled by the instructors. It was obviously supposed to be about breaking us down and then building us up as a team that would stand together, but it didn't achieve any of that. All it did was expose the weak guys who couldn't take the pressure. There were some young guys in our squad, with Derick Hougaard and Schalk Burger only 20.

We went from being announced as World Cup rock stars to being told to report to the bus with a pair of PT shorts, a pair of jocks, a rugby jersey, a gum guard, a hat, running shoes, and socks.

A lot of rubbish has been written and spoken about Kamp Staaldraad, so I'll tell you exactly what happened.

Before we set out, I got some advice from a mate of mine from Durban who was friendly with one of the instructors running the camp. He said that one of the drills required you to bury an egg and cook it underground, underneath a fire, and urinate on the egg so that the moisture cooked it. He told me we would only get one match, so I should smuggle in a lighter, which I did, lodged in the inside of my cap.

After about two-and-a-half hours in the bus, we were nearing Warmbaths (now Bela-Bela) when we were told to put on blindfolds. About 20 minutes later the bus stopped, and we were told to take the blindfolds off and get off the bus. It was pitch black and we were in the middle of nowhere. Then the shouting started.

Instructors, dressed in khaki, screamed at us to get into a formation, but none of us had been to the army so it was a complete mess. Eventually we got into some kind of formation, while these guys laughed their heads off at us. They then told us to get onto a truck that would normally transport cattle or sheep.

Before we climbed on we were searched for contraband, and I thought to myself, 'Holy shit, I've got the Bic lighter on the inside of my cap.'

We were told to strip naked in the road, in the middle of the bush. The okes hesitated in taking their kit off which resulted in such venomous obscenities that we realised it was no joke.

There we were, 30 okes standing naked and being searched, basically spreading our cheeks and opening our arms. The instructors started going through all our clothes, but somehow they missed the lighter strapped inside my cap.

After 10 minutes of marching down the road in the dark we were stopped alongside a bunch of poles at the side of the road. What followed was horrible. There were two guys to a pole and off we went down the road. Every now and again the instructors would tell us to swap partners – 'Poles down, swap!' Victor Matfield and Bakkies Botha would just find another pole, because they are the same height and they wanted to stay together, but the instructors spotted their little trick and our punishment was to leopard crawl through the fire brush.

It was ridiculous, but typical army stuff about everyone paying the price if individuals stepped out of line.

The theme of Staaldraad was that if an individual stuffed up, he would have to watch while the rest were punished with push-ups, sit-ups, or whatever. 'Don't let your *maatjie* [mate] down,' they kept on saying.

At that stage we were surprised at what was going on, and obviously knew it was no joke, but no one had a clue how long it was going to go on for.

Werner Greeff had made the Springbok squad by the skin of his teeth because of an ankle injury. He had arrived at the camp wearing an ankle brace and was marching in the dark with a tractor tyre when he stepped into a hole and hurt his ankle. He completely lost it. The whole party came to a halt and one of the instructors said: '*Wat is jou probleem* [what is your problem]?' He said '*Nee, nee* [no, no]', took off his ankle guard, threw it into the bush and added: '*As dit breek, dan breek dit* [if it breaks, then it breaks]'.

About an hour-and-a-half after that, we entered a little enclosure in the bush. Dawn was breaking and Rudolf was now on the scene (up until then we had only been with the instructors). He sat on a little ledge and on the ground before us were boxing headgear and gloves.

'Form a circle,' he said. '*Ja*, we need to get to know each other. There are a lot of rivalries here, and in the World Cup only certain guys can start. Players will be competing for the same positions. We need to understand the dynamics of that, so we must fight.'

First up was Thinus Delport against Werner. Now, Werner, who can be a difficult fellow at the best of times, had just thrown his toys and his sense of humour was gone. He's a good but tough guy, who's had a lot of personal upheaval in his life, and doesn't take any shit. We could see he wasn't impressed with this camp at all and now the first fight was between the fullbacks.

Werner wasn't really interested in fighting at first but then he took a few shots from Thinus and realised, 'OK, I'm not really proving anything, I'm just getting a *klap*.' He got angry and that's when the fight really started.

The rest of us watched the two of them climb into each other like there was no tomorrow, with the bout lasting three minutes. Jaws dropped. Selborne Boome, our quiet intellectual, thought he was in a time warp. He went to De Wet Barry and asked, 'Is this for real?'

That was the typical type of match-up but there were also some strange ones. After the likes of Dale Santon against Lawrence Sephaka, Faan Rautenbach against Richard Bands, and myself against Christo Bezuidenhout, there was the un-called for bill between Corné Krige, the captain, and Schalk, the 20-year-old.

In another fight, Derick got punched in the nose by Breyton Paulse. He came out of the ring yelling '*My neus is af* [my nose is off]! *My neus is af!*' Rudolf threw him back into the circle and said, 'Keep on fighting, your three minutes are not up.' Derick kept on taking a beating for the remainder of the time.

None of the 15 fights were uncontested. In each of them, the guys got stuck in – you had to fight. The first one was obviously going to be the most difficult because the guys didn't know what to do. Werner had taken the high ground at first, saying, '*Ag*, this is pathetic,' before angrily switching to, 'If you want a fight, I'll fucking give you one.' Rudolf obviously knew these were the two guys to put against each other to set the tone.

The instructors were egging everyone on like mad. They were loving it. The purpose of Kamp Staaldraad was for Rudolf to see what kind of characters we really were. By then he knew what the rugby capability of each guy was, but he wanted to see how tough we were.

That's why I say I wasn't traumatised by Staaldraad, as I learnt a heck of a lot about myself and about the individuals around me. None of it helped me or South Africa in the 2003 World Cup, but would I do it over again? Yes, I probably would, because I had never done something remotely like it. I realised that you can go without food for three days – as long as you have got water, which we always had access to – and that you can function without sleep.

I was 25 and I had done a hundred fitness sessions before, where I thought I was going to die, but Staaldraad made me realise that your body and mind can be pushed much further than you think, and that no matter what a fitness trainer does, he can't kill you. You learn that you are more of a machine than you realise, your mind is there to hold you back physically, and as tired as you are, you can go further.

For me, Staaldraad was an educational experience and I quite enjoyed the challenge. Look, it wasn't pleasant. My fight with Christo was like a Clash of the Titans, all the fights between the big boys were. It was pretty much three shots for you, two for me – boom, boom, boom!

Apart from the heavyweight clashes, there were the athletic match-ups where a guy like Gcobani Bobo, throwing jabs, knocked Louis Koen out twice.

On the first night, the winners of the tug-of-war had been promised food. Our group won and they brought a box, which contained two live chickens.

'There's your supper, there's the fire, do whatever you want,' said Rudolf.

The Afrikaans guys said, '*Lekker*, we can sort this out and share the meat.'

But Rudolf said: 'No, no, no! Joe [van Niekerk], you must kill the first chicken.'

Now, Joe was the type of guy who thought chickens came from Nando's. He had never considered how they got there, so he started to panic and hyperventilate.

'No, I can't kill a chicken!' he said.

'Joe, kill the chicken, just wring its fucking neck,' Rudolf replied. 'It's easy.'

Joe had never killed anything in his life, and wrenched the poor creature's neck, without too much conviction. I can't explain how horrific it was. We all stood there like bloody barbarians watching poor Joe hyperventilate and reluctantly torture the unfortunate fowl. He just didn't want to do it and didn't know how. Eventually Joost van der Westhuizen had to intervene by grabbing the chicken and putting it out of its misery. It had suffered so much that when we braaied it later on, it was too tough to eat because of the stress it had been subjected to.

Now we were down one chicken. Rudolf had cottoned on to the fact that the English guys in the squad had no clue about stuff like this and that the other English oke – me – would be equally useless.

The finger was indeed pointed in my direction. I knew what was coming. I had seen the horror and the panic, and like Joe, I had never done anything remotely like this before.

Without thinking, I grabbed its legs with one hand and the head in the other, and before I knew it the body was in one hand and the detached head in the other. I had ripped the head clean off, the body was twitching, and there was blood spurting all over me.

I had been so worked up by what I had seen with Joe, and could not bear a repeat. I took everybody by surprise, including myself, because they thought there would be another fiasco, but it was over in a split second.

When Staaldraad broke in the press, one of the photos used was of me with a headless chicken. We used to joke and say Nando's should capitalise on it and say: 'The craving has spoken!' Seriously, though, this was something I never would have known I was capable of doing.

I plucked the chicken and braaied it. That night we stood around the fire in an exhausted stupor. I remember being next to Christo, a great guy, and you could see the players standing with their eyes closed, but unable to sleep. The next thing I knew, Christo had caught me inches from the fire. I had fallen asleep. If I'd had the strength, I would have thanked the lucky stars above me that I had been next to the strongest guy in the squad.

I recall another group somewhere along the line won two Bar-One chocolates, which were shared among 30 players. Each guy took a little bite and passed the chocolate on. It was about sharing under stress.

The instructors then took us to a dam and it was off with our kit again and into the water. We had to wade in up to our chins. It was the coldest water I had ever experienced and I had never felt so frozen in my life.

We were given a drill where we were each handed a rugby ball that had to be pumped full of water, and when all the balls were full, we could come out. You had to find the ball in the water that had your number on it – there were no names on this camp, each guy had a number, as this was about taking your identity away and then building you up again as a team.

I can see the philosophy behind what they did, but you can't do basic army training in three days. You can learn things about yourself and your limits, but that's about it.

We were never ever going to pump our balls up with water. We had bike pumps with little nozzles and you had to suck the water into the pump and then push it into the ball. The nozzles broke after two minutes.

'Make a plan!' screamed the instructors, who basically just wanted us in the water. We had been in for an hour-and-a-half when I saw that Stefan Terblanche was turning blue. His jaw was clattering away and he looked as if he was about to freeze solid.

It was a bit easier for us big boys, because we have got some insulation, but I hated every second of it. I have still got real hassles with cold water, and I hate ice baths to this day because of that futile exercise.

While we were freezing our bollocks off, Rudolf and the instructors were having a braai in front of the dam, making boerewors rolls with tomato sauce and mustard, and drinking beers. The next thing they accidently bumped the braai and a hot coal fell out, which started a veld fire. They blew the whistle and told us to put it out.

'Problem! Get out of the water; you've got 30 seconds, we're timing you!' they said, trying to make out that it was part of the drill. We put out the fire and were then ordered back into the water.

The guys were *gatvol* (fed up), and began to talk about a rebellion. Corné came to me and asked me what I thought. I replied: 'Whatever we do, we've got to do it together because if we're disjointed … Maybe they actually want us to make a stand together.'

We started walking out of the water, but one guy stayed in. Faan Rautenbach is one of the most decent okes you will ever meet, and it's not in him to challenge authority. It's just the way he was brought up. But by him remaining in the water, our insurrection was dead in the water, so to speak.

Faan just stayed there, chin deep, not budging, while the instructors went mad. '*Julle is nie 'n fokken span nie, klim terug in die water* [you are not a fucking team, get back into the water]!' Then they shot two rounds past us into the water. We shat ourselves. And so we got back in … and we flipping froze.

After an eternity, the command came: 'Out of the water, line up.'

We always had to march in a formation of three and had to sing as we marched. The big singers were Louis Koen, De Wet, Corné and myself.

The guys were really tired – we hadn't slept for 40 hours – so we didn't give a flying continental about being self-conscious about whose member was hanging out or shrivelled up. We also didn't know we were being filmed because Dale McDermott, our technical analyst, was a part of the team and always had a video camera with him, as he did at the camp.

It wasn't cool being naked, but I would rather have been naked in the dam than have had clothes on and had to walk wet and chafe.

When we got out of the dam, Corné asked the instructors: 'Do you mind if we get dry first, even if we just keep our clothes off until we're dry?'

They said: 'OK, you don't want your clothes, leave them.'

Corné never thought an innocent question like that would result in us leopard crawling, with our schlongs hanging on the bloody burnt grass.

Eventually we were told to put our kit on. It was nearly dusk and the next challenge was to stay awake through the second night.

The instructors told us they were going to drop each of us off on our own in the bush. We would have one match to make a fire, and then we would have to do the egg thing (as described earlier) and cook a drumstick. But we weren't allowed to eat the food when it had been cooked.

It was late winter on the highveld and really cold. They told us that if our fires went out, we couldn't get help from anyone else and if they found tracks from us walking away from our camps, the team would pay.

When they dropped me off at my spot, I knew I was safe. I didn't give a rat's arse about the fire, because I had the Bic lighter in my hat. I even decided to be cheeky and try to start my fire with my match (it worked, so I didn't have to use the Bic). I made a nice clearing, got lots of wood, and got my fire going. I was sorted. I dug my hole, put the egg in it, and waited for the fire to make a few coals. I pissed in the hole so that the moisture would go down to the egg, put all the coals over it, got a stick and braaied the drumstick. I was pleased with myself. I was MacGyver, I was running the show!

I was ready to sleep, because I thought the egg would be done by the morning. I fell asleep but soon woke up freezing.

Being a *soutie* from the city, I had stupidly not realised that, if you want to stay warm, you have to make two fires and sleep in between them. So I lay there until my backside froze, and then I turned around until my front froze, and so on. I didn't actually fall asleep again properly.

Next thing, a bakkie pulled up. It was Rudolf.

'How's it going?' he asked.

'Not too bad,' I replied.

He checked out my little fire, and asked me what time I thought it was. I looked at the bright moon overhead and estimated it was 1am.

He told me it was only 10pm. It felt like I had been there for six hours, because I had been on my own, had no one to talk to and had done my own thing. It also takes only so long to make a fire.

Rudolf was going from camp to camp asking each of us what we thought about the World Cup – this was his one-on-one time with us.

In the morning we got picked up one by one. We all smelt like braai smoke and hadn't really slept, but we were happy to see each other after being on our own for 12 hours.

The instructors lined us up in a formation and we had to put our egg, wood and drumstick in front of us for inspection. 'Is your drumstick cooked?' they asked. 'Very nice, eat it. Egg? Cooked?'

They tested the egg by banging it on your forehead, and if yours wasn't cooked, you literally got egg on your face. If you had got it right, you could peel it and chow it.

My egg was half done, so I got half the egg down my face and I chowed the rest.

We had also been given a piece of wood on which we had to carve or burn something that we thought should symbolise our World Cup campaign, and a piece of wire we could use for decoration or as a tool. I don't remember what I did with my piece of wood. I had all these ideas, but the wood was so hard that I couldn't do anything with it.

There were quite a few failures with this carpentry exercise which resulted in punishment on an obstacle course. It was the usual 'over that, under that, climb-the-rope, through-the-tunnel' course, which wasn't too bad, except you had to do it within a certain time. If one guy didn't make it in time, the whole team had to go again. We were on the course for an hour-and-a-half, which I suppose was always the plan. We kept going – marching, carrying tyres and pushing ourselves through boundary after boundary.

That night the staggering troops were told that the next exercise would be 'staying awake'.

The instructors lined us up and we had to lie *lepel* (spoon) to keep each other warm, and retain body heat. So there we were, 30 okes in *lepel* formation watching the stars, with the instructors (who were taking hourly shifts) telling us about the stars and other boring stories in order to try and make us fall asleep. Our job was to keep each other awake.

A couple of okes got bumped, but we stayed awake. Then we got up, marched, and were instructed to lie down again. Now, there were serious temptations to go to sleep – after all, this was our third night of the camp.

We all made it through the night, though, and the next morning they told us we had a fun day ahead. They said we were going to go abseiling and jump out of helicopters into the water, but we had to get to the top of the mountain first. By now we didn't care about anything around us – we were just putting one foot in front of the other.

The grand finale saw us all flown out in a big army chopper and dropped into the water. However, each group had one or two guys who couldn't swim, so we had to make sure there were enough swimmers in the water to catch them and guide them through the water.

We were then given materials to make rafts in groups of seven or eight, and told we had to use them to go across the dam and back. We had 20 minutes to build the raft, which had to be done in the nude in the water.

When our time was up, they told us to move one group to the right. For example, the last group moved to the first boat, so the boat you built was no longer yours, you had to sail on the boat that another team had made. So we sailed and some of the guys made it, while some didn't. It was a colossal mess. The boat my team made was the worst one and came back in about 14 pieces. The one we sailed, won!

Afterwards, an instructor's whistle went and we were back in formation. We marched and did push-ups. We marched again, and soon the water was behind us. We were thinking to ourselves, 'Holy shit, is this it? Is the camp over?' But then they marched us all the way to the middle of the bush, gave us GPS navigators, and said: 'Here are the co-ordinates, you guys get yourselves back to base.'

But before we got going, we were told that Danie Coetzee had left his ball at the dam (we had all been given a ball for the duration of the camp, and weren't allowed to leave it anywhere, like a rifle in the army). Danie, Victor and De Wet went to find Danie's ball, while everyone else collapsed in a heap. They returned 25 minutes later with the ball.

We had been left in the middle of nowhere and it was getting dark and cold. We wanted to make a fire but our allocation of matches had been used up the previous night. I had my Bic and I wanted to pull it out but I knew the instructors would then wonder how we started the fire.

Neil de Kock decided to look for matches. He saw a tree that had a ladder going up to a platform, and he thought maybe they had left the matches up there. So he climbed up the ladder and as he got his head over the top there was the guy in charge of the camp, Adriaan Heijns, pointing a 9mm to his forehead, with Rudolf next to him. Neil just froze, then went back down. And as he did, they threw down matches, so my lighter was saved again. In fact, I never used it, but I did show it to the guys proudly on the way home.

Then the instructors said: 'OK, you've got 30 seconds to fall asleep in that tent.'

It was probably a 15-man tent so we had to pack in like sardines. I promise you, I was lying on my back, the one half of my body was on someone else's half, and his half was on mine. We were told to sleep, which wasn't a problem. We slept for about an hour-and-a-half, before the instructors woke us up with gunshots and told us to get into formation.

'Congratulations,' they said. 'It's all over and there's a braai on the go for you.' We all tucked into lamb chops and guzzled beers – it was the best braai I have ever had. There was an immense sense of relief. We were alive! These okes had nearly killed us, they had broken us, and here we were having beers with them.

The smaller players like Derick and Breyton had struggled because of the physical strain. Schalk got through a lot easier than the other youngsters because he's a big guy.

The vibe was really good on the bus, the guys had a feeling of togetherness and felt a sense of achievement. Rugby was the last thing on our minds because we were just so amazed at ourselves and were talking and telling 'army' stories. We still talk and laugh about Staaldraad to this day.

As our bus neared Pretoria, we saw the newspaper signboards. 'Geogate' had broken, big time.

When we arrived, the media were all over us, requesting interviews. We said they could talk to every single one of us, but we would be there as a whole team, as we had just come through Staaldraad together. They could walk in one at a time and ask whoever they wanted a question. I have never seen journalists so scared. None of them could get any dirt because they were too afraid to ask any real questions.

From there we travelled straight to the Drakensberg Sun in KwaZulu-Natal to meet our wives and families. We were spoilt and were not shy to lap up the luxury.

I went into Staaldraad weighing 118kg and came out at 111kg. I lost 7kg in three days, but I reckon I put it all back on at the Drak Sun buffet.

9

HUMILIATION AND TRAGEDY

There was an episode at Kamp Staaldraad on the second night that I reckon summed it up in terms of the relevance of the exercise to the 2003 World Cup. It began with us getting pulled into formation, and the instructors calling us out one by one to insult us and highlight our 'flaws'. For instance, Victor Matfield was mocked for his hair and his good looks. They would also shout out somebody's attributes and say: 'If you think you're this person step forward.'

Then they led us in total darkness to a hole in the ground, and we were told to crawl through the tunnel. I only just fitted into the hole. I could barely crawl and I really struggled. I'd try and look back to see some light and I couldn't see past my body because it was covering everything. We didn't know how long the tunnel was so we started to panic. But eventually we got through, and arrived in a black space, where we couldn't see our hands in front of our faces. It was like a big box that had been dug into the earth. The instructors then told us to find a space, sit down and be quiet as the next guy came through and the next and the next. By this time, we were like zombies and claustrophobia was the least of our worries. There were a couple of guys who did panic, and they were ripped through into the black hole.

We all sat there naked and huddled up, our dicks hanging over each other's shoulders – it was that tight a space. The instruction then came that if we had something to say, we should say it. This, we were told, was the time to share something because it would just be voices. We couldn't see anyone, so we could say what we needed to. Ashwin Willemse spoke about being a coloured man and having to go through this army-style torture. He said that he had certain ideas about certain people and he wanted to get rid of those in the interests of team-building. A lot of guys spoke their minds, and obviously Rudolf Straeuli and his team were above the hole listening. We didn't know that there was a tarpaulin covering just above us, we thought we were in the middle of the earth.

The next thing we knew, the All Blacks' haka started playing on a tape deck. We stopped talking. A voice from above said: 'Ah, the haka makes you go quiet, now what do you do?' The only thing we could think of was to start singing the South African national anthem. When they turned up the volume of the haka, we would sing louder. They would turn the volume up again, and we would respond, and so on. Suddenly they ripped the tarpaulin off and threw ice cold water on us. And when I say ice cold, I mean freezing!

There's a video tape of the whole episode, because Rudolf had set it up for use in the World Cup. We were confessing all these private things, everyone had been opening up … and they were recording it. There would be a break for a while and then the tape would start again: 'Ka mate, ka mate …' and we would sing again as our defence mechanism, and they would throw more buckets of ice water over us. There we were, a naked ball of 30 guys, singing the national anthem, in the middle of the night, in a hole in the ground in the middle of nowhere. They played the haka 10, 15 times over. I'm not exaggerating. The water just kept coming, making us colder and colder.

Let's cut to our 2003 World Cup quarter-final against the All Blacks in Melbourne. We had decided to counter the haka by singing the national anthem, as we had done in the pit, so we lined up bristling with intent. As the All Blacks started to perform the haka we kicked in with the anthem but when they had finished, we weren't even at the Afrikaans part of the anthem. Nobody had thought this through. We really were brainwashed troops! So there we were – arm in arm – singing the anthem, with the All Blacks – who were waiting for kick-off – looking at us like we were idiots. When we realised it was a complete stuff-up, we started to sing a bit more quietly and then aborted it. By the time we got into position to receive the kick-off, the wind had been taken completely out of our sails.

All that suffering in the pit had achieved nothing, in fact it had set us back. That epitomised the whole purpose, or the lack thereof, of Staaldraad. Yes it bonded us, yes individuals found out more about themselves, but it achieved nothing on the rugby field. Rudolf had good intentions. He wanted us to get closer as a group, and we did get closer in those three days, very quickly. We gained resilience as a group, but we didn't have enough time to become a good rugby team, to discover a miracle game plan. The most unfortunate part of Staaldraad was that it didn't stop in the bush at the braai on the fourth day. There was a ripple effect that extended into the World Cup.

I've mentioned Adriaan Heijns, who organised Staaldraad. He was also Rudolf's chief lieutenant on matters of security and mind games. As a former undercover agent in the South African Police Force, he was a hardcore guy who was reported to have been involved in some serious military action. We nicknamed him '007', because he was like James Bond – always checking the perimeter of the hotel for bad guys, for instance.

We soon started calling him '000' (double-o-zero), because it was embarrassing how he would case a joint before we could enter.

We were based in the dozy seaside hamlet of Fremantle, near Perth, for the World Cup, but before we could go into a pub for a drink after a game, he would stop us at the front door, go in, do a search and then tell us it was fine to go in. It was utterly bizarre. We sometimes felt like we were trapped in a movie that was a cross between a comedy and a horror. He and two of his assistants would follow us down the Fremantle cappuccino strip, keeping a distance of 100m, so you couldn't ever escape.

On the Sunday before our quarter-final match, Rudolf called myself, Joost van der Westhuizen and Corné Krige to a meeting in his room to discuss the important week ahead. We knocked on the door and he let us in. His hi-fi was playing at close to full volume. I couldn't hear a thing. There was no way we could talk to him or hear him because the music was so loud. We were thinking, 'What the hell?' He pointed to the chairs and conspiratorially said: 'Shhhhh!' We held the meeting with the music blaring, in case '000' had missed any bugs. It was so funny. Really, who wanted to spy on us or steal our game plan? We were so shit!

Guess what our supper was on the Monday before that quarter-final? A bowl of drumsticks and boiled eggs. The flipping humour collapsed, and a lot of okes lost it. I can take plenty but even I refused to eat it. I went and ordered room service. They just took it too far, and didn't know when to stop. They killed a lot of the good that had been achieved in the bush by not knowing when to back off. I think they psyched themselves out – the paranoia was off the scale. Rudolf probably got sucked in by the bad advice he was getting, and '000' was a big part of that.

Staaldraad ultimately had the most tragic aftermath. Dale McDermott, who had videotaped the events, was made to feel that if he didn't expose what the camp was about, he would be doing South African rugby a disservice. Whether it was a camp that needed to be public knowledge or not is debatable. Whether or not the camp was a complete failure is also debatable. The bottom line is that the Boks were never going to do well at that World Cup, Staaldraad or not. The way Staaldraad was exposed gave the rugby world a reason why we were such a bad team at the World Cup. But if we'd won, it would have been heralded as the secret of our success and '000' would have been the saviour.

I was shocked when I heard Dale had leaked the tapes. I knew him well and I thought there was just no way he would do something like that on his own. He was too much of a good bloke and not a guy to make waves, so he was obviously pressurised by somebody. Or maybe there were other circumstances that we weren't aware of. I don't know. It was so unnecessary.

I had to watch *Carte Blanche* (a Sunday night investigative show on M-Net) and see my bloody dick hanging out. I was very angry at *Carte Blanche* because it was in bad taste and our dignity was just tossed around – if you'll pardon the expression. The next week *Carte Blanche* had an exposé on prisoners who were being rehabilitated by sending them on safari, and they had the decency to block out their private parts. I had to watch myself naked, trying to build a raft and get it across a dam. The prisoners' dignity was protected, yet ours wasn't given a second thought.

Dale committed suicide. I went to his funeral at Durban High School, which he had attended. It was just so sad. A bad situation had been made tragically worse by the death of a wonderful guy like Dale, who loved the game, had a bright future and was a great teacher at a lovely primary school. He had been pressurised into doing something that he couldn't live with.

10

FIGHTING A LOSING BATTLE

After Staaldraad, there was more pain at a fierce pre-season camp at the Natal Technikon in Durban. We did three sessions a day based on physicality and fitness. I can't remember what our game plan was for the World Cup, but I know we were supposed to be the fittest team in Australia – that was set in stone, as if it was the only thing we could cling to. We had to tackle bags covered with England jerseys – with 'Wilkinson', 'Johnson' and 'Hill' written on the back – and weren't allowed to stop until we had ripped the jerseys to shreds.

It's easy to make Rudolf Straeuli the scapegoat for all our woes in 2003 but if you look back at 2002, he wasn't that far off from having a successful season. Yes, the two Scotland Tests at home were abysmal, but Rudolf had a real chance of winning the Tri-Nations. We were looking good in the Test against the All Blacks in Durban until Springbok fan Piet van Zyl tackled referee David McHugh. Ironically, the momentum was with us when that happened, but it changed when McHugh was replaced by Chris White. If Rudolf had won that Test, we could have won the Tri-Nations that year, so he didn't have a lot of luck.

The bottom line, though, was that he had the rugby world on his shoulders going into 2003. His defence during all this adversity was 'Judge me on the World Cup', and here he was, about to be judged.

If you look back at that Springbok squad, it wasn't the most gifted, but there was talent. The big problem was the maturity and balance of the squad as a whole. Schalk Burger would soon become the best player in the world, but he was only 20 then. Jaque Fourie, Juan Smith, Bakkies Botha, Victor Matfield and I were starting our careers. There were a lot of babies – the right guys at the wrong time.

But there were also some shockers, and you can't compare that Springbok squad to the 2007 one in terms of quality. You would look at 10 of the 30 players in 2003 and wonder if there was no one else. As they say, sometimes you can get a bad bunch of grapes, and then you have disappointing wine that year.

We were based just outside Perth in Fremantle, a famous stop on the international yachting circuit because of the strong prevailing wind – the Fremantle Doctor – which sailors revel in.

It's a lovely town but there was little enjoyment for us, as the Kamp Staaldraad theme just wouldn't go away. Every single minute of the day was accounted for in a military-style regimen. It was this colour T-shirt for morning training and another for afternoon training. We would have to arrive at breakfast or dinner at this time in our tracksuits and say grace in them. We couldn't take a dump without seeing what the programme said.

De Wet Barry was my room-mate at the World Cup. We had become good friends since making our Bok debuts together three years earlier. Occasionally we would go for walks to get out of our 'prison' but would be followed down the road by one of Adriaan Heijns's mates, and we would return even more pissed off. It was so disappointing to have dreamt of the World Cup for so long, and then, having finally got there, to see it was nothing like I thought it would be.

When I returned to South Africa, I didn't want to talk about the Boks. Roxy and I got engaged in our post-World Cup holiday in London (more on that later), and that far outweighed anything that happened in Australia. During those five weeks I took comfort in designing Roxy's ring and faxing possibilities to my mother for her opinion. It was a cool thing to do amid the utter tedium.

There was one other highlight – captaining the Springboks for the first time, against Georgia. I felt a real sense of history and honour at being made the 51st captain of the Boks. I began the World Cup as the second-choice hooker behind Danie Coetzee, but captained the team in the Georgia game and then started the rest of the matches.

For me, 2003 was a horrendous year from start to finish. I had an injury up until August and then Rudolf went out on a limb to get me to the World Cup, and I'll always be grateful to him for that, even though the tournament was no fun at all.

What did I enjoy most about the 2003 World Cup? That's a tough one, but probably the little Sony camera we were each given to make a personal record of the tournament. When I look back on the 2003 and 2007 World Cups, the experiences are incomparable, and not just on the rugby field. I'd like to think that those of us who were there in 2003 made sure lessons were learnt on how to create a happy and healthy team environment, and made sure those mistakes weren't replicated over the next four years.

In our pivotal 2003 World Cup pool game against England in Perth, our starting XV had a combined Test cap tally of 256. For our 2007 World Cup pool game against the same opponents, we had 547. In 2003, we competed well for about 60 minutes of that match. England only scored one scrambled try in their 25-6 win, but their experience wore us down. They would get into a good field position and Jonny Wilkinson's boot would do the rest (he kicked four penalties and two drop goals). By 2007 that was how we would beat teams in tight games. In 2003, England as a team were where we were in 2007 – at their peak.

In any sport, if you win, you've got good players. If you lose, the coach is rubbish. People don't want to believe there is such a thing as a poor Springbok team. 'We are South Africa, we should win every game,' they say. That expectation is ultimately a good thing, but it makes life really tough when you are short of key ingredients. In 2003 we were trying to bake a cake with no baking powder.

Rudolf can't be blamed for everything, but he shouldn't have allowed himself to get led astray by '000', who created the paranoia. It's so easy for that to happen in a job that is a minefield of politics and deception.

The deficiencies in our team were exposed in our 29-9 quarter-final defeat to the All Blacks. It felt like our ship had sprung holes all over the show. We spent the game running around trying to plug them, but there just weren't enough hands to prevent us from sinking.

11

JAKE'S CALL

In early 2004 my wife Roxy and I were visiting friends in Jo'burg when Jake White phoned. 'I've got the Bok job,' he said. 'We need to talk.'

We met at the Mugg & Bean in Sandton City, where he dropped the bomb: 'Smitty, I need you as captain.' I immediately had mixed emotions. Firstly, I completely shat myself at the prospect of the responsibility and all the drama that goes with the job, and secondly, I was concerned about my poor form. I was having my worst ever Super 12 season, I wasn't in the best physical shape of my life and my performances were inconsistent. There had been pressure on my position at the Sharks from Lukas van Biljon and on the national front from Gary Botha, who was playing well for the Bulls.

I told Jake that I would love to be his captain, but there was the issue of my form and I was still hurting from what happened in 2003 with the Springboks. The last World Cup year had been terrible for everyone involved. I explained that I wouldn't want to be Bok captain unless there was a workable plan to get the Bok machine back on track, and then I would happily do it for nothing.

When it's going really well as a Springbok, it's fantastic – your phone rings all the time, your mates SMS you non-stop and you hear from friends you didn't know you had. Everyone gives you a slap on the back. But it's the complete opposite when it's going badly. You can't go to a restaurant without getting chirped. You can be in a restaurant at 8pm and some wise arse will come past your table and say, 'Shouldn't you be training?' It's not advisable to do your grocery shopping on a Sunday if you've lost the day before, because the snide comments will fly.

We are public property and I understand that people treat us that way. It goes with the territory. When it's good, it's really good, because we're popular public property, but when it's bad, it's awful, and our private lives have to be sacrificed. We become recluses because it's not worthwhile going out – people want to give us their 10 cents' worth, they want to let us know how they feel. They don't figure that we're feeling 10 times worse than they are, because we're the ones who are responsible for what went wrong. We're in the thick of it.

When the Boks crashed out of the 2003 World Cup at the quarter-final stage, we certainly didn't have people waiting at the airport saying, 'We still love you', like the All Blacks had after their exit in 2007. I don't think that would ever happen in South Africa.

We feel embarrassed and ashamed when things go badly wrong. We can lose a game here and there, we can go down to the All Blacks by a few points in a good game, and that's OK. But the heavy defeats and those five losses in a row (like in 2006) are a different story.

We talk about the ramifications of defeat as part of our motivation before every game. We say, 'Guys, we're playing for each other but we've got the weight of the nation on our shoulders. We can make a lot of people happy by winning.'

Fans don't mind going to work on Monday when their team has won because they can talk about how the Boks punished the All Blacks, Wallabies or England.

We get hate mail regularly, and it's not always related to how the Boks are performing. For example, I have criticised those idiots who take the old South African flag to rugby matches. Now there's a guy who continuously sends me a photocopied image of the old flag to my mailbox at Kings Park, with the caption: '*Ons is vir die ou Suid Afrika. Fok jou* [We support the old South Africa. Fuck you].' It's become a joke because I know the guy's handwriting and I give his envelopes to other people to open. There's another chap who used to write once a month throughout Jake's tenure to tell me how useless I was, and why, and he would call Jake 'Joker White'. That kind of mail obviously becomes more frequent when you're not winning.

Early in my career as Bok captain – in 2004 and 2005 – a loss meant I struggled to sleep for a few nights, but I learnt some perspective. When I talk about people abusing us, it's not John Smit the person they are angry with; it's John Smit the captain – the guy in charge of the national hope, the Boks. And when they see me in the street their reaction is: 'Smit, fix it, sort it out!' You realise over time that it's not unjustified. People support the Boks because they are proud of their country, because we're a champion brand, and their emotion gets rewarded every weekend when we win. But if you don't reward emotion, it becomes a double-edged sword.

It became easier for me to deal with the pressure once I was able to differentiate between John Smit – the person – and John Smit – the captain. I realised that while I have a massive responsibility, my life wouldn't end if I got dropped. The Springbok captain might die and get dropped or fired, or whatever the case may be, but that's not the end of the world (although it would probably feel like it at the time). That's one of the most valuable things that I came to grips with.

When we lost 49-0 to the Wallabies in 2006, Roxy went out to the garden at half-time when the score was 30-0 to get some fresh air, as she was pregnant at the time. She thought the game couldn't get any worse, only to go back inside three minutes before full-time and see what would be the final score. She knows a reasonable amount about rugby and, because of how I'd prepared her for how quickly the captaincy could come to an end, the first thing that went through her mind was, 'My husband is going to get fired.'

The reality is that it's amazing that I've got this far and I've got all these Test caps. My Bok career could easily have ended when Lukas exploded onto the scene or when I got injured in 2002. So many things could have ended it.

The other thing that gave me perspective was that I saw the captaincy as a job to be performed to the best of my ability, not a celebrity thing or a prestige reward. It's not like being given a sports award at school – a pat on the back – it's more like being made head boy or president. You've got to make sure that you do the right thing all the time. It's not a reward – it's a job, a responsibility.

In the old days, the best player in the team was handed the captaincy and it was seen as his due. I was lucky when I began my career as an 18-year-old at Natal in '97 because I got to learn the art of leadership from genuine legends such as Gary Teichmann, Mark Andrews and Wayne Fyvie. In terms of the Boks, André Vos and Bob Skinstad were very different leaders and had their unique qualities, and I had my time with Corné Krige as well.

Corné was a killer of a player, and I think he wanted to be captain just about more than he wanted to win. I'm certainly not like that. To this day, I say to any coach or player that if me sitting on the bench or carrying tackle bags will give the team a better chance of winning, then I'll do it. It's got nothing to do with my personal ambition, which is to be the best. But when it comes to a team, the only success I've ever gained is when I've put the team first, and I've been good at what I do through that. Other guys don't work like that, as they want to be the best individual and the team to fit around them.

I don't think that when my career ends after 10, 15 or 20 years, the public will say, 'Wow, John Smit was South Africa's most brilliant hooker or prop. What an awesome player!' I'll probably hold a couple of Test records – and I've certainly had my moments – but I'm not a Frans Steyn, who's just an unbelievable, irreplaceable talent that's born, not created.

I have a humble opinion of my status as a player. I certainly believe I'm the best at what I do, but not everyone has agreed with me or taken cognisance of that, which I've had to deal with. Half the people think I'm average to crap, and the other half think I'm the bee's knees.

I think people have sometimes done me a disservice because they haven't understood that there are many contrasting types of hookers.

When I was a kid, Springbok hooker Uli Schmidt was all the rage because he was so athletic and scored tries from the wings. But he was half my size. If we had to do a 3km run against each other he would probably lap me.

My strengths are obviously very different to what his were, but mine aren't always recognised. I've had to capitalise on what I'm good at. I'm a 123kg hooker/prop so I want to make sure that whoever scrums against me pays. I want to make sure that I hurt opponents in the tight exchanges, defend well on the blind side, and throw well into the lineout. So when I wasn't side-stepping and scoring tries, and my rivals were, the pressure was on.

But I can't be a Gary Botha or a Schalk Brits, I can only be the best at what I've got to offer, and then it's up to the coach to choose what type of player is best for the team. Furthermore, I believe that what I've brought to the table allows an athletic lock to perform, a flank to break away a little bit earlier, and other players to excel and have a second or two somewhere else. I pride myself and get a heck of a lot of satisfaction out of doing things that people don't see, like irritating the opposition and creating an environment through subtle, unseen actions, that benefit the team. I'm talking about the tricks of the trade in the scrums and the tight-loose. And it's been rewarding to hand them down to a youngster such as Bismarck du Plessis. I don't want to die with all those secrets inside me.

It's very difficult to be rated as a captain in rugby in the same way as, say, Proteas captain Graeme Smith is in cricket. He can go out there and score 50, 100 or 150 and he's seen to be leading by example. A golfer can shoot 64 and 65 on consecutive days, and he's a legend.

For a hooker, if you win your lineouts it's because you've got good locks; if you lose them, you've been crap. If you're scrumming well, it's because you've got really good props; if you're not scrumming well, you aren't pulling your weight. There's no tangible way to say, 'John got 7 out of 10'.

I had to be quite harsh on myself and open to the opinion of people I trusted. Jake was always very honest with me, and Roxy would be the first one to tell me if I had played badly. But once you've played a number of games, you know whether you've been good or bad.

Jake asked me to be Bok captain at a time when I wasn't playing well, so I said: 'Jake, I want to be the one who helps sort out this mess but you can only pick me if I'm the best.' And I guess, to be fair, he had to lie to me at that stage and say, 'Definitely!'

Thankfully my form got a little better as the Super 12 went on and when the Boks had a three-week camp before our first Test together, against Ireland, I trained extremely hard. I played some good rugby in those initial Tests – where it counts most – which took a little bit of pressure off, but it was a tough time for me because being asked to captain South Africa means taking on a massive managerial role.

12

THE JOURNEY BEGINS

I was almost sick to my stomach with nerves before the first Test of 2004 against Ireland in Bloemfontein. We had a new team, a new coach, a new captain and a new beginning. We desperately wanted to brush away the debris from 2003 and lay a strong foundation for the future.

But we were facing a settled, successful Six Nations side. They had won the Triple Crown by beating the other Home Unions and had made it clear through their arrogant public utterances that they expected to beat us, which was ideal motivational fodder for us.

Jake White's team talk before his first Test has gone down in Springbok folklore. He completely floored us with the angle he took. He started talking about the World Cup – not the one that had just passed but the next one, in France – in four years' time. Jake never mentioned Ireland. He told us we were about to play the first match on our road to the World Cup. We looked at each other in bemusement, thinking this guy must have been smoking dope, because it was the furthest thing from our minds, but it was an inspirational thing to say because it made us feel that we were starting a special journey.

Jake had picked a really good Bok squad. As I have often said, his greatest gift is understanding people and knowing how to pick the right individuals so that the sum ends up being greater than the parts. In 2004, we had players with strong personalities, but not conflicting ones. We were young, driven and ambitious.

My first team address was a far cry from my team talks now. There was nothing smooth or commanding about it. I spoke with sheer emotion and heart, and that was OK because we were all in the same boat in terms of youth and inexperience. I think these players needed something that was genuine, passionate and applicable to the situation we were in. I don't think I reduced anyone to tears in 2004 or 2005 with powerful rhetoric – that part of my captaincy took a long time to develop and it came as I got more confident in my ability to lead. You can be instantly confident as a player, but it takes a long time to gain confidence as a captain and that comes from how your players respond to you.

For a start, you don't know whether the captaincy is a flash-in-the-pan or long-term thing, and you don't know whether you'll do a good or a bad job. It took me two seasons of being a captain to feel at ease in my role. The more comfortable I became, the more the guys reacted to me. In my first season especially, I'd spend the night before the team talk thinking about what I was going to say, what special thing I could do to motivate the guys, what points I should bring up … It was like preparing a speech and I'd be more nervous about how I was going to prepare the team than I was about my own game. In time, it started to come naturally to me. I'd pick up on things during the week and know when to drop certain hints and pointers.

After 2005 I started worrying less about captaining and more about playing and strategy. In 2004 and 2005 I relied completely on Jake, our game plan, and what we'd practised, because I was too nervous about being the captain and my own game to think about assessing the situation on the field. It was only in 2006 and 2007 that I began manipulating our game on the field according to what was unfolding.

When we first assembled in 2004 I was especially nervous about how the Bulls players would respond to me – as they were from the strongest South African province – but my fears were unfounded.

From day one in 2004, I've never been questioned as Bok captain by any player. Besides Luke Watson (more on him later), I've never had one guy even half-challenge me or half-criticise me, or question anything, which is quite bizarre. I've never had altercations or a challenger who's tried to ruffle my feathers. This isn't because I'm 'Captain Fantastic', it's because I've never wanted to lead on my own. I'd say that's what defines me as a leader. From the start, I put Victor Matfield in charge of lineouts and Juan Smith in charge of the loose forwards. Os du Randt had a big role up front, and Fourie du Preez, Jean de Villiers and Percy Montgomery were in charge of specific elements of the backline. I had half a dozen micro captains – experts in their fields – and got them as involved as I possibly could, so the macro situation took care of itself. There have been Tests against tier-two opposition where I didn't make one strategic call, but in bigger games I would take on more strategically because the pressure would force the guys to focus more on their own games. I think this sharing of responsibility saved me. I've always felt that I had the support of the guys because I empowered them.

We took a lot of confidence out of beating Ireland twice (31-17 and 26-17), Wales (53-18) and the Pacific Islanders (38-24), while winning our contractual dispute with SA Rugby boosted morale immeasurably.

Our opening Tri-Nations match was against the All Blacks in Christchurch. While they were more experienced than us, we were probably the better team on the night, but lost 23-21 when Doug Howlett scored their solitary try in the last movement of the match (we had scored three).

In the change room afterwards, we were absolutely gutted, irritated and angry all at the same time. Jake was the only one who was calm. He said we had lost because we didn't believe that we could win, while the All Blacks had the belief that they could. We weren't sure how to take that. In effect he was right because the All Blacks had won so many times before as a team and they expected to beat us, especially at home. After being taken by surprise, they rallied and came through at the end. That was a sign of a quality side, whereas we were still finding our feet as a team. We realised that we had gone into the match hoping for the best, and had been almost happy to say, 'Damn, almost'.

The same thing happened in Perth the following week when we lost 30-26, with former SA U21 captain Clyde Rathbone ironically scoring the match-winning try.

We returned home upbeat because the Springboks hadn't been so competitive Down Under for some time.

Our first match back was at Ellis Park – our favourite ground – where we produced a classic Bok performance against the All Blacks. We were all over Andrew Mehrtens like a rash and forced him into making mistakes.

Ellis Park is such a special place for the Boks and hell on earth for the visiting teams. It's no secret that they feel like they are stepping into a lost valley in hillbilly country. Opponents have told us over a beer how they get a sinking feeling as the bus gets further away from the comfort of their Sandton hotel and passes through the dodgy, run-down areas surrounding the stadium. We've heard of fans spitting and banging on their bus as it enters the ground.

Inside, the stadium is so well designed that the crowd sits on top of you and gets totally involved in the game. The fans really let rip and at the risk of sounding snobbish, there's something scary about a lot of them. The Aussies reckon

Ellis Park is straight out of *The Jerry Springer Show* and that the fans look almost capable of murder.

Opponents are definitely intimidated and on top of all this, they battle to breathe. We deal with the altitude much better because we train and play a lot on the highveld and half our team is invariably from the Pretoria-based Bulls.

If it was possible, I would have all our Tests played there. Every Springbok – whether from Durban, Cape Town or Bloemfontein – will tell you that Ellis Park is his favourite ground and that's because of the instant and sustained lift you get when you take to the field.

That 40-26 victory against the All Blacks – which included a hat-trick of tries for Marius Joubert – set us up for what was essentially a Tri-Nations final in Durban against the Wallabies, with the winner taking the title.

That was one of the biggest weeks I can remember in my rugby career. The hype was off the scale as the public happily embraced us after having endured a few years of misery. You could sense their relief that the Boks were back on track.

The frantic clamouring for Test tickets was something I'd never experienced before. A farmer contacted me through a friend and offered to buy me a 4x4 if I gave him 10 tickets. I'd never get involved in a deal like that but I reckon even if I had fancied a new vehicle, I wouldn't have been able to provide the tickets.

When it became apparent that the Boks could win the Tri-Nations, we asked our employers if they would consider giving us a bonus. Saru president Brian van Rooyen said he would be glad to reward us if we brought home the bacon. A few days before the Wallabies finale, Bok manager Arthob Petersen climbed on the team bus before training and said: 'Gentlemen, I'm pleased to inform you that the South African Rugby Union has agreed to grant you a bonus of R10 000 each if you win the title.' After tax, it would be the princely sum of about R7 000 for winning South Africa's first major trophy since 1998. But that wasn't the point.

The guys were more amused than anything else at what the administrators thought was an adequate reward, and this match was all about the rugby.

We made a good start, but trailed 7-3 at half-time. I recall the Wallabies whipping themselves into a state after Lote Tuqiri's try, shouting over and over again: 'Let's steal it from them, boys!' That was like a bucket of ice water over me. I called the guys in and demanded that we refocus. We did, scoring two tries soon after the break – through Victor Matfield and Joe van Niekerk – which gave us a 17-7 lead. They hit back with two late tries but we held our nerve to win 23-19.

I recall leaving the stadium in the bus with 'We are the Champions' blaring – it was the sweetest feeling ever. Only Os du Randt and Percy Montgomery had experienced this kind of success before with the Boks. Quite a few of the guys had won the Currie Cup but this was on a different scale.

On our Grand Slam tour at the end of 2004, there were very different expectations of the team because we were the Tri-Nations champions, even though we had got over the line by virtue of the two bonus points we had picked up overseas. The lack of expectation at the start of the year had given us breathing space to grow and improve but mentally we still had a long way to go.

We began with a 38-36 win against Wales in Cardiff, after leading 38-22 with 10 minutes to go, and arrived in Dublin thinking we were better than we were. We controversially lost 17-12 to Ireland and got whacked 32-16 by England at Twickenham, before finishing strongly at Murrayfield with a 45-10 win against Scotland.

The Springboks had gone on that tour uncomfortable with the expectations and weighed down by the prospect of achieving a rare Grand Slam (consecutive wins against the four Home Unions).

The mindset of South African rugby teams is that they'd much rather be in a corner, and fight themselves out with an attitude of 'there's nothing to lose, let's go show these bastards what we're made of!'

The hardest thing for me as Springbok captain was to get the players to believe how good they were and not to let their supporters or themselves down by underperforming. In 2005 we had to sit down as a team and decide whether we were one-hit wonders or a good side that now had to kick on to another level. But changing the team mentality didn't come overnight; it took a heck of a long time to get the guys to understand that each individual had to work that extra bit harder if the team was to move out of its comfort zone. The challenge was that we couldn't be satisfied with what we did in 2004; we had to repeat that success and achieve something else. We had to win our next game, not because the opposition had beaten us 10 times in a row, but because we had beaten them twice in a row.

I mentioned that there was controversy in that Dublin Test in 2004 and we didn't react well to it, another sign that we were still relatively immature. That week had started on a bizarre note when Jake uncharacteristically lost the plot in a press conference. He was asked how many Irish players he would pick for the Springboks and, in a lapse of reason, he said: 'None'. He was being honest, but you just don't say those types of things, and Ireland were instantly provided with priceless motivational ammunition for the week. Just as a player can lose concentration and drop a pass, so can a coach in his dealings with the media.

The match itself produced the weirdest moment of my captaincy. We had been under pressure in our 22 for some time when referee Paul Honiss blew for a penalty against us. He then called me over and said we were overstepping the mark. He added that I had to go talk to the players because the next time it happened, there would be a card. So I turned around and called the guys over, and as they started approaching me, Ronan O'Gara tapped, ran and scored, in front of Honiss, who awarded the try.

I lost it. I've never felt such anger. I wanted to knock him out, I was that angry. I ran to him and screamed at him like I've never done in my life before or since, remonstrating that we were following his instructions to take time out to talk about our infringing. He just ignored me. He looked away like I wasn't there and that he couldn't hear me yelling. Then he put his hand up like a school teacher and told me to go away. I was either going to hit him or leave it. The devil on my one shoulder was egging me on, but the guardian angel on the other won the day – but only just. That's the closest I've ever come to completely losing control. It was the first time I'd been blatantly cheated in my rugby career.

When I went back to the team, I could see the anger in their eyes and they could see the state I was in. I said: 'We will not lose this match, let's win it in spite of the referee,' but as the words were coming out of my mouth I could see this was one speech that wasn't going to hit home. The guys were too shocked; they were beyond rallying against this outrage. They had never seen anything like it. I knew the game was over, and so was the dream of the Grand Slam.

A year later Honiss came up to me and apologised – well, sort of, because he also defended himself to the hilt, saying no captain should turn his back on the referee. But how was I supposed to go and talk to the players? On the tape I could clearly hear him saying, 'Go speak to your players', so he wasn't going to weasel his way out of this one. He got it wrong. It's as simple as that. It can easily happen to referees at Lansdowne Road because the crowd puts pressure on them. When O'Gara tapped and scored, the crowd erupted. They went crazy, and Honiss didn't want to incur the wrath of 49 000 Irishmen by calling the try-scorer back. It wasn't his intention to cheat us, he was just too weak in the moment to make the correct decision.

In a Super 12 game the next year, Honiss was the touch judge. We kicked the ball out from a penalty and he put his arm out in error for the opposition to throw in. I ran up, got in his face and said: 'Paul, this isn't Lansdowne Road and they aren't Ireland.'

Childish maybe, but it did give me a little satisfaction.

13

HIGHS AND LOWS DOWN UNDER

As Tri-Nations champions, the Springboks went into the 2005 Test season full of confidence, despite our mixed results on the end-of-year tour. We won our series against France in June – drawing the first match 30-30 in Durban and then beating them 27-13 in Port Elizabeth.

We had a settled team and the goal was to be the first Bok side to win back-to-back Tri-Nations titles, without relying on cultivating our underdog status as our primary form of motivation.

Before the Tri-Nations, though, we had to play two Tests against the Wallabies for the Mandela Plate. We lost 30-12 in Sydney but bounced back with a 33-20 win at Ellis Park (we had a record six players of colour in the starting XV for that second match, and nine in the match 22).

A week later, we beat the Wallabies 22-16 at Loftus in our first match of the Tri-Nations.

Our next match was against the All Blacks at Newlands, which is their favourite ground in South Africa and our least favourite when we are playing them because of the disappointment we feel when we see so many locals wearing All Blacks jerseys. We sympathise with the history behind the coloured population supporting the All Blacks, but our feeling is that this country has come a long way and that rugby fans should move on too. It's a slap in the face for the Springboks, and annoying because there has been nothing remotely racist about the Boks for a long time now.

This Test was one to savour for us. We beat the best team in the world 22-16 and then had the added satisfaction of seeing their partisan local supporters trooping off home in their black jerseys with their tails between their legs.

I recall not wanting to leave the Newlands change room. I just sat there … savouring the victory. We had played really well, and we had disrupted Byron Kelleher and Dan Carter to the extent that the All Blacks could not get any rhythm. We roughed them up good and proper.

Having beaten the Wallabies in Pretoria without too much drama, we faced the significant psychological challenge of beating them again in Perth in our next game. The Boks had not won an away match in the Tri-Nations since 1998 and this was the next big challenge for our evolving team. We won 22-19, with Bryan Habana scoring two breakaway tries, and a major psychological hurdle had been cleared.

The second-last match of the Tri-Nations was in Dunedin against the All Blacks and it was basically a final as New Zealand were heavily favoured to beat Australia a week later in Auckland. The winner would not only land the title, but would also secure the No 1 spot on the IRB world rankings (the Boks had been at No 6 when Jake White took over).

It was a week drenched in rugby mania in this freezing South Island city, as the old Springbok-All Blacks rivalry was restored to full bloom by the enthusiastic locals. The streets were decorated in the colours of the teams, we were heartily greeted by the locals when we strolled about town, and the media loved us. On the eve of the match there was a heart-warming headline in the *Otago Daily Times* that read: 'Welcome back Springboks', and the editorial was all about how the All Blacks had missed their old foe during a period in the professional era when they beat us with monotonous regularity and we stumbled from one crisis to the next.

That week confirmed what I had long believed – the All Blacks need the Springboks, and they need us to be at our best. We validate the All Blacks in a rugby world where the only other consistent force is the Wallabies and to a lesser degree, France and England.

The guys fed off the hype that week by digging deep into history, focusing a great deal on our traditional rivalry with the All Blacks.

We went in-house for our jersey presentation on the Friday, with our most capped backline player, Percy Montgomery, presenting to the backs and Os du Randt doing the duty with the forwards. It was stirring stuff. Keeping the ceremony among ourselves pulled us closer than ever.

An excellent week of preparation amid very enjoyable Test fever produced a brilliant Test, and we did exceptionally well to fight back from 21-10 down in the first half to be ahead 27-24 after a try from Jaque Fourie in the 65th minute.

The defining moment came with four minutes to go, when we had a defensive lineout near our 22. I threw to our banker – Bakkies Botha at the front – but it went straight through his hands and we lost the lineout, which was unheard of for us at the time. The All Blacks kept the ball until Keven Mealamu eventually spun over for the try that decided the match, the Tri-Nations title and the No 1 ranking.

If we'd won that lineout we would have kept possession, worked the clock and kicked it out. The throw was on the right trajectory, the jump was perfectly timed, but the ball sped through Bakkies' hands. It was just one of those inexplicable things. It all came down to that moment. We were absolutely devastated, but we were consoled that fate had decreed it wasn't meant to be for us in a classic Test.

We travelled to Sydney on the Sunday and were in the mood to blow off some steam because the Tri-Nations was over. We had a fortnight off before we had to start playing in the Currie Cup. It was time to let our hair down.

We hit a few local pubs before ending up at Hugos, a well-known destination for the who's who of Sydney sport. We were running the show, and having a great time. I had my credit card behind the bar – running a tab – and the drinks were flowing. Dwight Yorke, the former Manchester United soccer player who had signed with Sydney FC, was also there and we had a drink with him.

At one point, I turned away from the bar to go to the toilet and bumped a guy who had a drink in each hand. He spilled one over his clothes, and was seriously pissed off, despite my sincere apology. He called the bouncers and said I was out of control. Now, in Australia they are extremely strict about over-indulgence, so the bouncers took the guy's word for it, took me by the arms and escorted me out.

Outside on the pavement, I remonstrated: 'Can I just go and get my credit card?' But they weren't interested, and the more I reasoned with them, the more emphatic they were that I wasn't going to put a foot back in the club.

I'll admit that I was impolite to these guys, called them idiots and said they were being unreasonable. I was irritated, aggravated, intoxicated, and just wanted my credit card. They probably got this every weekend, and the more I argued, the less they listened to me.

Bryan Habana and Hanyani Shimange, who had been with me for most of the night, had followed me out, and they pulled me towards a cab, saying, 'This is going nowhere, we will cancel your card on the way back to the hotel,' which we did. I then sat in the foyer with Victor Matfield for about an hour-and-a-half – just chilling and chatting – so we would be tired enough to sleep on the plane.

On arrival in Jo'burg, our media officer Rayaan Adriaanse called Jake and me aside.

'We have a situation,' he said. 'A story has been published in an Australian newspaper about one of our players being involved in a racial incident.'

'Who's the clown?' I asked.

'Well, you ...' Rayaan replied, explaining that Peter Jenkins, an Australian rugby journalist, had written an article about me racially abusing a Tongan bouncer after I had been asked to leave the club.

To put this into context, before we left on this tour, Jake had addressed us on the subject of behaviour. He had got wind that Aussie reporters were working in cahoots with the Wallabies with the aim of disrupting us with negative stories. Jake told us they would be watching our every move, wanting to catch us out drinking, womanising, or crashing cars (which is what their players usually do), so he said anybody who misbehaved would be on the first plane home.

Our behaviour had been impeccable, and nobody was out of control on that last night – tipsy yes, but in control.

Racism isn't in my nature. I wasn't brought up in the apartheid era. I went to Pretoria Boys High which is multi-racial. I don't see things in terms of race. I could easily get angry with a bouncer, but I wouldn't see his skin colour.

I went into shock, and so began the longest three days of my life. I slept badly, and I lost my appetite, which says a lot about the state I was in.

Thank goodness Bryan and Shimmy were with me during my unceremonious exit from the club and they could vouch that I hadn't made a racist comment. I queried the bouncers' intellect, sure, as an obnoxious drunk would, but there was absolutely no racial abuse.

Luckily my South African friends living in Sydney knew the club owner and it was arranged that the Tongan bouncer and the owner would have a conference call with me to sort the matter out directly. Jake and I were both anxious to see this cloud over me blown away. By the Wednesday, I was in a heck of a state, as Roxy will testify. This type of incident is the worst thing any national captain can get involved in, but especially a Springbok rugby captain.

Jenkins had found out we were out on the town and had trailed us all night, up until the last place. The bouncer said he had been pressurised by Jenkins into speaking about my ejection (I suspect a payment was made).

During the conference call I could tell the bouncer was not enjoying it at all, that this was the last thing he wanted to be involved in. I apologised to him for being difficult that night, but was adamant that I hadn't racially abused him, and he was happy with that.

To this day, the actual nature of the abuse – the offensive words I was alleged to have uttered – have never surfaced, and that's because there weren't any. At no stage did the Tongan guy say, 'Hang on, you did actually say something that offended me.'

I've never spoken to Jenkins and never will. He makes my blood boil. He was a veteran reporter before climbing over to the other side of the fence and taking up a position with the Australian Rugby Union. He has visited South Africa many times and knows race is a touchy subject in this country, yet he happily created a storm to sell newspapers.

I got calls from Bryan and Shimmy to support me, which helped when the local media were giving me a grilling. A journalist from the *Daily News* in Durban called me 10 times between 5am and 6am when the story was breaking, leaving messages that my silence was confirmation of guilt, but I couldn't speak to reporters until it was sorted out.

This sorry saga was my worst nightmare. I would drive through Durban, with my name emblazoned on the side of my car, and see newspaper billboards screaming: 'Bok captain in race row', and wanted to pinch myself to wake up.

Our end-of-year tour in 2005 produced mixed results. The match against Wales in Cardiff was memorable for me not only because of our commanding performance in winning 33-16 – with Bryan scoring two tries – but also because it was my 50th Test. Before kick-off, I had run out onto the field with Wales flyhalf Stephen Jones alongside me, as it was also his 50th Test, and I was taken aback by the deafening roar of 75 000 Welshmen celebrating the achievement of one of their popular players. The Millennium Stadium has no peer when it comes to atmosphere on the days when the Welsh find full voice.

Perhaps a big reason we played so well in Cardiff was because we'd just had a fantastic holiday of sorts at a ski resort in Argentina. We had beaten the Pumas 34-23 in the first week of the tour and then had the curious problem of having a tour 'bye' before the Wales match.

Jake sensed that making us train all week would piss us off and, to his credit and our enjoyment, we had a brilliant week of relaxed *spanbou* (team building) in the mountains.

We lost 26-20 to France in our final tour match and in the change room afterwards Jake gave us a pep talk regarding our long-term plan.

He said: 'The next time you guys are in this Stade de France change room after a match you will have the Webb Ellis Cup in here with you. But only if over the next two years every one of us makes an extra effort to improve mind, body and soul. We have to make sacrifices if we are going to do it, whether it's time away from home for training camps, your diet, or extra time in the gym – whatever it takes to make you a better rugby player. Each of you knows where you can add a bit of polish, and you all have to commit to that now.'

That loss to France was particularly disappointing for me because I got suspended for six weeks for accidentally fracturing French captain Jerome Thion's larynx with my elbow. I'd never been yellow-carded and had no record of dirty play whatsoever and all of a sudden I had this lengthy ban. For me that was bizarre. I'd never in a million years tried to aim my elbow into his throat. I was simply running with the ball in my hand and accidentally collided with his throat.

14

SHARKS SHENANIGANS

While the sun shone on the Springboks in 2004 and 2005, they were winters of discontent in the Shark Tank.

Kevin Putt had decided that the group of players he had inherited wasn't good enough so he drafted in half a dozen Pumas players from Witbank, as well as a sprinkling of other guys from smaller unions. We had lost to the Pumas in the Currie Cup, and whoever played well for them that day got a contract with the Sharks. We had an influx of players who didn't understand the Sharks culture and the balance was thrown off kilter.

The fans couldn't understand why the Sharks were buying nobodies and we lost a lot of support. Lessons hadn't been learnt from what happened to Hugh Reece-Edwards in 2000 but at least we got some quality players in Albert van den Berg, Gaffie du Toit and Philip Smit out of the Griquas guys who came to Durban that year.

Putty never recovered from his 'no-name brands' buying spree. Of the 10 players he brought in, only Jacques Botes and Skipper Badenhorst came through. My feeling is that if the Sharks contract someone, he should either be the best in his position in the country or have the potential to be the best, because we aim to be the leading side in the country.

It didn't happen that year and Putty was stuck with these guys from a selection point of view because he had promised them starting positions. It caused frustration for him and he found it difficult to be honest with everybody involved because he still had the older Sharks guys who he had to be loyal to and who still had a role to play.

Putty was caught between saying one thing to one player and something else to another, hoping they wouldn't consult each other. He was doomed because players talk and he was always going to get caught out.

I had first-hand experience of Putty being economical with the truth. When Ollie le Roux took the Sharks to the CCMA (Commission for Conciliation, Mediation and Arbitration) because they wouldn't renew his contract on the grounds that he was out of shape, Putty asked me if the players thought Ollie still had something to offer. I told him he was putting me in a difficult position but that I'd ask the team as long as it remained confidential.

I said that while Ollie was a great player with plenty of experience and ability, he had cooked his goose with a lot of the players. They didn't have the time of day for him. He would park next to the training field and not go inside the stadium with the other guys (he would get our kit master to go on the cart to fetch his jersey). He would train, take his jersey off, put his T-shirt on and leave. He was also telling the kickers how to kick, and the backs how to pass. He would give marital advice, farming advice, you name it. He was an expert at everything.

I asked every single player involved what they felt about Ollie. I wanted the best for him and if managed well he could have added value. But not one player said they wanted him to stay, although they respected his ability as a player.

I relayed this confidential information back to the coach. But on the last day of the CCMA hearing, Putty blurted out that the captain had come to him and said Ollie no longer fitted into the team. That was the final word of the hearing, and I'd been stitched up by Putty, big time. Ollie phoned me and was obviously furious. Putty, of course, didn't explain what had happened and made me look like the bad guy to cover his backside. That was Putty.

His lack of loyalty explains why we no longer have Shaun Sowerby in this country. In that 2003 season when I was battling with serious injuries, he made Shaun the Sharks captain, and he did a fantastic job. He played really well, supported the coach and gave it his all. But the day I returned to the squad, Putty called me in and made me captain. Just like that. I said: 'Are you sure? I don't mind playing under Shaun, we've been mates since we were 18 and flat-mates for six years, and he led from the front for you. I don't think this is right.' Then Putty started benching Shaun, after he had been so loyal to him. It was very shabby treatment, and who could blame Shaun for taking up an offer from Stade Français? Well done to him for becoming one of the biggest names in French rugby.

The mixed signals Putty gave Lukas van Biljon and me led to Lukas cottoning on that he was being bullshitted, and there was one hilarious episode when he chased Putty around his desk like a raging bull. That epitomised Putty's tenure. Not a lot of loyalty and honesty.

I remember his last day as Sharks coach. Ian McIntosh called me to a meeting at Gary Teichmann's house on the Wednesday before we played the Brumbies in the Super 12. Dick Muir, John Allan, Mac and Gary were there, and they told me Dick was the new Sharks coach, with Mac assisting for that week, and they were taking over immediately. We had known it was inevitable because we were playing so badly.

I was never going to campaign for Putty because I wasn't a fan of his coaching or management style. His language would often offend the Afrikaans guys and he would blow hot and cold, ferociously crapping on the team and then wanting to be everybody's mate.

Tactically he was very good but for one vital area. He wanted a No 9 like he had been – a general who would call the plays, the lineouts, everything. We never had a No 9 like that. We had Craig Davidson, who was an instinctive player, not a communicator. Craig was very good on the break, he put his body on the line to the extent that it ultimately shortened his career because of concussion. But Putty got stuck on that issue, and wouldn't let it go.

Just after he had been fired and was living in New Zealand, he said on TV that I'd told him that 'Victor Matfield puts a steel plate in his arm guard so he can knock players out'. I was furious and slated him in the Kiwi media. I said he was lying and had made it up, which he had.

We beat the Brumbies in the week Dick took over – with 21-year-old Ruan Pienaar having a sensational game – but then went on tour and never won a game. Dick, though, didn't care about results, and after all the darkness of Putty's final months, he was the proverbial ray of sunshine.

Dickie is a warm, open, feel-good guy and the Sharks players loved him. He was big on the process of teaching us to attack. He wanted us to move the ball and be more aware of space. I used to ask him if we could play more conservatively and he would say, 'No, we have the talent, keep the faith.' That was the big gift he gave the Sharks. The players eventually came around to his line of thinking that when it was on, you had to give it a go, and we scored some brilliant tries during his tenure.

Dick doesn't have the organisational skills of a coach like John Plumtree, but he has the people skills and the vision to let guys dream big and think beyond the here and now. The Sharks pioneered this attack-from-anywhere approach because of his vision. He was outstanding and his positive attitude was infectious.

Most coaches struggle with paranoia, but not Dick. Every Friday before a match he would ask me if I wanted to go for a beer to discuss the game. 'Just one!' he would say with a smile. I skipped the beer, but we would chat, and it was always about winning the game through scoring tries. When he was under pressure at half-time and the guys were down, he would never panic and change the plan. Week in, week out, he stuck to his blazing guns. Dick brought a balance back to the team dynamic. He was very much about us playing and working hard, but also enjoying ourselves throughout.

The guys felt a lot less stressed about what they did for a living because they didn't have a horrible fear of losing. Winning was not the focus. We concentrated on playing and making progress in our game, with the idea that the wins would take care of themselves if we got Dick's game right.

Dick introduced going out as a team on a Tuesday, having a few beers and a lot of fun. All of a sudden, players came out of their shells, because they realised that they could be professionals and still relax, and get a balance between life and rugby. He encouraged guys to have a life outside rugby, to study and do part-time work. When a player sees that a coach is interested in him as a person and cares about what happens to him after rugby, he wants to reciprocate and do well for the coach and the team.

Dick was also refreshingly honest, but not harshly so. He knew who his first-choice players were, but didn't give them preferential treatment. If you weren't playing well, he said so, and if you continued to play badly, you got dropped. He liked the rotational system, which meant more opportunities for players and therefore less frustration, as he was keeping 25 players happy and not just 15. A lot of the things Dick did showed courage and conviction, and that rubbed off on the players. When he was picking 19-year-olds, the other guys started believing in themselves more.

Dick's recruitment of Plum as the Sharks' forwards coach was a masterstroke because he gave him balance. Plum is technically very good, excellent on defence, and he calmed Dick down on the all-out attack. Plum was outstanding from the word go and, being a Kiwi, there was automatic respect.

Plum's attitude as a coach is one I've never seen before. I've looked at the younger Sharks players and thought they don't know how lucky they are. His calmness is incredible – he doesn't get worked up – which is rare for a coach. He has perspective on everything. You can have the same conversation with him on a Friday before the game and on the Sunday afterwards.

It's hard to find a better coach than Plum, who took over from Dick as Sharks head coach in 2008 when Dick joined the Bok set-up. He's technically brilliant, very good with people, frank, and calm. He's mates with the guys – we all call him Plum – but when there's something that has to be said or done, he does it. Everybody knows he's in charge without him ever having to remind them. It's because he has a quiet strength and is at ease with his status; he's not constantly trying to prove he's the head coach. He gets the work done quietly and efficiently. Most coaches are afraid of how they interact with the team in case it affects their power or status; they are afraid players will lose respect for them.

Plum once told me how he wants to be his kids' mate but has to step in now and again to keep them on the right track. He's like that with his rugby players.

Plum is still a relatively young coach but he's learnt a lot through different experiences in places around the world – like Swansea and Wellington – in a short time.

After we lost to the Reds in one of the big shocks of the 2009 Super 14, Plum said to the guys that even he had started to believe he was a good coach, which was the worst trap to fall into. You don't often get a coach admitting that he's made mistakes.

Plum has a lot of pride but not a big ego. He knows it's not about him, but about the players, and he drives this all the time.

15

FROM HEROES TO ZEROS

After an impressive 2004 and a respectable 2005, the bubble burst for the Boks in 2006. Never mind the so-called second-year syndrome, this was third-year terror.

After having had a charmed run for two years we were thrown off balance when we had a sudden slew of injuries to key players. The team misfired, confidence took a big knock and we entered a downward spiral.

We started well with a 36-16 win over Scotland in Durban, but in Port Elizabeth we lost Schalk Burger to a serious neck injury and played badly, despite winning 29-15.

On a personal note, I should never have played that game because I had strained my calf in the captain's practice the day before, but Jake White was desperate for me to play as he was under increasing pressure. Jake always wanted me to play every single Test, which I understood because we were a partnership. But I don't know how I got through the game. My calf was strapped up dead and I played with my teeth clenched throughout.

While we were poor in Port Elizabeth, we had won, and the real drama erupted the next week when we lost 36-26 to France at Newlands. We were terrible and you could sense that the belief was ebbing from the side. It was the first Test we had lost at home under Jake and the whispering voices of the folk who had never liked him – but had held their tongues because we had been winning – found full voice.

Two weeks later we were in Brisbane, which has never been a happy hunting ground for the Springboks, but on this occasion it was a macabre cemetery. I still can't quite put my finger on why we got a 49-0 hiding. There are no excuses – you can't defend that scoreline – but there were some contributing factors.

It was the first time we had toured without the Incredible Schalk and there were injuries to key players in Bakkies Botha, Fourie du Preez and Jean de Villiers. We also had two senior players who were distracted from the task at hand. They were having major personal issues which I'm not at liberty to disclose. I spent the week in one of the player's rooms counselling him, which in turn didn't help my preparation.

Jake was showing obvious signs of stress over his job, and our performances against Scotland and France hadn't inspired confidence. Mentally we weren't in a good place while the Wallabies, for some reason, were in a vicious mood. It was Pierre Spies's debut Test and he got the ball from the kick-off. As he was running it up to take his first contact in a Springbok jersey, the Wallabies were screaming 'Fuck him up! Fuck him up!'

It was the ugliest Test I've ever played. In the post-match TV interview I didn't know what to say. I just stood there mouthing empty platitudes, inwardly begging the guy to shut up so I could slink off.

What can happen in rugby is that when one team is, say, 10% up and the opposition 10% down, it results in a thrashing. Everything the Wallabies tried that night came off, and everything we did was a stuff-up. Our performance was summed up by Jaco van der Westhuyzen dropping the ball and then kicking it in the same movement before it hit the ground, trying to pretend it was a drop goal.

The hardest part of being a captain is trying to right the sinking ship when it's taken a lot of water. I have learnt that if you have nothing profound to say, rather leave it. Say nothing. What the heck is there to say that's not going to sound plastic to hardened rugby professionals?

In the change room after the game, nobody said a word, and we had the shortest Kontiki ever (more on these fines meetings later).

We played New Zealand in Wellington the following week. Jake had finally realised that Jaco wasn't the answer at flyhalf and called up Butch James, who flew in on the Wednesday. It went a lot better. We scored a try in the first 30 seconds through Fourie du Preez, but ultimately we were never really in contention, and lost 35-17.

We were heartened, though, because the All Blacks were a better side than the Wallabies at the time, so we went to Sydney with the motivation and belief that we could turn it around. And we nearly did. We led until the 75th minute when Mat Rogers scored a try and Stirling Mortlock kicked the touchline conversion to give the Wallabies a 20-18 win.

My spirit was broken. There were tears in my eyes when I walked to the post-match TV interview and I had to take a minute to compose myself. I mentioned in that interview how cruel the game can be when it goes against you, and we truly felt the rugby gods had forsaken us. But at least we had something to work with when we returned for the home leg of the Tri-Nations – two Tests against the All Blacks and one against the Wallabies.

First up were New Zealand at Loftus. I was convinced we could resurrect our form of 2004 and 2005 at this famous Springbok stronghold but we suffered another dismal loss – 45-26. I'll never forget the boos that reverberated around the stadium as I made the dreaded walk to the post-match TV interview. The pain cut right through to my very marrow as I stood there as Springbok captain and had to raise my voice above a 50 000-plus chorus of derision.

The public condemnation at the time was unrelenting. The folk who had cheered us in 2004 now passed cheap chirps in the airport, in hotel foyers, in the street. Funnily enough, it was almost always the same thing: 'I hope you're on your way to practice, not home.'

Talk about going from heroes to zeros ... I remember wondering: 'Is this it? Is this the end of the road? Will any of us have jobs tomorrow?' But even in the darkest times, it's never a case of 'is it worth it?' because you know how good it is when you win.

When you are a Springbok, no amount of psychological spin doctoring can ever fully banish that fear of losing because you know that a defeat follows you around like a rotten smell until the next time you win.

It takes a while for a Springbok to register the staggering magnitude of what a Test means to many South Africans. Obviously you're aware of the multitudes at the stadiums, but over a career it sinks in that there are South Africans in Springbok beanies cramming into bars from New York to Delhi, and their happiness rests upon your shoulders, not just for that night but for a few days after. The result of a Test deeply affects so many people and you realise that it's hardly just a game.

We discuss it in team talks – how we can affect the psyche of the country on a Monday morning. As I said earlier, if we win a big Test, folk arrive at work with a spring in their step, and no matter how *kak* their job may be, their morning is brightened by exchanges about the game, about the try Habana scored, or the tackle Bakkies made. They feel good, and we are responsible for that, just as we are indirectly responsible for the oke who comes home from watching the game in a foul mood.

The more you play for South Africa, the more you realise that as good as it is when you're winning, it's 10 times worse when you're losing. It doesn't help that as a nation we are still uptight. There are a lot of different cultures and each has its reason to moan. Whites complain about reverse racism, and blacks that they were denied things for so long because of apartheid. Everybody has a lot to be negative about, but one thing they can all be proud of is the national rugby team.

People rely on us to provide them with good cheer. Our supporters will spend their last bucks of the month on meat and beers for a braai, and R650 for a Springbok jersey is a lot of money for the average working person. But on match day, our supporters gather in hope and excitement – the *kak* week at work is forgotten because the Boks are going to deliver. We know this. We know that the Springboks complete the 'we love *braaivleis* [barbecue meat], sunny skies' jingle.

But then we lose, and sometimes play badly in the process, and those supporters feel betrayed. The ice that melted in the *Klippies* and Coke freezes over again. These okes get seriously pissed off. They take it personally. I know because if I dare to venture out of my house after a defeat, I'm told how *kak* we are. People are not shy, trust me. I've often felt that the guy stopping me in a shopping mall would actually like to inflict physical pain on me to make me understand how much I've let him down.

It's quite a heavy thing to carry around with you, but you won't hear a Bok call it a burden because this responsibility is what makes us so proud when we win. When you play for South Africa, you accept that you sign away your privacy as part of the proudest deal you will ever make.

There was a sad postscript to that disappointing loss to the All Blacks in Pretoria. On the Friday, Frik du Preez – the Springbok Player of the Century – was invited to present the jerseys. The excitement among guys like Bakkies and Victor Matfield was something I've only seen with my three-year-old daughter at an Easter egg hunt, which is why I felt so deeply for them when Frik proved to be an unfortunate flop. He spoke about falling standards and how he wasn't prepared to hand out jerseys to losing teams. In his day, he said, they had never lost two in a row and we had just lost four. I eventually switched off. I just stopped listening. Bakkies and Victor were so disappointed. It was such a letdown.

There had been so much despondency in our camp after our run of losses and the guys had been cheered by the prospect of their hero handing out the jerseys, but he failed them. It was like meeting the president you voted for, only to find out he's not the person you thought he was.

16

GETTING BACK ON TRACK

After that terrible loss to the All Blacks at Loftus, Jake White got us the hell out of town as fast as he could. We were playing the same opponents in Rustenburg that Saturday, so he took us to an isolated resort in the Pilanesberg mountains.

I'm not a big believer in basing a rugby team in the backwaters but in this case it was a godsend. We had lost five Tests in a row and if we had remained in Pretoria to prepare for this match (it's only a 90-minute drive from Rustenburg) we would have run the risk of being spat on in the streets. But we had a fantastic week of isolation in the bush. Many of the guys had hunted while growing up and Mother Nature quickly revived their spirits. The feeling was that it couldn't carry on like this. Surely we couldn't lose six in a row?

We were *gatvol* and in the mood for a fight. We didn't give a damn anymore. We wanted war. The line from me that week was 'this is it' – there wouldn't be any more chances for this team, we'd already had two more lifelines than we should have had.

'They will fire our coach if we lose,' I told the guys, 'and when the new guy comes in, he'll change the team a year out from the World Cup, and everything we have worked for will be flushed down the toilet.'

This 'now or never' speech was a tough call for me to make because we were playing the All Blacks – not Italy or Japan – at their best and they had put 45 points past us the week before. And when you lose after a 'do or die' speech, where do you go from there? But it was a call I felt had to be made, as it really was do or die. We simply couldn't lose three in a row at home and the more I banged the 'last chance' drum during the week, the more the guys got worked up.

We wanted a war and we got one. The game was ferocious even by Springbok-All Blacks standards. From the first whistle this match was straight out of the amateur era in terms of the players wanting to sort each other out. Our second row started it when they gave their front row a 'welcome to Rustenburg' in the first couple of scrums. After one exchange, I watched with wide eyes as a crazed Carl Hayman chased Os du Randt to a ruck and split his head open with a punch.

The All Blacks, who had won 15 Tests in a row, played as if their lives depended on it. It really was a struggle in the grand tradition of our rivalry, despite the unlikely location.

And it all came down to Rodney So'oialo's brain fart when he came into a ruck blatantly from the side and referee Chris White raised his arm in our favour, with the All Blacks ahead 20-18 with three minutes left.

I don't know where the conviction came from but I just knew the game was over. I was in midfield and sprinted to the spot, calling for the ball before anybody could do anything rash. As I was running I was shouting 'Posts, posts, posts!' to the ref, but even before I'd opened my mouth I could see André Pretorius walking towards me, which was a good sign. I smiled at him and said, 'Rather you than me', which broke the ice and he smiled back.

That kick had to go over. I couldn't begin to describe my emotions as André lined it up from the touchline. A cloud of woe would lift if it went over. If it didn't, well, I reckon it would have been all over for Jake and that Bok team. It sailed through – with me roaring it on every millimetre – and when the final whistle went soon after, I collapsed onto the pitch and wept with relief. I had carried defeat on my shoulders for two months and in a flash of André's boot, the excruciating weight vanished.

The relief was reflected in our celebrations that night, but it took a while for the hostility between the teams to cool. The All Blacks were staying on one side of the Sun City hotel and we were on the other. Both teams went to the Traders bar that night, but there wasn't a lot of mixing. There was a distinct whiff of cordite in the air. Butch James made a comment – no one can recall what it was – to All Blacks assistant coach Steve Hansen which caused some drama and we decided it was best to move on to the casino.

On the way there, I stumbled across a dazed Dan Carter plonked in a bush, looking a little worse for wear.

'Dan, can I help you?' I asked.

'Thanks Smitty, that would be nice,' he said with a smile.

So there I was, after that ill-tempered battle, helping the All Blacks flyhalf along, arms around each other's shoulders, comrades in intoxication! I found him a quiet table in the casino, sat him down and left him to it.

Chiliboy Ralepelle and I gambled the night away. We won some good money, so it really was my lucky day.

I got back to the hotel at about 9am, as did quite a few of the guys, and it was chaos in the corridors. It looked like a schoolboy rugby tour, with fire hydrants in naughty hands and the guys generally blowing off steam. We don't normally behave that way but after being in the pressure cooker for so long, you could cut us some slack.

I got into my room and showered, and as I was changing my dad phoned: 'Hi, I'm outside. Are you ready?'

Clockwise from top left: I was selected for SA U21 in 1997; in action for SA U21 against a Free State XV; playing for the Sharks in the 1998 Super 12 and Currie Cup; celebrating my first trophy success with the Natal U21 team (we beat the Lions in the 1997 final)

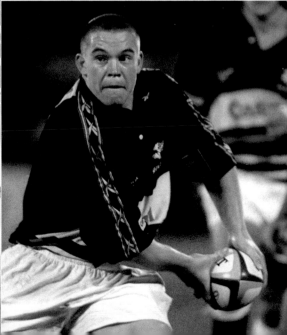

Clockwise from top left: Paddling down the Zambezi during the Sharks' pre-season Super 12 camp in 1997 (from left to right is Walter Minnaar, Shaun Payne, Gary Teichmann, the guide, John Slade, me and Joe Gillingham); getting ready to sing the national anthem before my Test debut against Canada in East London with Corné Krige on my left and Dan van Zyl on my right; I started my first Test against Argentina on the end-of-year tour in 2000 and wore the No 2 jersey again against Wales; with my good mate Shaun Sowerby in London during the SA U21 tour in 1998

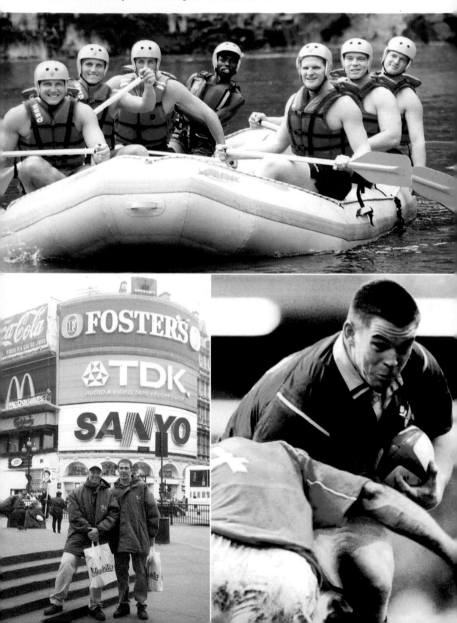

This page: Battling the Blues in the 2001 Super 12; Albert van den Berg congratulates me on my try against the Lions in the 2001 Currie Cup semi-final
Opposite page: Packing down against France in 2001 with Ollie le Roux and Willie Meyer also in the front row; trying to keep warm during Kamp Staaldraad in 2003 (with a few photoshopped rugby balls keeping our pride intact!)

Above left and below: I captained the Boks for the first time in our 2003 World Cup match against Georgia in Sydney
Above right: Tackling Jerry Collins during our World Cup quarter-final against the All Blacks in Melbourne

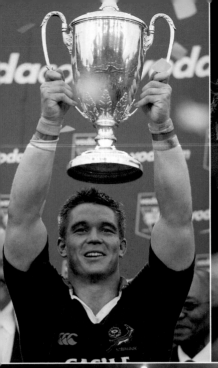

Opposite page: Scrumming down with Os du Randt and Eddie Andrews during our 2004 Tri-Nations match in Christchurch; urging the guys on during that game
This page (anti-clockwise from top left): Lifting the Tri-Nations trophy after we beat the Wallabies in Durban; celebrating our win with Jake White (who had a lot more hair then!); Butch James hugs me after my try against the Chiefs in the 2004 Super 14

Clockwise from top left: Thanking our fans after we beat Scotland at Murrayfield in 2004; we drew our first Test with France in 2005 but won the second to clinch the series; beating the All Blacks at Newlands in 2005

Clockwise from top left: Taking on the Wallabies at Loftus in 2005; shattered after losing to the Wallabies in Sydney in 2006; hugging Breyton Paulse after our last-gasp win against the All Blacks in Rustenburg in 2006; helping the Boks to break our drought at Twickenham later that year; colliding with David Pocock during the 2006 Super 14

Opposite page: In action for the Sharks in 2005. We finished fifth behind the Bulls on points difference
This page: Devastation after losing the 2007 Super 14 final to the Bulls in the last move of the game

Right (clockwise from top left): A Sharks team dinner outing; my 29th birthday in Surfers Paradise; at a fancy dress party with BJ Botha and Eduard Coetzee; jet boating with the Sharks on a raging river at Lake Taupo *Below:* We thrashed England in our two home Tests in 2007

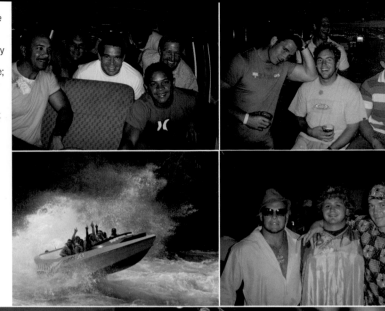

I'd forgotten that we had arranged a family day on our farm … In the car my dad took one look at me, or maybe it was one whiff of me, smiled and said, 'Don't worry, I'll do the braaiing, you just have to talk to your mother.'

After the high of Rustenburg, we were never going to slip up against the Wallabies at Ellis Park. We won 24-16 and the Tri-Nations ended on a successful note.

That took the heat off Jake and the team, but it would return with a vengeance that November when Jake gambled on his future by experimenting with new players, beginning with the centenary Test against Ireland in Dublin (the Bok emblem was first worn by South Africa in 1906 when they toured the four Home Unions).

Jake had consulted with the powerbrokers regarding his plan of expanding our depth ahead of the World Cup. He got consent and a promise that he wouldn't be judged on results, but the reality is that the Boks are always judged on results. He shouldn't have tampered with the team for that Dublin match, as it was a heck of an important occasion and we were playing in a replica of the 1906 jersey. We wanted to win in that historic kit to do justice to our legacy but understood that the World Cup was our ultimate goal.

Our back three were all making their Test debuts – Jaco Pretorius and Frans Steyn on the wings and Bevin Fortuin at fullback – and we had left the likes of Victor Matfield, Bakkies Botha and Fourie du Preez at home (Johan Acker-mann and Albert van den Berg were recalled to the second row with Ricky Januarie starting at No 9).

It was the most unsettled team we had fielded under Jake, and there we were at Lansdowne Road – an inhospitable venue – against a good Ireland team.

We emerged from the tunnel and were just about knocked off our feet by a gale force wind howling from left to right. Jake's philosophy on wind is that you play against it in the first half because the hype and the emotion will tide you over for a while, and teams tend to feel each other out in the beginning so you have the full advantage of the wind in the second half. I argued that because we had such an inexperienced team, we needed a good start. We needed all the help we could get, and if we could get our tails up I could get the youngsters to believe in themselves when we came in at half-time. But to my discredit, I didn't go with my gut feeling. Jake can give his opinion, but the toss is up to me. I won it and decided to play into the wind.

We couldn't do a thing with the ball in that first half – we couldn't kick it out, we couldn't move it wide – and then, Murphy's law (there would have been a few Murphys in the crowd), the wind died at half-time. Ronan O'Gara had played the wind like he was born in it and Ireland led 22-3. We never recovered from that first half, losing 32-15, and I never forgot a painful lesson about trusting my instincts. From that day I have always played with the wind in the first half.

I was fighting a lone battle from an experience point of view on that tour and worked really hard to fire the team up the next week for the first of back-to-back Tests against England. I played on Lansdowne Road being an aberration, a one-off stuff-up because of the wind. I said: 'Let's start the tour in England, last week didn't happen.' I asked who had been in a team that had beaten England and nobody put their hand up, and I said, 'None of the Boks at home have either, besides Monty, so what an opportunity. Let's bury the bogey.'

We played bloody well and Butch had the game of his life, but he got injured at the end of the third quarter when we were leading 21-13 and in complete control. Things then went horribly wrong, with Phil Vickery scoring a late try to give England a 23-21 win.

We were never going to lose the following week. The boys now knew they could win at Twickenham and wouldn't let it slip again. André's four drop-goal extravaganza gave us a comfortable 25-14 victory.

That win at Twickenham – the Boks' first since 1997 – was a massive psychological turning point for us and England. Jake had made victory at Twickenham the focus of the tour and hammered the point that beating England there would be the first step on the road to beating them in the pool game at the World Cup the following year.

And when we smashed them 58-10 in Bloemfontein and 55-22 in Pretoria in June 2007, the whole psyche of games between the teams had swung in our favour.

They brought an understrength side but it wouldn't have mattered who they'd brought. It was a World Cup year and we were primed for success. We were anxious to consolidate our drought-breaking win in London and wanted them to be in a habit of losing to us. We would have smashed whoever they sent.

Suddenly it was us who had the long sequence of wins and we knew we would not lose to them in France.

17

SUPER 14 HEARTBREAK

The 2007 Super 14 campaign was one of the most enjoyable periods of my career. The Sharks had great players, great coaches and played some fantastic rugby.

The whole campaign was such a pleasure. The guys got on extremely well with each other, and we had strong personalities such as Percy Montgomery, Bob Skinstad and Butch James. The chemistry was awesome. We loved touring, we had a lot of skill and pace and were extremely physical. We man-handled the opposition – we were that strong – and became the first South African team to top the Super Rugby log. All of this made the disappointing loss in the final – to the Bulls in Durban – all the more unbearable. I don't think I'll ever get over it.

The hype on the day of the game was something I had never seen. All morning there were flags flying from cars all over KwaZulu-Natal. We went to the Riverside Hotel near Kings Park and drove our cars from there to the stadium, but we nearly missed kick-off because of the carnival raging throughout Durban. We put on our hazard lights and drove down one-way streets and when the cops stopped us, we explained that we were the players.

In the change room, the guys were in complete control. We believed that we were going to win, that we were a better side than the Bulls and would come out on top if we simply did our jobs. As a captain, you pick up a mood, and I don't recall a more promising or positive vibe.

When we ran out onto the pitch, the stadium erupted. It was as if the whole country was cheering the success of our rugby in having two teams in the final. It was magical. The cheering just went on and on before kick-off, which gave the players a massive boost.

Early in the game, Bryan Habana took Monty out in the air. That really frustrated me because in any other match anywhere else in the world that would have been a yellow card at the very least. I should have known then that this wasn't a game where referee Steve Walsh and his assistants were prepared to make the big calls.

The game just flew by and I can only tell you about things that stood out, like that Habana tackle. We seemed to have it wrapped up at the three-quarter mark when I found myself being subbed, which was disconcerting because I wanted to be on the field to manage what went down at the death.

I watched from the sideline with a sick feeling that something would go wrong, but when Albert van den Berg scored a try with three minutes remaining to put us ahead 19-13, I reckoned I had been paranoid for nothing and I hugged the guy next to me, who happened to be Monty. 'What's he doing here?!' I thought, and that brought the first flutter of panic. Why the hell had our kicker been subbed? Who was going to take the conversion that would give us a crucial eight-point cushion?

With Monty not there, the kick surely had to go to Butchie, the one guy who could take shots like this with his eyes closed. He had the temperament and the experience. He had played in a Super 12 final. It was his kick. It was as simple as that. (In fact, it shouldn't have even been Butch's kick, as Monty should have been kept on for the full 80 minutes.)

But the next thing I saw was a toss-up taking place between Frans Steyn and Ruan Pienaar. AJ Venter was acting captain and Frans had gone up to him and said he wanted to take the kick. AJ felt that because he was so adamant, he should have it. Having just turned 20, Frans was the youngest guy on the field, and it didn't make sense in that situation for the least experienced player to take a kick that should have shut the Bulls out of the game. AJ got sucked in by Frans's bravado but shouldn't have had to make that decision.

The least Frans should have done was take his time and use up the full minute, but he rushed it and hooked it across the poles. I saw the Bulls' heads go up and they sprinted to the kick-off, as they knew they were back in it. We had opened the door.

Those last minutes were like a nightmare in slow motion for me. The infamous ruck where Wikus van Heerden illegally stole the ball from us was right on the sideline in front of touch judge Lyndon Bray and our bench. I screamed at Bray 'Hands in, hands in!' but the play continued. A few minutes later Habana went through our defence, Derick Hougaard kicked the conversion and we had lost 20-19.

I've never been so broken, and I'll never get over it. It's the worst I've ever felt. I wanted to cry but didn't want to do it in front of the guys, so I went into a toilet and sobbed for five minutes before I was able to pull myself together.

Dick Muir should never have subbed his captain or his kicker. If he had needed to freshen up the team, he should have done it around Monty and me. Dick had been subbing us throughout the tournament, so his gut feeling was to not change a winning formula. However, the lesson is that a final is very different to other matches of a tournament. You don't do things on a gut feel in a final, you stick to the basic rules that win finals.

It's a different world in a final. A World Cup pool match, for example, is completely different to a World Cup final. There's a reason why no tries are scored in finals – pressure. Nobody makes mistakes on defence, and the intensity of everything is multiplied by 10.

There was no respite from the pain the day after the final. The Boks were convening in Bloemfontein for a training camp and the players from both teams were supposed to go up in a bus from Durban (can you believe it?). I had decided beforehand to take my car and that blue Sunday morning, Monty, Butch, Bob and I drove to Bloem together.

I hadn't slept a wink. I couldn't deal with the defeat. It just burnt, and having to face the Bulls was the last thing I wanted to do.

Bob was playing DJ in the front of the car, telling jokes and trying to lift the funeral atmosphere. Eventually he told us to snap out of it and stop wallowing in self-pity, and the next thing we were singing songs, talking rubbish and letting off steam. But when we pulled into the car park at the hotel in Bloem my heart sunk again, and once more I was having visions of Jaco van der Westhuyzen swinging from one of the Kings Park crossbars like a monkey.

I thought the Bulls guys would be swaggering around with their shoulders back, grinning smugly, but I couldn't have been more wrong. They handled the situation in the most wonderful, humble manner. I don't know whether they had discussed it beforehand in a meeting or whether it was spontaneous, but their sincere humility diffused a potentially difficult situation.

I'll go so far as to say that the way they received and treated us – that hand of conciliation put out to us – was the first step to winning the World Cup. It unified us. It was a huge moment. They could easily have gloated but they chose humility instead.

18

ALTERNATIVE HEALING

In the Boks' first 2007 Tri-Nations game, against the Wallabies at Newlands, my right boot got hooked into the turf when a scrum collapsed in the 10th minute and my hamstring ripped in what felt like slow motion. Cold panic set in. Not being a speed merchant, I'd never had an injury like it, and I thought I could 'run it off'.

I got to my feet and tried to walk. When I found myself in the Bok defensive line, I realised I was a sitting duck – I couldn't lift my leg.

The worst case scenario screamed through my mind: No World Cup ... three years down the drain ... all the crap I took in 2006 for nothing. I sat on the sidelines with ice on my hammy and tried to block it out.

'Mate, you are going to France,' Jake White told me. 'You will have the best rehab possible and we'll sort it out.'

And, in fact, it healed pretty well during the Tri-Nations. Obviously I played no further part in the tournament and it was quite nice to hear people say that I was conspicuous by my absence (while we beat the Wallabies 22-19 at Newlands after two late drop goals from Frans Steyn, we lost 26-21 to the All Blacks in Durban a week later after leading 21-12).

It was the first Test rugby I had missed since Jake took over as Bok coach and I must admit it was encouraging to hear people saying I was integral to the team because they were underperforming without me. I had grown used to the only comment being that I should be dropped.

Jake stuck his neck out by sending a second-string squad to Sydney and Christchurch for the away leg of the Tri-Nations (the guys fought bravely in losing 25-17 to the Wallabies and 33-6 to the All Blacks). The Aussies and Kiwis were seriously pissed off, but it was a very clever move because it developed our depth while allowing the core of what would be the starting XV in France to be spared the possibility of injury.

It was two weeks of quality time for those of us who stayed behind in Cape Town. It solidified our decision-makers into a tight-knit group. The first-choice XV lived together, bonded, and got very fit. We got in some excellent training under Springbok shrink Henning Gericke, technical adviser Rassie Erasmus and scrum guru Balie Swart, and did a lot of technical homework on our kicking and mauling.

For instance, Rassie made the forwards do lineout drives against the backs, who had to try and stop us from 15m out. At first we thought it was a bit silly, and the backs were pussy-footing around. Then Rassie said, 'OK, now the forwards must defend against the backs' moves.'

Each division alternated between attacking and defending, with the losers having to do an extra fitness set (we were getting caned that day with sets of 400m sprints). As soon as it became a competition, things changed. Butch James was a maniac and I had to calm him down. I thought he was going to knock himself out, never mind a forward. Fourie du Preez had danced around the first couple of drives, before getting stuck in. He realised that the harder he went in, the better off he would be when he had to do a box kick behind the forwards at the World Cup.

After having mauled for 15m, the forwards then had to sprint back to the halfway line to defend against the backs, knowing we had to be in position or tries would be scored. It was a brilliant exercise because each group found out what the other actually does in a match, and we knew that we would be a better team at the World Cup after having got stuck into each other.

Rassie was instrumental in that period – he's very good technically – but he was in talks with Western Province at the time and when he got the job as the union's senior professional coach, he reluctantly withdrew from the Bok management team.

Jake then had another stroke of genius when he decided to replace Rassie with Eddie Jones, his good friend and mentor. Jake has based a lot of his coaching and ideas on Eddie's philosophies and the Brumbies' style of play under him. We would watch videos of the Brumbies and Wallabies (who Jones also coached) and focus on things like their lineout structures, and three-phase moves from scrums and line-outs. We weren't replicating what those teams were doing, it was more a case of Jake wanting us to see the benefits of a phase game based on our strengths. This resulted in a structured game based around our forwards.

Eddie had often told Jake in the past that he wished he had South African athletes to play the kind of game he wanted. Now he did.

I thought getting Eddie involved with the Boks just before we left for Paris was an excellent idea, because we'd get an injection of fresh ideas and energy from someone who had been involved in a World Cup final (only Jonny Wilkinson's boot prevented him from getting a winners' medal in 2003). Eddie was welcomed with open arms by all the players, which perhaps wouldn't have been the case with previous Bok squads when foreign coaches were viewed with suspicion.

At Eddie's first training session with us, we showed him some of our set plays.

'What do you think?' I asked. 'What would you give us out of 10?'

'If I'm being generous, about four,' he replied.

Ouch. We realised that we had been doing the same things every day but expecting different results.

Eddie fixed small things like running lines and fine-tuned here and there, and our backline play picked up. Stopping the Wallabies backline is one of the most difficult things to do in rugby, so our backs had a lot of respect for Eddie and were all ears.

Butchie and Jean de Villiers hung on to every word, but for Butch in particular, Eddie was a godsend. Even before we left for Paris, Jake wasn't convinced that Butch was the answer at flyhalf and he said to me in the week of the World Cup opener against Samoa that he thought André Pretorius would be his flyhalf for the big World Cup games. But in France, Butch just grew as a player under Eddie. He got better and better every week and was running the show by the time we got to the end of the World Cup final. At that stage Jake thought Butch was God!

My comeback game was the pre-World Cup Test against Namibia at Newlands (which we won 105-13 after scoring 15 tries), but horror of horrors, my hammy pulled again in the warm-up.

That was when the conjecture began in the media that I was seriously crocked and that Jake was covering it up. I was being written out of the World Cup and I was also getting disheartened. But Bok physio Clint Readhead was convinced I would be alright, and to tell the truth, I would have gone to France on one leg.

Our last warm-up matches saw us play a friendly against Connacht in Ireland and a Test against Scotland. The travel arrangements – from South Africa to Ireland, and Ireland to Scotland – were an unholy stuff-up. To this day I reckon somebody was trying to take us out of our comfort zone and test our resilience before the World Cup. We spent hours in airports, on buses and just standing around. It took us two days to make each journey. We were seriously pissed off. Maybe it wasn't a bad thing for us to experience a bit of the real world considering our travel plans usually run like clockwork, but we were flipping grumpy, especially when our journey from Galway to Edinburgh – usually an hour's direct flight – included a day spent hanging around at Heathrow airport.

I was now close to being fit and in Connacht I went for a slow jog to see if I could play, but my hamstring tightened up again. It was probably the worst thing I could have done after all the travelling and I was very annoyed with myself. For the first time I got seriously negative. I had set my sights on playing against Scotland at Murrayfield. I reckoned that game – two weeks before the World Cup – was my fitness test, and if I didn't make it, the dream was over.

Jake and Clint decided there and then that I would be a spectator in Ireland and Scotland, and I would return for the opening game of the World Cup against Samoa, but I was deeply worried.

We beat Connacht 18-3 but were terrible, before coming good against Scotland. We'd only had two days to prepare for that match as we had taken an eternity to get to our base in Peebles, and the talk was that Scotland had just come off the heaviest gym regimen in their history and were going to sort us out physically. But we bullied them. Watching in the stands, I had confirmation that we were serious contenders for the World Cup. We had been tested off the field with the travel, and on the field we made a mockery of Scotland's pumped-up physical challenge. We threw them around like rag dolls and won 27-3.

But I was living in panic every day. At the best of times I'm downright miserable when injured, because I'm frustrated. Roxy hated being around me when I was injured during the Tri-Nations that year. I felt that I was letting the guys down by just hanging around and being deadweight. The only thing worse than not being part of the action at all is still being part of the general picture but not being able to play. I was living in the Springbok camp and was part of the team and management meetings. Every morning at breakfast guys would ask me how I was feeling, and I just wanted them to shut up!

At the time, André was in Germany seeing Bayern Munich's doctor Hans-Wilhelm Müller-Wohlfahrt, who specialises in soccer players' hamstring injuries. I went to Bok doctor Yusuf Hassan and asked if I could be sent to him too, even if it was at my own expense. But Hassan is a good doctor and was adamant that I was getting the correct treatment with the Boks.

It was at this time that Roxy took some unusual action, by going to see Gladys Quinn, a friend of my mother's and a kinesiologist who believes in alternative healing by using the energy in your body. To be honest, I used to think this kind of stuff was mumbo jumbo. Not anymore.

While I was still in Ireland Roxy went to see Gladys to get a 'balance' reading. Gladys believes that your body and mind have to be one, and if they are in conflict, you won't heal.

Gladys said she could do a healing through Roxy because Roxy and I are so emotionally connected. She said the biggest problem wasn't my hamstring, but my mind. I was so scared of missing the World Cup that I was only interested in quick fixes. I had kept on trying to block the injury out, pretending it wasn't there. Gladys said that as soon as I accepted the injury, it would heal quickly.

Roxy told me all of this over the phone and it was like a dark veil lifting in front of me. I knew her words were spot on. I realised that Clint was doing his best but I was so negative and so panicky that I was fighting everyone, including myself. I changed my mindset immediately and Clint couldn't believe how I suddenly started getting better. He phoned Roxy and said, 'Thank you, thank you! I was starting to think he wasn't going to make it.'

When I heard Gladys's explanation from Roxy, the penny dropped. I realised straight away that I'd been in denial.

For our opening World Cup match against Samoa, I was strapped from bum to knee. I never felt any pain at the tournament and played the final without strapping.

19

PUTTING THE TEAM FIRST

Midway through our final pre-World Cup training camp in Durban, Pierre Spies began coughing up blood. Yusuf Hassan, our doctor, detected that something was seriously wrong and subsequent scans revealed that Pierre had a hereditary blood disease and could very well have died in the next six months if he had continued playing.

When players are named in a World Cup squad, a strong bond forms between them because you are united under the expectation of your country. You are acutely aware that you are carrying your nation's hopes. And Pierre was expected to make a big impact for us. He's a super guy, a magnificent athlete, and was in excellent form. So to say goodbye to a star like him, not knowing whether he would ever play rugby again, was very difficult for the guys.

Then came the whispers about drugs. I always shake my head at human nature when accusatory fingers are pointed at players because we get tested so often, even when injured.

I always say, 'Go and have a look at the player when he was 18. Did he have the physical framework then?' In the case of Pierre, I saw him playing for SA U19 in Pietermaritzburg when he was still a wing and he was a freak of nature then.

The thing with Pierre is that he comes from a family of athletes and almost abnormal training regimens were part of the deal. His dad, Pierre Snr, was superfit and was a champion sprinter and wing for Northern Transvaal, and he died from a heart attack at the age of 51. It made a lot of sense in hindsight that he could well have been suffering from the same affliction that his son now had.

The big question was who should replace Pierre in the squad. I was heavily involved with the decision and I told Jake White: 'I have a dodgy hammy. I feel under pressure, so the other guys feel under pressure. If I get injured there's only one other hooker – Gary Botha.'

So I pushed hard for Bismarck du Plessis' inclusion. He had been with me at the Sharks for a couple of years and I knew what he could do. He was a huge impact player for us in 2007. We knew he would be a phenomenal hooker from day one at the Sharks. The Boks needed a third hooker more than we needed a sixth loose forward. Jake understood that and picked Bismarck on account of my suspect hammy. It would prove to be a masterstroke because Bismarck ended up throwing in a vital lineout in the World Cup final when I was off the field for blood.

Gary felt hard done by as he was an original member of the World Cup squad, but his attitude after being leapfrogged by Bismarck was very good. He never spoke badly of him or me, and he remained positive. Those things make a big difference in a World Cup campaign.

The only other big selection issue came when we had to decide whether to play Bob Skinstad or Wikus van Heerden off the bench in the final against England. Bob had missed the birth of his son because he didn't want to disrupt the team, and got pipped at the post because Jake predicted that the final would be ultra tight and we would need someone who could play on the ground rather than a guy who could potentially break the line out wide.

Before we left for France, it was imperative that we sorted out all matters related to payment. Money is undeniably the root of all evil, and jealousy over it is the quickest way to splinter a sports team.

SA Rugby told us that it would offer us a pot of R26 million to win the World Cup and then took out insurance in case we did. The potentially tricky part was deciding who would get what if we did win it. I had a strong opinion on this and called in three or four senior guys and proposed that we simplify the matter by dividing the pot equally among the 30 players, no matter what roles they would inevitably play. My reasoning was that the guy playing 80 minutes every week and the guy spending most of the tournament holding tackle bags were both equal members of the same squad, and that if we had a few sour apples the whole barrel could end up polluted. In past World Cup campaigns, there have been complicated systems to determine how money would be proportionately handed out according to how much each guy played – a point for this game, half a point for that game – but it was ugly, it encouraged selfishness and bred resentment.

Not one senior guy fought me on my idea, and when I took it to the team, the reception was amazing, especially from the guys who knew they were on the fringes. They were touched that the senior guys cared more about the team than themselves. An astonished Ashwin Willemse came to me and said: 'You mean you and I will get the same money even though you're the captain and I'll hardly play?' It was a solidifying moment, just as the Bulls players' treatment of their Sharks counterparts had been when we arrived for the Boks' post-Super 14 camp.

My second piece of financial inspiration was to propose that we made sure injured players were taken care of. I said to the guys: 'There are going to be injuries so I suggest we take the money we got for the warm-up games against Connacht and Scotland and put it into a kitty, rather than our pockets, and make it an insurance fund. If nobody gets injured, the money goes back to you. But let's take it for now and cover each other. The pot is only so big. If 10 guys get injured, they will get paid pro rata.'

Again, there was not one dissenting voice, and I could feel we were drawing closer as a group as it became evident that it really was a case of all for one and one for all. Our three major World Cup casualties – Pierre, Jean de Villiers and BJ Botha – got paid out of that kitty.

Of the R26 million the Bok squad was paid as a bonus, each player received R800 000 and got out R480 000 after tax. It's decent money but not a fortune compared to other professional sports. In any case, during the World Cup I had the distinct impression that it wasn't the money driving the players. I had asked a number of guys what was important to them and the general answer was that the money would run out, and they would spend it on who knows what, but they would always have a World Cup winners' medal.

During that pre-World Cup build-up in Durban, I had an idea for an excellent team-building exercise and discussed it with Henning Gericke. I told him my holiday house down the KwaZulu-Natal south coast could sleep 30 people, and I wanted to secretly arrange a day that the players would never forget. He loved my plan, and he and our excellent public relations manager Annelee Murray got to work on the logistics.

The exercise began in a team meeting when I asked the players to write the names of the two most influential people in their rugby lives on a piece of paper and slip it under my door that evening. On the Wednesday, I announced on the bus that we wouldn't be training ... we were heading off for a surprise team-building exercise. The guys started joking about Staaldraad and called me '000'!

The day started at the Selborne Golf Estate driving range where cooler boxes of beers and cool drinks awaited the guys, and we had great fun in a longest drive contest. When Victor Matfield was opening his first beer he said: 'Are you sure I mustn't take my clothes off first?'

I led the guys through the lush coastal bush towards the beach and on the path was a sign saying '1995', and more cooler boxes. I had prepped Os du Randt to talk about the 1995 World Cup (although he didn't know he would be speaking about it during this exercise) and we sat in the bush in a circle listening to the legend talk about the amazing journey of that Springbok World Cup squad. The guys knew they were listening to a genuine hero, and were silent. It was just Os's voice and the sound of crashing waves in the background.

Onwards we went and arrived at a tee where two guys were about to tee off. I'm sure they'll never forget the day the Bok World Cup squad watched and cheered their shots.

Our next stop was a cove on the beach. More refreshments were served as Bob, Percy Montgomery and Albert van den Berg spoke about 1999. Bob spoke earnestly about a World Cup they could have won had there not been sideshows that prevented them from gelling as a team. He said they still managed to get so close, and now our team could go that step further.

I'd arranged with Nando's to have a 'halfway' tent further down the beach. The poor guy who was dressed in a Nando's suit got tackled a few times but escaped having his neck wringed! There was also a surf instructor with boards and some of the guys hit the surf for the first time in their lives.

A little further on was '2003'. Bakkies Botha and Victor said there wasn't much to say about that year's World Cup other than that it had been unpleasant for everybody. That stop lasted less than three minutes, and we didn't even finish our drinks. None of the guys knew where it was going to end, as they hadn't been to my holiday house.

It was dusk as we trudged along the beach and up popped '2007'. Now it was my turn to speak. I said we had heard about the Boks' three previous World Cup campaigns and that it was time for us to create our own story. 'We have a good team, we have self-belief, and we have trained well,' I said. 'The only thing that can stand in our way is individuals putting themselves ahead of team ambition.' I then gave them a rundown of the Sharks' 2007 Super 14 campaign, and said that while we'd had an amazing season, on one occasion one guy had worried more about himself, which could have cost us the title.

We spoke about how the needs of the team were paramount, and that if someone got dropped or injured, it wouldn't be about how the individual felt, but about what the team needed. All the guys chipped in and we covered a lot of ground, including our policy on alcohol. We felt that because we didn't have the drinking culture of the Aussies and Kiwis, we didn't require a blanket ban on drinking. We could be mature about having the odd beer and wouldn't compromise the campaign by cutting loose after big matches. As it turned out, not one guy abused alcohol in France.

We had a bonfire going by now and the players opened up about all sorts of things. My closing words were: 'The preparation is over. The next time we see each other we'll be in our No 1s on the plane to Paris. We have to arrive in Paris having won the World Cup already.' The guys didn't quite understand this at first so I explained it further. 'We have to decide right now that we have won it. It's done. We arrive in Paris like champions, train like champions, and behave like champions. Start preparing for how you will behave as a champion because you've done it already.' This power of positive thinking had a big influence on us and we kept referring to it during the World Cup.

After my speech, I told the guys to follow me and joked that our destination was only 5km away, but then we came across candles leading along the path. The guys had been thinking, 'That was great fun, but Smitty's Staaldraad is over and it's back on the bus to the hotel', but as they walked around the corner they arrived at the lawn of my holiday house and standing there were the mentors whose names they had written down.

Not one player had any inkling of this. Most guys, like me, had their fathers there, but there were also school teachers and current coaches such as Loffie Eloff and Heyneke Meyer. It was a wonderfully emotional moment.

What an evening! It was a spectacular success. There was crayfish and fillet steak on the braai, the bar was open and Durban band Sitter was playing. They did a brilliant version of 'Shosholoza' (which we played often in France), and Butch James, Jaque Fourie and Schalk Burger were up on the stage strumming with them.

At 11pm a bus came for the mentors. Each of them was given a Springbok jersey signed by the player concerned. We thanked them and told them we would return their favours by bringing home the Webb Ellis Cup.

I wanted the players to have time on their own to let their hair down, which they did. It was the most amazing night in the tropical splendour of the KZN south coast.

We had a supporters' golf day the next day in Pretoria, and needless to say, we were a mess!

20

FIGHT TO
THE FINAL

J ake White loves omens. It was dusk as our bus drove
into Paris from the Charles de Gaulle International
Airport and as we passed the Eiffel Tower, the lights
flicked on and the spectacular French landmark was
bathed in glorious green and gold. I still don't know
why they chose that colour scheme for the duration of
the World Cup, but good on them!

Jake enjoyed that, and when we turned into the road of
our hotel – Avenue St Jacques – Jake triumphantly saw it as
another omen: 'Check the road sign, boys, it's St Jake!'

Before we left South Africa, Roxy and Springbok shrink
Henning Gericke had come up with an idea based on Lance
Armstrong's yellow armbands that raise cancer awareness.
Each squad member was given 25 green armbands to hand
out to family and friends, with the slogan 'Bok family energy
– we believe in 47'.

The '47' referred to the number of people in our tour
group after Eddie Jones joined us, and we would also be
away for 47 days. The religious guys in the group also found

meaning in Noah being in the ark for 40 days before releasing a dove which returned seven days later with an olive leaf. After the World Cup, one of the guys also pointed out that we had played four pool matches and seven in total, while if you add four and seven you get 11, which is the jersey number of Bryan Habana, who scored seven tries, the most at the tournament.

It was quite a special thing and we slipped on our green armbands as soon as we arrived.

We were overwhelmed by the motorbike cavalcade that greeted us at the airport. There were half a dozen monster bikes with flashing lights and wailing sirens, and they would escort us around Paris each time we set foot on the team bus. We felt like pop stars.

Four members of the French Foreign Legion were assigned to us and we assimilated them into the Bok squad. They made sure every journey we made went smoothly. They were clearly exceptionally well trained and were so good at their job that we hardly noticed they were around (our old mate '000' could have learnt a few tricks from them). They became part of the Bok family and Jake paid for them to come to South Africa for our victory parade.

Our first World Cup match was against Samoa at the old French headquarters, Parc des Princes. I recall lining up in the tunnel next to them – as teams do at the World Cup – and thinking how bloody huge they were. Afterwards, the guys said the same thing. I reckon Samoa picked their strongest, biggest blokes to try and smash us physically.

They did too. The first 20 minutes of that game were the most physical of my Test career. Samoa tore into us, but at that stage of our growth as a team, we were too composed to be rattled. We weren't the smallest team either, and it was a case of rolling with the punches. Mentally we were too strong. There would only be one result once their ardour had dampened in the second half, and we ran in some good tries to win 59-7.

We went into the change room upbeat that the show was on the road, but the first thing I did was look for Jean de Villiers. I wasn't sure what had happened to him, as he left the field early in the second half. I found him in the medical room. He was sitting there having his arm scanned, with tears running down his face. He had missed the World Cup in 2003 because of a shoulder injury that required surgery and now he had been struck down in the first match of 2007. His father was trying to console him, but there was nothing anybody could say. His bicep was torn and he didn't have to wait for the result of the scan for confirmation. He was devastated.

It was a big blow to our camp but also a massive opportunity to evolve our game around the way Frans Steyn played. Jean was a more creative player but Fransie had the strength to take the ball up. By picking him we added new tactical arrows to our quiver because of his massive boot. We were mentally in such a strong place that while we felt for one of our vice-captains, we just picked up the pieces, moved on and adapted. Our resolution was too strong. There could be no dwelling on the negative.

Our much anticipated pool game against England is one of my all-time favourite Tests. If I have one regret it's that we didn't go for more tries to get to the 50-point mark (we scored three tries), but I kept opting for the penalties because in a World Cup there are no bonus points for scoring four tries and you have to get into the habit of converting pressure into points. Still, a scoreline of 36-0 was pretty good and I have never felt so in control of a game in my life. Captaining was easy, and the control and decision-making of our backs was brilliant. It was seamless momentum.

On the team bus before that match, Henning had played us an extraordinary music video. It began with the stirring Juluka classic 'Impi' – which is about the Zulus fighting the English – and then went into Bok van Blerk's 'De La Rey' – which is about the Boers fighting the English – so you can imagine what buttons were being pushed. It then went into the patriotic 'Ons Vir Jou Suid Afrika', sung by Robbie Wessels and Van Blerk, just as the Stade de France became visible to the bus. It was powerful stuff, and that medley became the norm for each bus trip.

This may sound *windgat*, but we felt that England didn't have the attack to penetrate our defence, so we didn't want to give them scoring opportunities by being flamboyant. They were lacking confidence going into the game and had their injury problems (Jonny Wilkinson was out, with Mike Catt at flyhalf after Andy Farrell was originally supposed to start there), so we didn't want to give them anything to get their tails up. We only ran the ball in their half and when we did, we kept it close, and only went wide when we had taken their inside backs out of the game.

It unfolded perfectly. Fourie du Preez's performance was immaculate, and their pack didn't amount to the threat they could have been.

That match was like adding the ribbon and red wax to our World Cup package. I felt great throughout and when I saw the belief in our players – the confidence just oozing – my job was to make sure we didn't get ahead of ourselves.

Afterwards I reminded the guys that England had several players missing and that the senior players had no confidence in the coach, Brian Ashton.

For our third pool match, against Tonga, we travelled up to Lens in the north of the country by TGV (Train à Grande Vitesse). I recall sitting on that high-speed train thinking that the World Cup was going like precision Swiss clockwork. We had a few compartments to ourselves and the vibe was extremely positive as the guys listened to music, played PSP and chatted while we whizzed through France.

The Boks' big guns were originally supposed to have been completely rested for what we knew would be more rough and tumble from another Pacific Islands side, but Jake's sixth sense told him to put some insurance on the bench.

I thought it was still a very good team, captained by Bob Skinstad, and it was important that the back-up guys got game time as they had a role to play. But that match got increasingly complicated with every kick that the struggling André Pretorius missed. He had made the World Cup by the skin of his teeth because of injury problems, and it was his first game in two months. He didn't fire at all, missing four attempts at goal, which sentenced us to a fight to the death, because if you don't put Pacific Islands teams away, they linger, and then strike back.

Four minutes after half-time Tonga scored to take a 10-7 lead and the crowd sensed that the underdogs were in with a good shout, and got behind them. At half-time I'd said: 'We have to tighten up, we have to snuff the threat out now before the crowd warms to them ...'

Jake came storming down to the touchline after Tonga scored that try. He was furious. 'Smitty, you guys [the first-choice players on the bench] are on.'

The replacements made a substantial difference and we turned the game around to lead 27-10, but then relaxed and Tonga came at us again to cut the deficit to five.

I made a massive error in that period. Bryan Habana had been yellow-carded and I stupidly called the kick to the side of the field where we had no chaser. Tonga took the kick-off and went and scored. Bob came to me and said with a rueful smile: 'We are missing a wing, so why not kick to the other side?' I felt very stupid.

We eventually won 30-25 thanks to the bounce of the ball. I remember watching a Tonga kick heading for our 22 with a horde of red shirts chasing it. The ball bounced into touch and the final whistle blew. If it had bounced infield, they would have scored and drawn or won the match.

After the high of England, this close call was just what we needed. It was like the rugby gods were orchestrating our campaign for us and giving us a timely reminder that we were not indestructible.

An unfortunate postscript to the match was the citing of Frans for a ridiculous biting charge on Joseph Vaka. As had been the case with Schalk Burger after the Samoa game, the citing came just before the 24-hour citing period was about to end.

Schalk had been cited and banned for four matches for a dangerous tackle on Junior Polu, which we had thought wasn't anything too serious. Schalk's hearing went on until 3am, which was a major disruption to our preparations and focus. Fortunately, his sentence was reduced to two matches on appeal.

When Fransie was cited, we began to suspect there was a conspiracy designed to make life difficult for us. Vaka had clearly made up the accusation to deflect attention from him after he had tried to break up a big scuffle between Bakkies Botha and Inoke Afeaki, and it really upset Frans (who had run in when Vaka had become involved). 'People at home will think I'm a dog!' he said to me.

Just before Frans's hearing was about to take place, the charge was suddenly dropped. But a lot of time and energy had been wasted. We told each other that we were being seen as a threat, and people wanted to derail us. Conspiracy theory or not, those citings pulled us even closer together.

The big decision for our final pool match against the USA in Montpellier was whether Jake should play the first-choice XV or mix and match. He raised the issue with me and I suggested he call in the leadership group of Victor Matfield, Os du Randt and Percy Montgomery. It was unanimous. We said the top team had to maintain momentum going into the quarter-finals.

While we won 64-15, the Eagles gave us a good workout. Later, we had great fun teasing Bryan about how Takudzwa Ngwenya, their Zimbabwean-born wing, had run around him for one of the tries of the tournament. On a very sad note, though, we had lost BJ Botha to a serious knee ligament injury (he was replaced by Jannie du Plessis).

Onwards to Marseilles, the jewel of the south of France, for a weekend of the most unforgettable quarter-final action. We stayed in the hotel that the All Blacks had been in and when we arrived we saw that they had left their luggage behind in anticipation of a return to France from their quarter-final in Cardiff, where they were playing the Tricolores. We wondered if they were tempting fate ...

The hotel was stunning, straight off a postcard. It was right on the beach and you could have cast a fishing line out of your room window into the bright blue Mediterranean if you wanted to. Yet again we had an ideal week of preparation and the sea and sunshine was a refreshing change after the fog and smog of Paris.

We were playing on the second day of the quarter-finals and watched the first two quarters with extreme interest.

We were shocked when England beat the Wallabies 12-10, and pleased because we knew we had England's number while we just never know with our Tri-Nations rivals. And when the All Blacks lost 20-18 to France, there was an instant eruption in our hotel. The guys were supposed to be in bed resting but the result caused such a buzz that everybody was out on their balconies discussing the game animatedly. Yet another door had been opened, another major obstacle had been cleared from our road to the title.

The biggest task for me the next day was to dispel any doubt that we could also be knocked out – by Fiji, who had beaten Wales in the pool stage. There was no way we were going to complete the most unlikely of trifectas.

We almost did get knocked out, though, and our perilous position at 20-20 after 60 minutes induced one of my better, off-the-cuff speeches.

Fiji had drawn level through a sensational try by Sireli Bobo, and the crowd went absolutely berserk. The Islanders seemed to grow another foot taller and wider as they celebrated. My heart began to sink and then I thought, 'No way! It will *not* happen to us too.'

Being a tight forward, I was near the middle of the field taking this all in. I had the minute it would take for the conversion attempt to be taken and perhaps a few seconds afterwards to pull the team together. I got there in a hurry, instructed Bryan and JP Pietersen not to try and charge down the kick – it missed, thank heavens – and called the guys into a huddle.

I said: 'Not a word from anybody. Listen to me. We have to understand what we are faced with here. South Africa have never lost to Fiji. We are the Springboks, we believe we should win the World Cup, but we have got ourselves into a grave situation where there are two options. We can continue regarding Fiji as a threat and go into the last quarter with fear, or we can regard the glass as being half full and that means we have 20 minutes to play the game we planned to play instead of this loose rubbish that has given them their attacking opportunities.

'Guys, we watched the other quarter-finals. We saw the All Blacks getting knocked out; we saw them with eyes like saucers, rabbits in headlights, not knowing what had happened. They were forced into situations, panicked and didn't play to their strengths. Remember those close-up TV shots of Richie McCaw and Dan Carter looking like they had just seen a massacre? I'm seeing the same look on your faces. Your four-year dream is about to be obliterated unless something dramatic changes immediately.

'The difference between us and the All Blacks right now is that when their World Cup lives passed before their eyes, they didn't have it in them to stop the horror show. They are going home now. They can't fix it. But we still have time. We can still fix it, and we damn well will!

'This is the plan. We are going to kick deep. Bryan, you will chase and catch the receiver. Our forwards will arrive and put pressure on them until we turn the ball over. We will be awarded a scrum near their line and we will score from that. Alright?!'

And that's exactly what happened. The guys had understood the consequences of falling victim to fear and their response was superb. We then kept the game watertight, Fiji never got another opportunity and in the end we won comfortably – 37-20.

It had been another vitally important lesson. It had taken 60 minutes and a lot of sweat before we implemented the game plan that had been on the drawing board all week, and then it was a relative cruise. Fiji had been rampant at one stage with the whole world willing them on, but as soon as all 15 of us switched on, they were powerless.

I'm convinced that the battles we had all the way through the World Cup made us stronger and stronger. The three Pacific Islands teams rattled our skeletons in every tackle they made and it was such a contrast to the big yawn the All Blacks had through their pool games, so when they hit stiff opposition for the first time, they froze.

You have to be continually tested to stay ahead in life. If you don't fight battles, how can you be battle-hardened? It's like a bully teasing you by holding your head under water, and you think 'how much longer?' You come up just before you drown but you have tasted the fact that he could have killed you. You don't want to be in that situation again, so you stay away from the bully and you get more careful. That's exactly how teams are tested in rugby.

We had a flawless pool game against England but otherwise we fought all the way through the World Cup. Every challenge we overcame made us more resilient.

Take our defence, for instance. As the World Cup wore on, our belief grew that nobody would get through us. Defence became a good habit. We felt that teams would have to bring a shitload in terms of attack to get through us. You can have confidence, but there's nothing like the confidence borne out of consistently overcoming challenges. The more you do it, the more the team grows, and the bonds get tighter and tighter.

We reached the stage where we thought we could only lose the World Cup final – we could give it to somebody but nobody could take it from us.

That World Cup was like life in South Africa, where we survive against the odds. We have challenges in our country, and a lot has been thrown at us. In 1994, some whites were storing tins of food, and building underground cellars in anticipation of a bloody civil war, but Nelson Mandela helped the country prosper. Then Thabo Mbeki became president and the economy got stronger. At one stage we had interest rates of 25%, but we soldiered through it all.

South Africans' lives are about tolerance and adapting. It's all about attitude. If you are a white male who can't get a job, you can decide to go and make one for yourself. If you are a black guy whose dad had no opportunity, you can decide to make the most of yours.

The French people embraced us. We understood the crowds getting behind the underdogs but in general, they loved us. That was accentuated when England beat France 14-9 in the first semi-final. We were the tournament favourites and suddenly the world's favourite team, because if we got past Argentina in our semi-final, we would surely beat England.

The French simply couldn't bear the thought of the English winning their World Cup. Each morning when I woke up in Paris, I would open the curtains and look at an enormous sign on the windows of the office block across the street that implored: 'Go Springboks!'

As a team, the Pumas were having one heck of a swansong for their stars who were about to retire. They had got through to the semi-finals on a lot of emotion and a very basic game plan that saw them upset France and Ireland in the pool stage and Scotland in the quarter-finals.

But we knew we would beat them in the semi-finals. We had the pressure game to choke them out of the World Cup. I told the guys that we were like a massive python that you can see but want to keep at a distance. If you get too close, it wraps you up slowly and starts squeezing. After 50 or 60 minutes the opposition have had no ball, penetration, or opportunities in our 22. We have stolen their lineouts, and tackled them backwards. They can't breathe, and then they die.

That is what we did to Argentina at the Stade de France. We were called 'boring' by people who saw the game on a superficial level, and who didn't appreciate the subtlety of what we were doing.

Yet the suffocation approach almost always produced tries for us, and we scored four to beat the Pumas 37-13.

21

WORLD CHAMPIONS

In our last huddle before we leave the change room for a Test, I always look around the circle for eye contact to gauge the mood of the guys. In the Stade de France dressing room – from young Frans Steyn to a veteran in Os du Randt – I saw nothing but utter resolve, total focus, and steely determination.

'South Africa, let's go,' came the call from the IRB official and we lined up in the tunnel next to England.

This was it. Os got in behind me, CJ van der Linde behind him … and we started walking down the tunnel. At the front, just before we reached the grass, the Webb Ellis Cup sat glistening on a table. I saw it out the corner of my eye. I was aware it was there but I wouldn't let myself focus on it. When I watched a replay of the final, I saw that every Springbok did the same. Nobody so much as glanced at it. No eye contact. It wasn't ours. Not yet.

I had stopped sleeping well in the week of the semi-final against Argentina. I would stare at the ceiling of my hotel room telling myself to think about all the things that would go right and stop trying to find things that could go wrong. We had an exceptional team. Everything was in place.

I'm not normally a guy who worries but my record in finals was horrific. Since I had joined the Sharks in 1997, I'd lost three Currie Cup and two Super Rugby finals.

Roxy was more wound up than I was. If we had lost the World Cup final, she didn't know how she would be able to console me. The 2007 Super 14 final defeat had taken a lot out of both of us!

In turn, I was worried for Jake White. He had put his entire life into this.

Only Os knew what a final week could be like. Afterwards he said the hype and pressure had increased tenfold from what he remembered of 1995.

The first media session of the week was mind-blowing. Jake and I sat at a table surrounded by a towering conglomeration of cameras, microphones and lights. Recorders were piled up on the table. 'Welcome to the World Cup final,' Jake said.

Our hotel provided no refuge from the unrelenting hype. In fact, it was the centre of it. It was choked with administrators, supporters, sponsors – you name it, they were there.

World Cup sponsor Visa was also using our hotel, so its ambassadors – including England's World Cup-winning captain, Martin Johnson – were in our faces.

We had to have a secret corridor to help screen us from the chaos. We would come out of the lifts, go through the kitchen to our team room and then security had to open up a path for us through the people so we could get to the bus to go to training. Our training sessions were in the quiet and strangely named suburb of Noisy le Grand at a fenced-off sports club, so they were blissfully private.

Jake came up with the inspired idea of inviting the 1995 World Cup-winning team to do the jersey presentation. A few of them came in the end, including Francois Pienaar, James Small, Chris Rossouw, Joel Stransky and Morné du Plessis, who had been their manager.

You would have understood if these guys hadn't wanted their glory deflected, but the strong feeling from them was for us to take over the baton and create a whole new chapter of Springbok history. 'We need new stories, we need new pictures of a Springbok captain holding the World Cup,' Morné told us.

On the Friday morning, Jake told me that SAA (South African Airways) was flying in President Thabo Mbeki to wish us good luck the next day.

This was an interesting development because the Bok emblem, which we knew was under serious threat, had been a large focus for us. We believed that more than a century of the Springboks could end after this World Cup and that we had a huge responsibility and duty to the Springbok to win the 2007 World Cup and hopefully buy it time or even convince its strongest critics that it should stay. Each player understood the gravity of this situation. If we lost the final, the negativity of failure would invite the usual political interference. And victory would shut them up.

It was a powerful message. It gave us a sharp focus and banished the sideshows. It set the tone for the week. We felt we were playing for the future of the Springbok rugby team. And then came the news that the president was on his way.

Some of the guys had thought that the government wasn't supporting us, and didn't give a damn. Jake and I were a little overwhelmed at first at the prospect of a presidential visit on the most important match day of our lives. It was a fantastic honour, of course, but you want it to be a motivational visit, not a distraction.

There was no need for concern. Thabo Mbeki's message – that we had unconditional backing from the government – was short, sweet and emphatic. He said he wasn't there to take up our time on such a big day, that he simply wanted to tell us that the country was totally behind the Springboks. We had been worrying about the future of our team and here, on the day of the final, the president had flown in and said 'We back you'. That had a big impact on every player. It was the tying of the bow on our preparations.

What do you do with yourself on the day of a World Cup final, with kick-off at 9pm? It's the longest day of your life. You have to do your best to relax and stay off your feet. You have lunch and then go back to your room. Eventually, at 6:30pm we got together in the team room.

Jake, in his No 1s, went through his key points (we were in our tracksuits, with our No 1s on hangers and our boots in our kitbags next to us). Jake reminded us about what he had said in the change room after we had lost to France in 2005 at this ground. He said when we returned to the change room that night, the Webb Ellis Cup would be in the middle of it.

He emphasised again that the final was for us to lose, that we had to focus on our game and commit England to playing the same game as us, and that would shut them out. 'They can't beat you,' he concluded. Jake then played a highlights video of our World Cup campaign – nice, feel-good stuff – and then we were on the bus to meet our destiny.

In international rugby, it doesn't get more serious than the bus ride to the stadium. It is silent. I used to listen to music, but stopped when I became captain as I like to listen and get a feel of what's going on in the team – the atmosphere, the vibe, who's chatting, who's listening to music who doesn't normally, who's not listening who normally does, and who's whispering nervously. I pick up small things – things out of the ordinary – like a guy with wide open eyes, or somebody rubbing sweaty palms on his tracksuit.

Later, I'll make sure I stay close to the more nervous guys in the warm-up and give them quiet and subtle words of reassurance without them picking up that I've noticed their nerves. I enjoy that fatherly role, and I have a knack for it. Early in the match, I make a point of bumping into those guys after they have been involved in play – good or bad – and say 'well done, keep it up', or 'don't worry, keep going'.

Henning Gericke once again played DJ at the front of the bus as we neared the stadium and when we got off – with 'Ons Vir Jou Suid Afrika' ringing in our ears – we were ready for battle. The cocktail of adrenalin, motivation and determination coursing through my veins was like nothing I had experienced before. I felt truly bulletproof – and this was all before the warm-up.

The change room had all our home comforts. Our colours and flags were draped all over the show. Our names were on the lockers, the quotes placards that had travelled around with us for four years were on the walls. Everything was perfect. I was so ready, more ready than I have ever felt for a game.

After the warm-up it was my turn to speak to the guys. I had purposefully not prepared a speech – I wanted the situation to draw out of me what needed to be said. Looking at the players, I knew less would be more as motivation levels were overflowing. I spoke briefly about where we had come from as a team, and how we had got there. I said we had put one hand on the World Cup by beating Argentina, now it was time to put the other on it. Boom, done.

The game itself is a blur, apart from the odd big moment such as the Mark Cueto 'try' just after half-time (when he put a foot in touch before grounding the ball). I'm often asked about that incident, which resulted in a penalty and three points to England but even if they had got seven, I honestly don't think it would have affected the result.

While that 'try' was being adjudicated by the TMO, Stuart Dickinson, I knelt down and spoke to the guys. Everyone was totally focused. Sometimes when I speak I can see eyes wandering and I know we're in trouble, but not that night. If England had been awarded that try, I know we would have ignited to another level.

Another moment was the long-range penalty by Frans Steyn on the hour mark. I gave the ball to him and said 'Why not have a go?' and he replied 'Ja, bru'. He lined it up, had a look at the poles, and thump! Over! We led 15-6 and I knew

England were gone – that they didn't have enough to beat us – and from there we squeezed them out.

I got a stray boot in the face in the 72nd minute and had to leave the field to have my eyebrow stitched up. At the World Cup, you have to be stitched up by the stadium doctor. This fellow didn't speak any English and pulled me by my jersey down the tunnel into the medical room.

I reckon the urgency he showed must have had something to do with the French 'fondness' for the English. He practically ran me into the medical room, threw me on the bed, wiped my brow with Dettol and started stitching me up. No anaesthetic! Only by the third stitch did I know what was going on. It was like we were at war. Stitch, stitch, stitch, double knot and then he was racing me back out.

Now, the Stade de France is soundproof. Inside it you are in a cocoon. As quick as the doctor had been, I was terrified of looking at the scoreboard. I kept my head down, then looked up with half an eye as Bismarck du Plessis came off, and said my first 'Thank you, God'. England hadn't scored.

I was in a maul when the final whistle went. I dropped to my knees and praised the Big Man upstairs. It was so incredibly special. Most people only have a few really special moments in life, and the only time I have felt something like that mixture of overwhelming emotion and euphoria in Paris was when my daughter Emma was born. You can't control your emotions, and the tears come. There's relief, satisfaction, elation and gratitude all at once. I was in and out of the celebrations on the field because of TV commitments, but every single guy came and put his arm around me and thanked me for the four wonderful years.

When I saw Jake, we didn't say a word. We didn't have to. The biggest thing we had ever prepared for had been realised and we had been there from start to finish. He had tears streaming down his cheeks.

Our change room was chaos. We had the president, we had music blaring, we were singing, laughing, yelling and whooping like mad men. Each guy had whipped out his camera and there were endless shots taken with the Webb Ellis Cup (this is the only time you get to touch the actual trophy, as a replica goes around the world). We were in the change room for two hours. Nobody wanted to leave.

Back at the hotel, the champagne flowed with friends and family in the team room until 4am. South African business tycoon Johann Rupert presented each of us with a Cartier watch that had our name inscribed on it – that's how confident he had been that we would win.

On the flight home we expected there to be excitement at the Jo'burg airport but what we encountered was off the scale. It was completely manic. We were mobbed even before we got to passport control. In France we had been insulated from the atmosphere at home and now the full magnitude of our achievement exploded in our faces.

Our road trip around South Africa took the satisfaction to another level. When you see people without shoes chasing your bus in the pouring rain, waving little South African flags, it's humbling beyond words. The tears well up with the gratitude that you have been able to do a service to your country.

22

FRENCH ADVENTURE

I was back in France three weeks after the World Cup reporting for duty at my new club Clermont Auvergne; my Sharks and Springbok careers seemingly over.

Midway through 2007, I had made a decision that no matter what happened at the World Cup, I needed a change. I had been at the Sharks since I left school – I had cut short my matric holidays to go on tour with the Natal U21s – so after a decade in Durban it was time to move on and experience something new.

London Harlequins had made me a strong offer, which I considered very seriously, but I decided I wanted to experience something completely different and in the end I had to choose between Toulouse and Clermont.

I looked at the star-studded Clermont squad and made a rugby decision, assisted by my old mate Shaun Sowerby. He said Clermont was an ordinary town but had a very good rugby team, and I figured that with them having a Kiwi coach in Vern Cotter, it would be easier for me to make the transition (Vern had been one of Robbie Deans' assistants at the Crusaders and the backline coach, Joe Schmidt, had been at the Blues).

There are two things in the town of Clermont: the Michelin factory and the rugby team, which is owned by Michelin. Because of this, the locals accept you in a flash as soon as they have seen that you are serious about the club and have bled for the jersey.

Roxy and I hadn't done an extensive reconnaissance, we just made a decision. The club had sent us photos of where we would live, and during the 2007 World Cup I had visited Clermont and mailed photos to my wife.

The club couldn't do enough for us. When we arrived at our house, there was a car parked outside, the beds were made, and there was food and milk in the fridge.

We had a lovely three-bedroom townhouse just outside Clermont, with a little garden that was covered in snow in winter. There was a village down the road that had a typical French market on Sundays, and I enjoyed stopping in the village on my way home from morning training to pick up baguettes, ham and cheese for lunch.

We were there for nine unforgettable months and tried to get as much out of the experience as possible. We went for French lessons twice a week with Marius Joubert, my old Bok team-mate, but didn't learn the language as quickly as we would have liked. By the time we left France, I was starting to pick up what was being said in team meetings.

The most interesting thing for me initially was that I had come from an environment where I had been the captain for a long time and in control of what was happening, but now everything was said in French. Vern had been there for nine years and spoke the language perfectly. Every meeting, every video session was in French. At practice, I would go to the back of the queue and hope that I had worked out the drill by the time my turn came.

We had 11 different nationalities in our club, so I learnt to greet players in half a dozen languages. Vern is a stern coach and was not shy to *kak* on the team for substandard play, and it was interesting to see how the different nationalities reacted to that.

Clermont's change room was probably quite different and less intense than other French clubs because of the Anglo-Saxon flavour and Super 14 experience of the coaches, but some change rooms over there are crazy places, pre-match. The guys go berserk, headbutting and kicking each other. It's not uncommon for blood to be spilt before the team has even left the change room.

Our guys were relatively tame except for the one lock who liked to headbutt everybody. You learn to avoid the guys who are snorting up and down.

This chest beating and sabre rattling is understandable because of the violent way the game is played over there.

It was fascinating to travel around France playing rugby. Each weekend would provide a different type of contest. The weather has a major influence. You can go from trench warfare in rain and mud to a fast field under blue skies. You can have a captain's practice in mild weather on the Friday and then have the game called off the next day because of a frozen pitch.

There are only five or six teams that play good rugby in the Top 14 and the rest are ordinary. You can go as the top-of-the-log team to play a weak team and when you win 6-3 you celebrate like you have won the tournament because referees don't believe in away sides winning. It's unheard of. The refs get intimidated by the home crowd.

Remarkably, there are only two professional referees in the Top 14 – for the rest it's just a hobby. And this in the most expensive rugby league in the world where the players get the highest salaries.

My first away game for Clermont in the Top 14 was against Bourgoin, Grant Esterhuizen's former team, at a shabby old stadium. The change room was the size of a toilet in an average house and 22 of us were squeezed in there. It was so small that I had to wait for the guy opposite me to stand up before I could put my socks on.

I have a pre-match ritual of going to the toilet before the warm-up. When I asked where the toilet was I was pointed in the direction of some holes in the ground. I had never seen anything like it and asked Grant, who had moved to our club, what was going on. He said it was the toilet ... Turkish style. 'You have to squat as wide as you can and take good aim, and when you flush make sure you get your boots out of the way so that nothing is washed onto them,' he said. I refused. I may be from Africa but this was too much for me and I bit the bullet until we got home.

The variety of contest you get in Top 14 matches sets it apart from the Super 14, where you get more or less the same type of game every week. In France it can go from an arm wrestle to champagne rugby, from tactical kicking to a heavy focus on scrumming. Each week you have to come up with a different way to win the game.

I played 19 games for Clermont but it could have been a lot more considering I injured knee ligaments at a training session on New Year's Eve and was out for eight weeks.

When I had signed my contract with Clermont, I made it clear to them that I was coming from a demanding four years of rugby, and didn't want to have to start every game. They were happy with that because Mario Ledesma, the Argentine international, had been a big part of the team for a long time and had a year or so left on his contract, so we shared the hooking duties.

Mario and I were next-door neighbours. The day I arrived he invited me over to his house for a cup of coffee and gave me all the lineout calls. He was helpful and there wasn't any uncomfortable rivalry. He played good rugby for Clermont and I respected that.

Vern also saw me as an option at tighthead prop and he was never shy to move me there when needed, which was invaluable experience for me given that I would move to that position permanently when I resumed my career with the Boks.

Sadly, I was part of a Clermont team that continued their astonishingly unfortunate tradition of losing finals. They have lost all 10 of the Top 14 finals they have played. We lost 26-20 to Toulouse in the 2007-08 final after having beaten them home and away in the league. Our big-name players just froze. It was a pure pressure thing, given the team's history of failure in finals. The team choked, no question.

I would equate the occasion to a Super 14 final. The Top 14 final is played at the Stade de France in front of a sell-out crowd of 80 000. It's almost impossible to get a ticket.

When I had gone to Clermont, I had to make peace with the fact that in all likelihood I had played my last Test, but I got a call from former SA Rugby CEO Rian Oberholzer in February 2008. He had heard I was back in South Africa having rehab on my knee and asked if I would mind coming to Cape Town to meet Peter de Villiers, who I had no previous experience of. Rian was Peter's agent and had put together his job application for the Springbok coaching position.

Peter said he wanted me to captain the Boks but explained that it would be very difficult to do that if I wasn't back in the country permanently. He said SA Rugby would negotiate with Clermont to get me out of my 18-month contract. I was impressed with Peter's plans for the Springboks and my answer was that I would never turn down the opportunity to play for my country.

I might have battled to get out of my contract at any other French club but Clermont were appreciative of the fact that I had been open about the Bok development. Vern was very good about it and asked me what I wanted to do and whether I was done with the Boks. I had got on well with him and he had big plans for me regarding the leadership of the club, but I said my hunger to play Test rugby was undiminished and that the upcoming Lions series was a big factor. He understood and the agreement was that I would go back to South Africa to play the two Tests against Wales but miss the Italy Test and return to France for Clermont's semi-final and possible final.

Living in France was a good experience for us as a family but a tough one too, especially for Roxy. It's easy for us players to settle in because we have an instant support group in our team-mates and have a busy day of club commitments, so our lives don't change that much. But Roxy was in a country where she didn't understand the language, had no friends or family, and Emma was only one year old.

We had been there for three weeks when Emma got sick. At 4am her temperature was raging and we decided to take her to the hospital. We got lost and when we eventually found it there was no paediatrician on duty. Three doctors were examining her but none of them could speak English. They eventually managed to communicate that we should give her a bottle and feed her, and Roxy replied that she wouldn't feed, which is why we were there! It was a very frustrating experience.

Roxy also had to drive around to try and find a crèche but this was a problem because working moms have priority. Roxy certainly bore the brunt of our negative experiences of France.

In a way it was an unfinished chapter in that we didn't achieve all our goals there, but it was also nice to know that I was wanted to captain the Springboks.

The Boks' first Test of 2008 against Wales in Bloemfontein was my 50th as captain. I was very emotional when I ran out. I couldn't believe I had come so far, and that a whole new chapter was starting. SA Rugby honoured the occasion by giving me a specially embroidered cap and an all-expenses paid holiday for my family in Mauritius, which we hoped to take at the end of 2009.

23

A ROCKY RETURN

I t was one thing to come back to South Africa to play for the Boks, another to find a provincial home.

The Sharks initially didn't want me because they had planned their future at hooker around Bismarck du Plessis. There was a lot of talk about a real or imagined clause in Bismarck's contract that would permit him to leave the Sharks if I came back. I'm not sure what the real story was, maybe verbal assurances were made to Bismarck, I honestly don't know. But the bottom line is that the door to the Shark Tank was shut and I had to look elsewhere (this had its difficulties because mid-year is the worst time for unions to find money to contract someone).

I wasn't crazy about joining Western Province because they didn't have a strong team but I like Cape Town, so it became an option when WP's senior professional coach, Rassie Erasmus, approached me. He asked if I was willing to play prop as well as hooker, and said I should submit a salary request through my agent. Two days later, I read in the press that WP couldn't afford me because I had asked for too much money, but when my requirement – which was very reasonable – had gone through to them, they'd had no issue with the amount.

I think Rassie just changed his mind and chose not to be upfront with me about it. He had been very excited, telling me I was a big part of his plans, but that I should keep it hush, hush. Then he suddenly went dead and the story that I was too expensive was dropped to the press.

The Bulls suddenly expressed interest but said that as much as they wanted me, they were cash-strapped. They said they would try to make a plan because there was a chance a couple of their guys would give up their contracts and move on. They asked for three days' grace to see what they could do, but phoned back and said that while my offer was reasonable, they had been unable to find the money.

The Bulls were the most honest party I dealt with during this whole process. They never once gave me a false story or promise. How ironic that they were so accommodating when they had chased me away all those years ago.

Around that time, my good mate at the Sharks, Johann Muller, asked me when I would be back in Durban and was amazed when I said I could be going to Pretoria. He raised this with John Plumtree who, in his typical calm, sensible manner, eventually sorted out the issue with Bismarck.

I wasn't that hurt by the Sharks' initial cool response. Roxy was furious but I understand that there's no place for sentiment in the professional era. You expect the unions to make a business decision. I was 30, Bismarck, 24. He was the future. In the modern game, when your time is up at a union, that's that, whether you had been with them for one year or 10. There's no loyalty card. It's business, and I didn't lose too much sleep over it.

My move back to the Sharks was sorted out when Plum flew to George where the Boks were based ahead of the mid-year Tests, and the three of us had a sit-down. Bismarck has always been respectful to me, and there was no bitterness from him. I never held anything back in teaching him the tricks of the trade, and he knew that. He was a very good student. Perhaps he thought it was his time to go from apprentice to master, but there was never a personal issue between us. Plum was the mediator, and he said he would give us both game time. Bismarck wanted enough starting opportunities to give himself a chance to impress for the British & Irish Lions series, and Plum agreed.

I got the impression that Bismarck didn't want to compete with me again, but healthy competition is essential if you want to be the best. I had my share of rivals at the Sharks, such as Chris Rossouw, Morné Visser, Federico Méndez and Lukas van Biljon. Rudolf Straeuli, for instance, never asked whether I minded if he brought Lukas to Durban. Lukas just arrived and we went hammer and tongs for two years.

I'm very proud of how Bizzy is turning out. I think he's going to be one of the greatest hookers the world has seen. He's a freak of nature, immensely strong.

I remember attending a Sharks training session a few years ago, when I had time off from the Boks. I saw a guy with rippling muscles running with his shirt off.

'Who's the new centre?' I asked Piet Strydom, our manager.

'No, that's the new hooker from Free State,' he replied.

I knew then that Bismarck had a big future ahead of him.

Initially Plum wasn't keen to play me at tighthead when Peter de Villiers decided after the 2008 Tri-Nations that that's where he wanted me to be, so I played hooker in the Currie Cup that year. Then he and Peter sat down at the end of 2008 and Plum agreed to give me time in the position.

After the two-Test series against Wales (we won 43-17 in Bloemfontein and 37-21 in Pretoria), I flew back to France to fulfil my commitments to Clermont and then joined up with the Boks in Wellington ahead of the first Tri-Nations Test. It was an epic journey – I flew to Paris, then London, Sydney, Auckland and Wellington, arriving on the Tuesday to incredible hype.

The Test was being touted by the Kiwis as the 'real' World Cup final and the Boks wanted to prove a point by winning a match on New Zealand soil for the first time since 1998. I had been carrying a groin injury for some time in France, but as a foreigner, I felt obliged to play to earn my salary (it's the one drawback of being an overseas professional in a team). The conditions for rugby in Wellington were appalling, which hardly helped my injury. It was flipping freezing and we had to cut short our captain's practice on the Friday because of heavy rain.

I had a good feeling about the match but that changed in the sixth minute when I encountered Brad Thorn at a ruck. He's the All Blacks' version of Bakkies Botha, our enforcer, and he tends to have a short fuse. He was at the bottom of the ruck and I put my hand in his face – just kind of rested on him. I wanted to agitate him so that he would do something silly but didn't expect him to react as badly as he did. His switch flipped, and he up-ended me in front of the referee. I have a photo of Stuart Dickinson looking shocked at what had happened only a metre in front of him, yet in his post-match report he said he didn't see it. Anyway, there was no yellow card but we did get a penalty and three points. I was happy with the outcome, although a yellow card would have been ideal, considering how Thorn lost his temper, but I did antagonise him, I admit that. I pushed the button and he reacted. People assumed that Thorn had injured my groin in this incident but if you rip your groin you can't walk, never mind play rugby, as I was soon to find out.

The game continued and obviously there was now some needle between us. I saw him in another ruck and was going to clean him, just to keep him on edge. He didn't see me … and I didn't see Rodney So'oialo. As I moved my weight off my right foot to launch myself at Thorn, So'oialo picked me up and twisted me in the opposite direction, ripping both abductors off my pubic bone. I knew in an instant that I was seriously injured. I thought I was going to have to call for a stretcher but managed to hobble off. In excruciating pain, I watched the Test deteriorate from great to terrible (Bryan Habana scored just before half-time to make it 9-8 to the All Blacks but a try from Jerome Kaino soon after the break helped them to a 19-8 win).

I knew I wouldn't play another Tri-Nations match that season and guilt set in. SA Rugby had gone to a lot of trouble to get me back, spending a small fortune on transfer fees and on trips to France to negotiate with Clermont.

The immediate fallout in the media was that Thorn had injured me but he actually had nothing to do with it. There was no bad blood between us. He was concerned that he had been responsible and found me after the match. He started apologising but I stopped him and said: 'No mate, I started it, you finished it.'

The media obviously jumped on the incident, and we were happy to let them run with it to try and influence the judiciary, but it didn't work, as he only got a one-week ban.

Roxy drove up from Durban to meet me at the airport and took me straight to hospital in Jo'burg where one of our country's top surgeons, Mark Ferguson, reattached the groin muscles with titanium pins (he's a brilliant surgeon and has prolonged the careers of half the Springbok team). After the surgery, we flattened the seats in the 4x4 and Roxy drove back to Durban with me flat on my back for six hours. In fact, I wasn't allowed to move at all for three days, and I even had to pee in a bottle. It was a terrible time for me, because besides the physical pain and discomfort, I felt guilty that I was unable to repay the faith shown in me by Peter.

After less than 40 minutes of rugby, I was out of the Tri-Nations, but before I left Wellington, Peter asked me to record a message for the team for the following week's Test in Dunedin. One of the SuperSport guys, Russell Belter, filmed me saying: 'I might be leaving but I will be with you in spirit. You guys are far greater than any other team in world rugby right now, so forget about who or where you are playing, and just play for each other …' I spoke about each individual and described his value to the team. I was choking up while doing it.

I heard later that this had a big impact on the guys on the eve of the Dunedin Test, so I was pleased to have made some kind of contribution.

I watched the match flat on my back in Durban and almost screamed the roof off when Ricky Januarie scored his chip-and-chase try to give the Boks a 30-28 win. I was so happy for the guys but at the same time annoyed that I couldn't be part of it. At the time, winning in New Zealand was the one thing I had never done and it was top of my 'to do' list.

However, the Boks then lost 16-9 to the Wallabies in Perth the following week, and 19-0 in depressing fashion to the All Blacks in Cape Town (it was the first time the Boks hadn't scored a point against them in a home Test).

As soon as I was mobile, Peter asked me to rejoin the Bok squad, which I did before the Test against the Wallabies in Durban. The Boks produced another poor performance to lose 27-15, and Peter and Victor Matfield (who was captain in my absence) were booed off the pitch after the post-match TV interviews.

I was shocked and disappointed at the viciousness with which the public and the media reacted. It got really ugly. All the talk was about confused game plans and incompetent coaching. It was a story the prejudiced media wanted to write because of the scenario of there being a new coach with an old team, and the team was losing, so they presumed it had to be the coach.

The truth is that there was a fair amount of adjusting going on, which there had to be with a new coach. The old systems that the players were used to had to evolve with what the new coach was introducing. To Peter's credit, he didn't try and reinvent the wheel when he took over. We had to get used to what he thought of the game and how he wanted to manage the players, and then find the happy medium. The problem was that there was never going to be enough time to sort it all out before the Tri-Nations and it hardly helped that I got injured so early because I could have played a big role in managing the process.

Peter was giving the message in the media that we were going to play more expansively, but to the team it was more a case of him telling us that we needed to better appreciate the attacking opportunities given to us, wherever we were on the field. The players were happy with that because we had become very structured under Jake White, but we weren't sure exactly how adventurous Peter wanted us to be. With Jake, you could anticipate every single move from the Boks and Peter wanted us to play off the cuff if the opportunity was there.

So I went from watching my team-mates win in Dunedin and losing with honour in Perth to being ridiculed after two home defeats. Selfishly, I wondered if I had done the right thing in cutting my career in France short.

24
KILLING
THE CANCER

Before our last Tri-Nations Test of 2008 – against the Wallabies at Ellis Park – Peter de Villiers told me his gut feeling was that the team wanted me to talk to them about what had been going down and the way forward. I was nervous as hell. I had been making speeches for a long time, but I was afraid of failing the guys. I gave it a lot of thought, and realised that Luke Watson was the principal reason why the team was off colour. He was there under duress, he didn't enjoy his team-mates, he didn't participate in team meetings, and he basically did his own thing.

Our Kontiki in Durban had been very emotional. The guys were hurting and there were a lot of heart-to-heart discussions, before the guys relaxed. We had Adriaan Strauss playing the guitar and there was some really good bonding. At this point Percy Montgomery asked to speak to the squad.

'Guys, I have decided to pack it in,' said Monty, who had played his 100th Test against the All Blacks at Newlands. 'Please, I need you to keep this confidential. I've had a great career and it's come to that stage now where I've got to make a decision and, well, this is it. I'm retiring.'

We were all taken aback, because Monty had become part of the furniture.

I had the misfortune of sitting next to Luke while Monty was pouring his heart out to the 'family' he had spent most of his adult life with, and Luke was on his cellphone – SMSing the whole time – showing complete disrespect to a Springbok legend.

That was a really big let-down for me, and it summed up Luke's time with the Boks. He never tried to become a part of us. I think he really wanted to play for South Africa but couldn't stand the environment, and the truth is that he irritated the living shit out of the guys. I had players in my ear about him every flipping day. He was referred to as 'the cancer' of the team.

There were times when I tried to understand Luke, who I think is a victim of circumstance. He grew up amid endless family politics. I don't think he had the easiest upbringing, and he's come a long way since he allegedly said – after a speech at UCT – that he had wanted to vomit on the Bok jersey. He got back to just playing rugby and had a very good 2009 season. He led Western Province well and rarely talked to the media.

But in 2008 he was a spanner in the works and I can't defend his attitude in that period. This brings me to my speech at our hotel before the Test against the Wallabies in Jo'burg.

I didn't single Luke out in my talk, but I said to the match 22: 'There are 21 guys here who will bleed for each other, and you have to understand that you can't let one guy disrupt everything we have worked for as a team. We are bigger than this one guy, and he shouldn't be allowed to affect how we feel about each other. The 21 is still strong enough to play the way we want to play.'

The team blamed the bad environment on Luke, not on the new coach, which is what the public erroneously thought.

How can you function as a family when one guy doesn't give a rat's arse? He was polluting the environment.

I was getting seriously worked up as the speech unfolded and I picked up a glass that was on the table in front of me. I yelled: 'Passion is not enough. You can talk about passion until the cows come home. Do you want to see passion?'

And then I threw the glass against the wall as hard as I could. It exploded like a bomb, the glass showered over some of the players and there was a shard stuck in the wall.

Their eyes were like saucers. 'That is passion, and it's gone already, it's over in a moment,' I continued. 'You have to stick together for 80 minutes, not just for moments of passion.'

I watched the game from a suite. At kick-off a mate asked me how I thought things would go. I said: 'Trust me, we are going to annihilate the Wallabies today …' In the end, we won 53-8 and scored eight tries (four by Jongi Nokwe).

After that Tri-Nations roller coaster ride, I was part of an awesome Currie Cup campaign with the Sharks. I played a lot off the bench in my comeback from the groin injury and that gave me a good platform for the end-of-year Bok tour.

I enjoyed that Currie Cup so much because the Sharks were playing brilliant rugby and for once I didn't have the responsibility of being captain. I love captaincy but it's also nice to have a break from it. My mate Johann Muller had continued captaining the Sharks after my return and was doing a fine job. When we beat the Blue Bulls 14-9 in the final at Kings Park, I never for one second wished I was up there being presented with the Currie Cup I had tried so hard to win over the course of a decade. I was just ecstatic that we had won it at last.

It was a really special night in Durban, and people were deliriously happy, hugging each other in relief. I'm not sure how the Sharks fans would have handled it if we had lost yet another final.

We spent at least two hours with the trophy in our change room. It went into the jacuzzi with us and we drank lustily from it. Change rooms after finals are usually pretty much the same, but this was different. The Sharks had not won the Currie Cup in 12 years, despite often being the best team in the competition. I had resigned myself to the fact that I wasn't destined to get my hands on it. It had been like hunting for the bloody Holy Grail.

One of the goals on the Boks' end-of-year tour was for me to make a successful transition from hooker to tighthead prop (in order for Bismarck du Plessis to be accommodated at hooker). It had gone well enough when I helped out in the position at Clermont and played for the Sharks in the Currie Cup, but international rugby is another story and first up was a formidable Wales pack.

A lot of coaches had helped me – Balie Swart and John Plumtree were very good – but none more so than my fellow players. Bakkies Botha – who scrums behind me with the Boks – and Juan Smith – who's next to me – said from the word go: 'Don't worry, we will look after you. We will help you.' They are absolute champion blokes and I felt I was being backed up by two brothers.

The Wales match was interesting for me in that it was the first time in years I was more concerned about my own game than the team's. We won 20-15, despite the Six Nations champions making out before the game that we would get our backsides kicked. Wales always come with that story but it never quite happens for them.

I was very pleased with my performance, but it would be a one-hit wonder start to my new career as a prop because Bismarck snapped his hamstring in the first minute against Scotland, and I was back at hooker.

The Scotland match at Murrayfield was a complete dog show – we were terrible. We were down 10-0 at half-time and I told the guys in the change room: 'There's nothing going on here. Do you know what's about to happen? We are 40 minutes away from one of the most embarrassing defeats in our entire history.'

We turned it around just enough to scrape home 14-10. The whole week the media had asked if there was a danger of us being complacent, and despite our protestations, subconsciously we probably were.

England at Twickenham is never a problem in terms of commitment. At training I threw in comments here and there about how we were being written off again, and how England were talking themselves up as usual, so the pot was simmering all week.

On the morning of the Test I asked Peter if I could do things a little differently. I wanted him to take all the management and substitutes out of the change room so that I could have an extra five minutes alone with the starting XV.

Usually we get in a circle just before kick-off, say a prayer, have a little psyche-up chat, a squeeze and a shout and then move out onto the field. But this time I told the guys to sit down at their bags.

One by one I spoke directly to each player in front of the rest of the team, so it became a personal thing. Often in the past before big games I have written letters to the guys and put them under their room doors for them to read privately.

I cut to the bone with what each guy meant to the team. I told Bakkies, for instance: 'You're responsible for whether this team comes out of the blocks or not. When you fire, everybody fires, when you don't, we battle. I'm telling you right now that if you haven't decided to get out there and fire on all cylinders, we're going to struggle. So I'm asking you now, in front of everybody, to lead us into battle.'

With Victor Matfield I tapped into his leadership ability. I told him he's as much the Bok captain as I am, that his leadership is invaluable and that he must go out there and lead – he mustn't be afraid to take control or worry about stepping on anybody's toes.

Bryan Habana hadn't been in good form and his place in the team was under pressure, so I told him: 'Bryan, you're still the best wing in the world. Your talent hasn't suddenly diminished. I believe that and I need you to believe it too. I want a try from you today. You *will* score.'

He did. Bakkies played like a mad man and Victor was magnificent. But those were only three examples. Each guy got a similar address and by the time we were finished we didn't need an open door to get to the field, we could have run straight through the change room wall!

We thrashed England 42-6 on their hallowed home turf. It was beautiful.

25

SMASHING THE LIONS' SCRUM

On the Monday after the third Test against the British & Irish Lions, my body went into shutdown mode. I broke out in fever blisters, the glands in my throat swelled up and full-on flu ensued. Roxy called it. She told me I'd get sick in the week after the Lions series, as I usually do after a prolonged period of stress.

I honestly believe my subconscious doesn't allow my body to feel pain or get sick when I have vitally important games ahead of me. I won't let it happen, I have to play. But when the pressure is off, that self-defence mechanism relaxes.

I felt more anxiety and pressure for the 2009 Lions series than I did for the 2007 World Cup because of the massive sense of occasion, the rarity of the event, and the incredible hype generated by the huge British and Irish media circus.

The pressure cranked up a notch almost every day of the six weeks the Lions were in the country. The Lions are a one-off, you don't get another chance to play them in your career. You have to win.

The preparation for a World Cup is done piece by piece over months, in fact years, but for a Lions series you come in ice cold.

We hadn't played a Test in six months but fortunately the two teams that made up most of the Springbok side – the Bulls and the Sharks – had played well in the Super 14, although the Sharks fell away at the end and failed to make the semi-finals.

The last match of the Super 14 league stage, between the Bulls and the Sharks in Durban, was a classic. Never mind the fact that we lost 27-26, it was one of the most enjoyable games of my entire career. Both teams played brilliant, high-tempo attacking rugby in a wonderful advertisement for the South African game.

After the Bulls thrashed the Chiefs 61-17 in the Super 14 final at Loftus, there were only about three weeks left before the first Test in Durban, which gave us very little preparation time because the Bulls guys desperately needed a break.

To Peter de Villiers's credit, he understands better than most coaches that when it comes to training camps, less is often more. Even so, we only got together as a team 10 days before the first Test. We had been in Pretoria for a few days (without the Bulls guys) and done some fitness work, but nothing team-wise.

We usually have a training camp of between two and four weeks before the start of the international season, so by the time the first match comes you can't wait to play because you've been training for so long.

I think the minimal preparation added to our freshness for the first Test against the Lions. We got together on the Tuesday the Lions were playing the Sharks in Durban. We agreed that because we only had eight sessions before the Test, our accuracy and energy levels had to be excellent in every session. And they were.

I have to take my hat off to Peter here. It was a big call to allow the guys to rest after the Super 14. Most coaches would rather be over-prepared than anything else, but we weren't at all, and that's a brave thing for a coach to do.

Yes, we did have the warm-up match against a Namibian XV in Windhoek on the Friday night before the Super 14 final, but that was more about the coaching staff having a look at our back-up players.

It was also a stressful time for me, as my son Tyron, who was then eight months old, had fallen sick while I was doing the fitness sessions in Pretoria. He went into hospital on the Monday with a raging fever and was put on a drip.

On the Thursday morning Peter came to me after training and said: 'I can see you're very worried. Your family is more important than rugby. I've booked you on a flight back to Durban. Go and see your son, make sure everything's OK. You can join up with us tomorrow in Namibia.'

We didn't know what was wrong with Tyron at the time but his lab tests later revealed that he had a strain of the rotavirus that causes stomach flu.

When I arrived at the hospital, I could see Roxy was at the end of her tether, she had no gas left in the tank. She was due to sit her Masters exam in tax on the Monday and she had been in hospital each night of that week trying to study by torch light. Roxy is really bright – she is a qualified CA and a brilliant student – but she had never been under so much pressure. I relieved her at the hospital and she went home and slept until 2am. Then she returned because I had to sleep the remaining four-odd hours of the night and then race to the airport to fly to Namibia for that night's match.

I had to be reasonably fresh because I knew that the captain of the Namibian XV and my direct opponent, loosehead prop Kees Lensing, would be eager to prove a point after having been such an unhappy camper at the Sharks (he was Rudolf Straeuli's most expensive signing but ended up playing for the Wildebeest).

At the hospital, the paediatrician came through and said: 'Your son was pretty bad but he's over the worst. Go and play the game. You can leave him with us, he'll be OK.' That gave me peace of mind.

The game was a predictably ugly affair, as they always are when you're playing an invitation team in the middle of nowhere. We won 36-7 and I was very happy to get on the plane to fly home. That was the start of those eventual fever blisters, for sure!

We went to Kings Park as a team to watch the Lions play the Sharks. The tourists were very impressive in winning 39-3 and we picked up that it was pretty much their Test team in action.

We knew that the Sharks' backline was makeshift at best, but John Plumtree had put together a good pack, including Springboks in Jannie du Plessis, Johann Muller and Deon Carstens, Emerging Bok Steven Sykes and regular loose forwards Keegan Daniel, Jean Deysel and Jacques Botes. But the Lions gave them a hiding and we had a sobering realisation that we were in for one heck of a series, as we believed they could make their tight five even stronger.

When the Lions selected their team for the first Test, I thought they were having us on, because it was the team we would have wanted to play if we could have picked a line-up from their squad.

I was quite happy to go up against Gethin Jenkins because I had scrummed well against him in Cardiff the previous November. We wouldn't have left out a bruiser like Simon Shaw in the second row for the more athletic Alun-Wyn Jones and were pleased they omitted Adam Jones and Matthew Rees for Phil Vickery and Lee Mears. It would have been great if they had left that tight five unchanged for the other two Tests!

The front row the Lions picked for Durban was never going to give them the edge in the scrums. They underestimated our scrum, purely because I was new to tighthead, which worked to our advantage. They wanted the mobility of Mears and Vickery – thinking they would still have ascendancy at scrum time – because of the attacking game they wanted to play.

I was sick and tired of answering questions about how I thought it was going to go in the scrums, mostly because I didn't have a bloody clue!

I was quite happy with how it had gone for me at tight-head in the Super 14 but I knew it would be a completely different challenge against the Lions because the northern-hemisphere guys love their scrumming. I was worried that I wouldn't be able to hold my own and that I was going to be the weakest link in the team.

The Lions weren't shy in declaring they were going to target me and it ended up being to their detriment. If they had shut up about it, we might not have been quite as obsessed about scrumming as we were in the build-up.

That week was the most worked up I've ever been about a game and the most focused the guys have ever been about scrumming. Contrary to public belief, scrumming has never been a massive priority for the Springboks, we normally just try and do what's necessary.

But the Lions had come to our country and said they were going to hammer us in the scrums and we said, 'OK, that's fine, let's see what you've got.'

By being so cocky, they succeeded in pumping us up like I have seldom seen before. I don't think we have ever seen, or will ever see, a performance like that in the scrum from the Boks again.

On the Thursday before the first Test, we had an epic live scrumming session against the Emerging Boks (who would go on to draw their midweek match against the Lions). It went extremely well and was a big part of our success in the first Test. I was up against Wian du Preez from the Free State. He's a very good scrummager, is technically sound and has a couple of tricks up his sleeve.

That session was colossal, so tough in fact that I picked up an injury. We were hitting in so hard that my right lat was going into spasm, but I couldn't do or say anything. I wasn't going to crumble against the Emerging Boks. We were supposed to be the big boys!

I don't think Wian will ever know how much that session helped me. They had a solid scrum and Bok forwards coach Gary Gold told them to get stuck into us. Wian was amazing because he hit me with everything he had, and then after every scrum we would chat and he would tell me what he thought I had done wrong and what I could do to make it right.

I was stiffer after that session than I was for any of the Tests and it definitely helped me cope with the Lions.

The Boks' jersey presentation on the Friday was done by business tycoon Johann Rupert. It was an interesting choice from Peter because the year before Johann had been accused of being part of a 'third force' trying to remove him, and here they were sitting together. It's amazing how perceptions can change.

Johann's message was very powerful. He picked up a jersey and said: 'Guys, I have been fortunate to have made all the money that I could possibly need but with all that money, I still can't buy one of these.'

It's customary for me to present our guest with a Bok tie and give him our consent to wear it, but Johann wouldn't accept it because he hadn't earned it.

Our jerseys had the King Protea emblem on the chest for the first time and its introduction wasn't an issue. We had obviously been adamant that we didn't want to lose the Springbok emblem but were more than happy to embrace the national flower.

When singing the anthem, we used to put our right hand on the Bok emblem, which was over our hearts. Now we had the interesting conundrum of which of the two emblems to put our hand on. Would we cover the Protea (which was now over our hearts) or would we cover the Bok (which had shifted to the right-hand side)? Whichever one we chose,

Left: My dad and I at the Bok heroes braai before the 2007 World Cup
Below: The Springboks' World Cup squad was announced at Canal Walk in Cape Town and broadcast live on SuperSport

This page (clockwise from top left):
In action during our first World
Cup game against Samoa in Paris;
tackled high during our last pool
match against the USA in Montpellier;
exchanging words with referee
Alan Lewis during our quarter-final
against Fiji in Marseille
Opposite page: Taking on the much-
vaunted Pumas pack in Paris;
offloading in the tackle

Clockwise from top left: The sign put up on the windows of the building across from our hotel before the World Cup final against England; I went off for blood late in the final; driving forward, with Martin Corry making the tackle; the final whistle goes and we're world champions

Opposite page: A moment I'll never forget – lifting the Webb Ellis Cup, with President Thabo Mbeki on my right
This page: Celebrating with Jake White; holding the 2007 IRB Team of the Year award; meeting Prince Harry and Prince William after the final

We took the Webb Ellis Cup on a nationwide road trip, and also let Madiba get his hands back on it

Right: I played only 19 games for Clermont because of a knee injury

Below (from top to bottom): Clermont went on a team-building trip to Spain and we visited FC Barcelona; at the launch of Ernie Els's first club in Dubai (along with Peter Schmeichel, Andrew Flintoff and Martina Navratilova); with my parents, Roxy and Emma in the snow; Roxy, my Clermont team-mate Marius Joubert and I had French lessons together

Left (top and bottom): We beat Wales and Scotland on our 2008 end-of-year tour
Below (from top to bottom): Wearing the special cap I received for my 50th Test as Springbok captain; getting into the spirit of things in Scotland; finally getting my hands on the Currie Cup (aka the Holy Grail!)

Clockwise from top left: Hunting with Jaque Fourie; playing for the Barbarians against the Wallabies in 2008 was a huge honour; getting physical against the British & Irish Lions; scoring an early try in the first Test against the Lions in Durban; the Sharks forwards paintball team

Clockwise from top left: Celebrating Morné Steyn's penalty at Loftus, which gave us a series win against the Lions; lifting the Unity Cup after the third Test at Ellis Park; getting to grips with Benn Robinson in Brisbane; packing down with Bismarck du Plessis and Beast Mtawarira; on the charge against the All Blacks during the 2009 Tri-Nations match in Hamilton

We capped off a superb 2009 season by lifting the Tri-Nations trophy and the Freedom Cup in Hamilton

somebody would have had it in for us, and we couldn't cover both and stand there like X-Men!

Eventually I said: 'Guys, there's a very simple solution. We go back to what we originally did – stand with our arms around the players next to us and show off the entire jersey.'

Everybody was pleased with that. Happy days.

From the first scrum of the first Test it was as if there was a guiding hand behind us because we kept getting perfect field positions for set scrums.

Unless you are a tight forward, you won't understand that there are certain areas of the field where you are under more pressure than others. For instance, if you're a tighthead prop and you're playing upfield, and your first scrum of the day is on the left-hand side of the field, that gives the opposition loosehead licence to have a full go and do whatever he wants, because there's no blind side for his loose forwards to protect. So the opposition doesn't have to give you a straight scrum, they can just hammer you down the tighthead and they will get away with it.

In the first half, we were playing towards the Umgeni end and the first three scrums were all on the right-hand side of the field. That meant Tendai 'Beast' Mtawarira could have a full go at Vickery – who was probably the weaker of the two props, scrumming wise – and Jenkins couldn't get stuck into me. Suddenly three scrums had gone by, the Lions had been savaged, I had gained a lot of confidence and Jenkins was probably cursing his luck (so often it's circumstance that decides who gets the ascendancy).

I haven't seen a side get scrummed like that for ages. In the old days you saw it often because there were no rules, but it will be a long time before you see a Test prop get a hiding like the one Vickery got from Beast. When Beastie is 'on', he's 'on' and nothing can stand in his way, and he was 'on' that day! I could see the shock in the Lions' eyes. They couldn't believe what was happening to them as they got shoved about or gave away penalties. They couldn't do anything.

To cap off that great start, I scored a try from a move called 'Sharks', which means we play the same way. We scrummed, set it up, ran it up, the ball came into my hands … and I literally fell over the line. I couldn't believe it. It was one of the easiest tries I have scored but one of the most pleasing after all the tension of the week.

Then we started mauling the Lions. We had always planned to use the maul but we never expected to march them 20m at a time. There are few better feelings for a forward than to be in an advancing phalanx. Our mauling was straight out of the textbook and it soon earned us three points from a penalty and then Heinrich Brüssow drove over to score off the back of a maul.

We had played almost perfect rugby to be ahead 26-7 after 50 minutes. Then came the controversial substitutions …

For coaches, sitting in the box watching a Test unfold can be a very stressful experience. Peter, Dick and Gary have to try and read the match situation and decide whether fresh legs are required.

Dick is a great believer in introducing fresh legs during the second half and was occasionally successful with this approach in Super Rugby, but he also made a few substitutions that weren't quite on the button (most notably when Percy Montgomery and I were pulled off in the 2007 Super 14 final), so it's not an exact science.

Against the Lions in Durban, the coaches believed it was time to speed up the game but it had the opposite effect, which showed them the intensity of a big Test. They bravely copped the criticism afterwards and when chatting with the players, admitted that they had made too many big changes at once.

The spine of our team was ripped off the field and the shit hit the fan, as the Lions scored two tries to make it 26-21. But with three minutes to go, Deon Carstens, who had only just come onto the field, went down with a shoulder injury, and I came back on. We held on for the win, but only just.

We made that series far more difficult for ourselves by allowing the Lions to finish the Durban match so well. If we had left the team as it was, and carried on driving the lineouts, stayed in their half, kicked more penalties over and made it a 25- or 30-point victory, we would have had a far easier time in the second Test at Loftus because the Lions lived off how they finished. That's all we heard about in the next week, not the fact that we had made a winning start.

26

MORNÉ'S MOMENT

In the short post-match function after the first Test, Lions captain Paul O'Connell said in his speech that while they were very disappointed to have lost, they were pleased that they had shown they could play attacking rugby. That sounded a bit odd to me, a bit like Western Province being proud of how they throw the ball around, even though they seldom win trophies.

Like the media, we had predicted a conservative game from the tourists, not the running rugby they produced. In the end, they played 75% of the rugby in the three Tests but lost the series.

The Brits and Irish have an amazing ability to pull out something positive from a defeat and they went into the second Test in Pretoria convinced that they had been robbed in the first.

Knowing them as we do, we thought they would hit Loftus in a state bordering on psychotic. They would take that last 15-minute period in Durban and use it to work themselves up into a frenzy.

We prepared ourselves to counter a manic onslaught from them in the first quarter at Loftus but the one thing we didn't anticipate was losing a player in the first move of the game.

We invited our old mate, Os du Randt, to present the Bok jerseys on the Friday. Os had been our father figure and the moral grounding of the team for so long. He was our go-to guy when we were unsure of what to do and after he left we would say in a difficult situation: 'What would Os do?'

It was very apt for him to be there for this massive match. When he arrived at the hotel we were boosted before he had even said a word. He's one of those guys who doesn't have to say much. When he did have something to say as a player, it was mostly about being humble and doing your best for your country.

He's a living legend and we were thrilled to have him with us on the eve of our most important Test since the World Cup final, which had been his last Test.

He spoke about how he missed the Boks, how he couldn't have it anymore, how once it's gone it's gone.

The theme of the week was that we were playing a final and the series was to be won at Loftus, 'finish and *klaar*'.

The bonus that SA Rugby offered us for winning the Lions series was just under 20% of what we earned for the World Cup. It wasn't substantial at all and amounted to an extra match fee. But that didn't really bother us. Money wasn't an issue in such a huge week for South African rugby.

People don't realise that our victory in the second Test at Loftus was a rugby miracle when you consider the bigger picture of that game.

We had spent the week firing ourselves up to win the Test in the first 10 minutes. The plan was to fly in from the first kick-off at 100 miles an hour and make everything happen from the word go. We were supposed to take the game by the scruff of the neck and not let go until the final whistle.

I told the team: 'The kick-off is going to go to Victor [Matfield], and we're going to drive it till they sack us. We will get the penalty and kick it out deep in their half. We're going to play a five-man lineout, we're going to go off the top, play a Sharks move and score the try near the posts.'

Boom, kick-off. Victor caught it, and we drove forward. The Lions collapsed the maul and we were awarded a penalty. So far, so good. But the assistant referee Bryce Lawrence had put his flag out, and Schalk Burger was yellow-carded 30 seconds into the game for making contact with Luke Fitzgerald's eyes at a ruck.

A large chunk of our week's preparation was chucked out the window in an instant. That ultra-intense start had to be scrapped because we were down to 14 men. At the first stoppage I had to say: 'Alright, change of plan. We now have to play the first 10 minutes of this game as slowly as we can. Walk to the kick-off, walk to the lineout ...'

That was in complete contrast to everything we had ever done throughout our time as a team and it should have been a fatal handicap for us. It wasn't only about getting over the 10 points but also about changing the mindsets of the players. We had been primed to go hell for leather, then at the flash of a card we had to slow it down to buy us time, and then had to try and lift the intensity, which we couldn't do because the Lions had taken full advantage of the situation and were in full flight.

The first half was unbearable for us but, running into the tunnel at the break, I realised that the best rugby they had played throughout the tour had yielded them only 10 points, and we had managed to respond with a try from JP Pietersen that made it 10-5 soon after Schalk had returned to the field.

It hadn't helped that we had suffered some shocking decisions from the referee, Christophe Berdos. I had never seen some of the things he blew that day in international rugby. To be quite frank, he was nowhere near a Test-quality referee and made as many mistakes for the opposition.

He burnt us at crucial times and that contributed to us having so few chances to launch an attack in their half. An example was when we implemented a planned move from the lineout involving Bakkies Botha, a play that we had been using since 2004. Bakkies came around the back of the lineout and ran straight at Stephen Jones, only for the whistle to go. Berdos said Bakkies had left the lineout too early. Huh?! He got the law completely wrong.

This type of thing adds to the frustration when things are going wrong because every single one of us understands the laws of the game. Victor and Fourie du Preez were fuming and Bakkies wanted to *klap* some sense into the oke.

There can quickly be a snowball effect in a Test, and trust me, it's hard to stop. It happens both ways, and there's nothing better than riding that snowball when you have launched it down the mountain and it's getting bigger every minute.

We'd had it in the first Test and the Lions couldn't stop it until our mass substitutions. Now it was our turn.

With three minutes to go until half-time I told the forwards, 'We have to get points before the break, whether it's three, five or seven. I want you to give everything to try and force something.' A minute later we won a penalty just inside their half. I turned to Fransie Steyn and said: '*Boet*, do your thing.' He did.

In the change room I told the guys: 'They have played the best they can possibly play, they have given us their best shot and we've been terrible. Yet there's only an eight-point difference [16-8].'

Schalk kept on apologising for being sin-binned and I said, 'No, that's over, we've got to move on quickly because we can't play at this level of intensity. We've got to flipping wake up, we've got to get stuck in, we've got to up the tempo, we've got to start this Test again. We've got to start in the second half like we wanted to start in the first. What's gone is gone, but we've got to make sure we put it right. I then finished off with some unmentionable words. I don't often resort to seriously *kakking* on the guys but sometimes the situation warrants it.

The Lions should have gone on to win that second Test considering the momentum they had going into half-time. Later I read that Lions coach Ian McGeechan had said that Saturday night and the Sunday was the lowest point of his life, and I can understand why.

We were really tenacious after half-time. We only had two opportunities and scored from both of them. Often our forwards have had to pull us out of a hole but this time our backs saved the day. The second-half tries by Bryan Habana and Jaque Fourie were all brilliantly taken, with Jaque's giving us a 25-22 lead.

The scrums had gone uncontested because of the injuries to their two props – Gethin Jenkins and Adam Jones – which changed the dynamic of the game because they got an extra lock on the field in Alun-Wyn Jones.

I wanted to suggest to the coaches that we do the same, but couldn't decide which tight forward should go off. Beast Mtawarira and Bismarck du Plessis are athletic and I'm the captain so I decided it had to be Bakkies because we didn't need his scrumming power anymore.

Ruan Pienaar had also missed three kicks at goal, so we needed a change at flyhalf. To stop play so that I could get the message to the sideline, I kicked my boot off and the Lions helped my cause when one of their players thought he would be clever and throw it 20m from me. I yelled, 'Ref, my boot!' He stopped the game and I got the message to the sideline. Five minutes later Morné Steyn and Andries Bekker were on.

I had been happy with Ruan as our starting flyhalf at the beginning of the series but I also put in a big punt for Morné to make the squad. After his sensational Super 14 he deserved the call-up and with Butch James gone, we needed someone like him around.

To be fair to Ruan, he was a big part of our victory in the first Test but was off form at Loftus and temperament-wise he's not the kind of guy who can turn it around on the day. The worst thing for Ruan is to miss an easy kick early on –

that's a big warning sign that he could be in for a bad day with the boot, and that's what happened in this Test.

That's why I suggested we bring on Morné. I knew it was his time to shine because goal-kicking was going to be vital in terms of getting us back into the game and we had already squandered eight points.

The changes began to work immediately but there was also a key moment in the second half where we had an attacking lineout in the left-hand corner, probably about 25m out. We were at the stage where we were kicking to the corners rather than to goal because we hadn't been getting much luck with the latter.

There was a lengthy stoppage so I called the guys together. Three of the Lions players were down injured, because we'd upped the tempo, so we had an opportunity to conference. I sensed that it was now or never in the game and also that our determination was growing.

I said: 'Guys, come on, we can do this now,' and then Victor added: 'We're going to commit to each other that we're going to win this game! We will do it.'

It was like a schoolboy rallying call but often rugby is simply rugby – no matter what level you play at – and this was a voicing of a commitment that no matter what we'd had to take in this game, no matter what had gone before, we were going to win. We would win the game because of sheer bloody-mindedness and, of course, *that* last-minute penalty from Morné after the full-time hooter with the scores level at 25-25.

It's hard to imagine there has been a more dramatic end to a Test between the Springboks and the Lions. Perhaps there has, but the Boks were on the wrong side of it in 1955 when, with the last kick of the match at Ellis Park to win the Test, Jack van der Schyff's conversion drifted wide to give the Lions a 23-22 victory in front of a record 100 000 fans. That famous picture of Van der Schyff's head slumped onto his chest in despair lives on in rugby immortality, just as those of us hugging Morné in ecstasy at Loftus will for the opposite reason.

I don't think I would have the mental composure to take a penalty like the one Morné had at the end of that second Test, just supposing I had the physical attributes, which I clearly haven't!

What added to the drama of that kick was that the penalty arose from bizarre circumstances. Ronan O'Gara, who was on for the injured Jamie Roberts, had fielded a deep kick and the Lions players screamed 'Kick it out, kick it out,' while pointing frantically to the touchline. But the rugby gods were wearing green and gold that day (as opposed to the emerald green of O'Gara's Ireland) and he had a complete brain fart, hoisting it up towards the centre spot and in chasing up probably the first bomb he had ever chased in his life, crashed clumsily into Fourie du Preez.

If he had kicked it out, the final whistle would have blown and the match would have been drawn. It was almost like it was match-fixing!

When the referee raised his arm for the penalty, I looked towards the poles to gauge the distance (about 55m) and wondered whether Frans – who can be a bit of a spray gun at times – should take the kick, or his namesake, Morné? I wasn't too sure how far Morné could kick, which was why I didn't give it to him straight away. I grabbed the ball and walked as slowly as possible so that I could mull it over.

However, Morné strode towards me, completely calm and took the ball (and the decision) out of my hands. I grinned and said, 'Welcome to Test rugby.'

He gave me a little smile. He was totally relaxed. There was no sign of nerves or stress. He put the ball down as he had done a thousand times at Loftus and struck it as sweetly as Ernie Els does off the tee.

As he lined it up, I said a prayer, asking the Big Man upstairs what he had in store for us … and then the kick just sailed and sailed and sailed. The first thing I look out for in this situation is the crowd reaction behind the posts, and when the Springbok fans rose as one, long before the assistant referees' flags, I had that giddy is-this-really-happening feeling that I imagine you must get when you see your numbers come up in the lotto.

The scale of relief that I experienced was similar to what I felt at the final whistle of the World Cup final. A sense of achievement mixed with utter relief engulfs you. You know that it's done, it can't be taken away …

Even more special was the fact that it happened in such dramatic style right at the very end, in the last seconds.

Those moments of unbridled jubilation sweep by in an instant but while we were whooping about and hugging, I noticed the sheer despair of the Lions players. To have come so close to winning the game only to lose the series in 15 nightmarish minutes had completely mortified them. They were the living dead.

One guy I wouldn't have minded bumping into at that final whistle was Lions scrumhalf Mike Phillips, who was undeniably their idiot of the tour. He was full of cheap and nasty chirps that didn't make the slightest impression and just made him look like a twit.

When the Lions were up 19-8 going into the final quarter – which was pretty much a reversal of the first Test – there was a scrum in their half and while the packs were getting ready, Phillips walked between the two front rows, ball in hand, turned to our front row and sneered, 'See you next week for the decider.' So I piped up, 'Mike, 15 minutes is a long time in Test rugby, buddy …'

Our change room resembled the Rio Carnival. The music was blaring, cameras were flashing, and we were singing and popping the bubbly. The fact that we had another Test to play really didn't matter at that stage. We felt euphoric and it was a raucous trip back to Jo'burg on the bus, with the cooler boxes being thoroughly pillaged. I knew it was going to be one of those great nights that we would never forget.

Os had joined us on the bus back from Pretoria and was a guest at the Kontiki, which was an absolute blast.

The way a Kontiki works (and I will explain it in greater detail later) is that the three most senior players, except for the captain, are at the head table and they run the show. The three most senior players that day were Victor, Bakkies and Juan Smith – who make a formidable team – and they were in great form.

First the coach says a few words, and then I talk. I told the guys how grateful I was for everyone's commitment and I congratulated them on their achievement because it had felt like the British and Irish media had tried to take the taste of victory out of our mouths at the post-match press conference by dwelling on the Schalk incident. We had won the Test series, yet all they wanted to talk about was his yellow card and possible citing, so I made sure that I emphatically congratulated the guys.

Once the formalities are over, the Kontiki is about having a good time and letting off steam.

There were a few down-downs of beers and then along came Craig Roberts, our team doctor, with a box of cigars that someone had dropped off in anticipation of us winning the series. The doctor, of all people, was handing out a cigar to each player! Here we were in the presidential suite in Monte Casino – which costs R20 000 a night – drinking and downing beers with a cigar in each hand. It's not something that I've seen many times at a Kontiki …

It was a special time, the party lingered on and on, and then the wives and girlfriends joined us. Things eventually went pear-shaped, a couple of beers were spilt and some cooler boxes got broken.

The presidential suite had been our team room. The staff had really looked after us and we spent a week up there like kings. I think we tore the backside out of it that night because for our next week at Monte Casino, ahead of the third Test, we were relegated downstairs to the lowest floor!

I had a photo taken with Percy Montgomery towards the end of that evening. One of Monty's goals had been to play until the end of the Lions series because he had made his debut against them in 1997, and he hadn't kicked well at goal in the second Test in Durban, which the Lions had won to clinch the series. It was a burning issue with him and he wanted to make amends.

Monty had retired from Test rugby in 2008 but a very good second prize for him was that he ironically played a big role as a kicking coach in the 2009 series.

Monty has had a massive influence on my career and it was fitting for him to be with us that night. He used to be an integral part of the Kontikis because he was inevitably one of the three most capped players and now he had graduated from the front row of the Kontiki to the front seat of the bus with the coaches.

We love taking the mickey out of Monty regarding his mouth, which is the smallest I have ever seen! We called him 'the chipmunk' because he was always on about having to eat seven meals a day as part of his weight-training regimen and every time we saw him he would be nibbling away, forcing food down that little aperture.

This also means he can't down a drink too rapidly, so every Kontiki we would manufacture a reason why he would have to drink, just so we could laugh at him trying to gulp a beer down his narrow throat. Our female masseuse, Daliah Hurwitz, who's my age, drills him every time in the boat races (a drinking game), and we take the piss out of him.

27

BAD BLOOD

It was a difficult start to the week leading up to the third Test against the Lions because Peter de Villiers and I differed on the selection policy. Peter wanted to look at our depth ahead of the Tri-Nations while I thought we should prioritise the 3-0 whitewash.

While I saw merit in his thinking, it wasn't the decision I would have made. Ten changes to the starting XV were too many and just as crippling would be the serious distractions of the Schalk Burger and Bakkies Botha suspensions.

After seeing the footage of the Loftus Test we realised that Schalk was in trouble.

I know Schalk well enough to say that he would never have set out to injure Luke Fitzgerald's eyes. It's not in his nature. I've never known him to intentionally hurt somebody with a cheap shot – in Currie Cup, Super 14 or Test rugby. He will tackle the stuffing out of you but he won't do something that's contrary to the spirit of the game. He's not the kind of bloke who would drop his knee onto someone, eye-gouge or bite. The manner in which he cleaned out Fitzgerald is very similar to how we train, where you've got to roll the player out, but he grabbed Fitzgerald in the wrong place. He got his hand in the wing's face, which was the biggest mistake he made. But perception isn't always reality. The hand in the face didn't prove intent to gouge.

I asked Schalk what happened. He said: 'Barney, I don't have a clue. I was so worked up in the moment [he had just run out for his 50th Test and the incident happened soon after the kick-off] that I wanted to clean the guy off the ball as physically as I could. I wasn't watching him and when I grabbed and pulled him off the ball, my hand went into his face. I never intended to put my fingers in his eyes. If someone did that to me I'd be disgusted.'

Schalk does everything on the edge at the best of times and maybe he was trying too hard in his milestone Test and because he was coming back from injury (he had missed the first Test because of a calf injury and had hardly played in the Super 14). Maybe he was also feeling under pressure because of how well Heinrich Brüssow had performed in the first Test.

I don't believe that Schalk was trying to eye-gouge Fitzgerald. I believe he got it wrong in that he recklessly got his hand into the guy's face, and he was duly punished. Who could really tell in a court of law what he was thinking or intending to do?

My major concern for him in that week was that he was made out to be the devil's child or a serial killer, and I know that's not Schalk. So I phoned him and told him that he needed to draft a statement that said he gravely regretted the incident which led to his banning. He was very down.

The same thing had happened to me in France in 2005, when I was banned for six weeks for accidentally fracturing Jerome Thion's larynx with my elbow. Again, it was a case of perception triumphing over reality.

The Schalk incident spiralled out of control when Peter made a hash of trying to defend him at the Monday press conference. It was the start of what was going to be an ugly week because of his outlandish comments.

To be fair to Peter, he's not comfortable speaking English in press conferences, but his reaction to the questions from the angry British and Irish media was unfortunate. They all believed that Schalk should have been given a red card, which I thought was slightly embarrassing on their part, because they were basically saying that the Lions could only have won the Test if they had played against 14 men.

The media were in a mean mood and trapped Peter in a corner. The only thing you can give him credit for was that he was trying to stand by his player, but in a misguided way. Sadly, he just gave too many answers. He could have squashed the entire issue in the post-match press conference by saying: 'I haven't seen the incident, so I have to watch the video tonight and then form an opinion. Whether Schalk's guilty or not is for the disciplinary committee to decide.'

That's the standard thing coaches say to avoid falling into the trap, but Peter was obviously still excited about the win and got emotional when they were trying to take the glory of the series win away from us by concentrating on Schalk.

Unfortunately, emotion and a press conference is a recipe for disaster and I eventually had to intervene because it was going from bad to worse. I told the media to leave the Schalk issue to the judiciary.

On the Monday, the press were waiting for Peter and to our dismay, he walked straight into another ambush, saying that guys who don't like the rough stuff should take up ballet. It made him look silly and ensured a very difficult week for us.

He didn't have enough media experience yet to realise that his comments would impact on the team because they'd created a negative mood. Peter still believes that what gets said out there is irrelevant – that it's what happens between us as a team that counts – but it doesn't work that way. And why throw petrol onto a fire when you've already got a disciplinary hearing pending for Bakkies; Schalk has been found guilty of serious foul play and you have made all these changes to the team?

It meant we were fighting a media storm at every press conference, with the coach giving out bizarre sound bytes.

On the Monday Peter should have said: 'Schalk's incident was unfortunate and we accept his punishment. I've seen the incident and it doesn't look good, but we will carry on with the team that we've got and make the best of it.' But it just kept on simmering.

I spoke to Peter about it later and he admitted that he had learnt a heck of a lot from that week. But how do you school someone who's in that position? It's like telling someone that he can be president of a country but mustn't speak in public. It's a tricky one.

To be fair to Peter, we all learn during our careers. I'm not the same captain that I was in 2004. Sure, I didn't drop bombs in 2004 but I used to *kak* myself before every press conference. The night before I would be worried about the next day's press conference, and would try to guess what questions would be asked and prepare answers. That's how much of an issue they can be to people new to them. Now imagine me in 2004 having to do my first press conference in Afrikaans – I would have *really* shat myself. Peter's not comfortable speaking in English. He speaks Afrikaans to me, and a lot of people have told him to speak Afrikaans to the media too.

That was one of the longest, hardest weeks of my career because I had so much to deal with. I had a new team and was putting out fires all over the show.

During the week the players had to respond to questions about the coach. We had all read the newspapers, although players say they don't read them, and it's difficult to drive to training and not see the posters on the lamp posts.

I quite enjoy reading the sport pages because I love sport in general and, of course, my eye always drifts to the rugby stories. But I did ignore the newspapers for my own good in 2006 when I was taking a lot of flak. Every week there was a different guy telling me that I wasn't good enough or I wasn't this and wasn't that, so it wasn't in my best interests to reinforce all that negativity.

Later in the week before the third Lions Test, Bakkies took over from Schalk as the biggest distraction, although there were many to choose from.

We were flabbergasted at the initial citing for Bakkies' 'illegal' clearout of Adam Jones at a ruck (the prop went off injured) and then even more so at the guilty verdict which saw Bakkies banned for two weeks. We took it for granted that it was going to be overturned in the appeal and Bakkies remained part of our plans the whole week, which is why Steven Sykes was only called up on the Thursday.

We never in a million years expected the disciplinary committee's ludicrous decision to be upheld twice. In hindsight, it was silly not to prepare for that eventuality. That's when we really got our knickers in a knot and we realised that something just wasn't right. We felt Bakkies was being victimised for his transgressions in the past and we struggled to accept it.

We had to stand behind Bakkies, who had done what he had been coached to do when clearing rucks. We felt that if we didn't challenge the decision, the game was going to be adversely affected for everyone around the world. Every season officials try to soften the game and we don't want rugby to end up as a game for softies.

For instance, an assistant referee on the touchline will say to his mate reffing the game, 'Rule 10.4 – charging in without binding on a player.' I'll bet he doesn't know three other laws in the whole book but he knows he can make a name for himself by highlighting this particular one. A referee can potentially penalise any player entering a ruck. Have you ever seen two guys, bound together, entering a ruck as the law says they must? Or binding onto a guy in a ruck and then carrying on cleaning?

I asked Peter how he felt about Bakkies' sentence and he was just as furious. As it turned out, all of us – from the coaching staff, to the management, to SA Rugby's acting managing director Andy Marinos – felt extremely aggrieved. And when I approached the players about making a stand against the ridiculous citing, they all jumped in, only too happy to defend Bakkies.

I chatted to Andy on the Friday about making a public statement and he was keen and said we should take it to Saru president Regan Hoskins. I wanted a consensus on this because we weren't only standing up for Bakkies, but for the future of the game too. I went to great lengths to ensure we weren't doing something on an emotional whim or being rash and irresponsible.

In 2004 our white armband protest had been miscon-strued as a tribute to an administrator, who had died that week, rather than our fight for contracts. So our actions had been lost in translation before and we wanted to make sure that it didn't happen again, which is why we had 'Justice 4 Bakkies' written on them.

I've never known a rugby week like that one and looking back, it's not surprising that our intensity dropped markedly. There were just too many sideshows in the build-up, too many changes to the team, and not even the Ellis Park factor could save us.

Somehow we were still in the game when we trailed 15-6 with 25 minutes to go, until Ugo Monye intercepted when we were putting pressure on their line and raced off for an 80m try. That pretty much closed the door for us.

I don't have any fond memories of that game. The Lions wanted it more than us and they got their selections right, with Shane Williams proving a point by scoring two blistering tries. We thought he should have started every Test.

The biggest disappointment of the whole tour for me was that there was no socialising between the teams, due to a fair amount of bad blood.

A week or so before the first Test we invited the Lions players and management to join us for drinks in our change room after each of the Tests so that we could create the friendships and memories that Lions tours of the past are renown for. The older ex-players talk about these memories all the time. For instance, Willie John McBride still visits Morné du Plessis whenever he's in South Africa. We realised that there weren't going to be many opportunities to mix and decided to be proactive and invite them for a beer after the final whistle. They declined.

This happened long before we had played each other, when there was no reason for anybody to be pissed off with anybody. Nothing had been said or done. I later heard that this stemmed from one of the senior Irish players who said that he wasn't interested. We don't know why they made a decision contrary to the ethos of rugby, but we do know that we made the effort. We thought 'to hell with them' and that snub added to the needle that was there in all three Tests and it made the series victory all the sweeter.

Another thing that irritated us about the Lions was their attempt to pull a fast one when we swapped jerseys after the first Test. When our guys got back to the change room, we realised that the jerseys we had been given were not the real thing. A genuine Lions Test jersey is embroidered with the player's name, number of caps, and the name and date of the fixture, but the ones they gave us could have come from any sports shop.

It's a major thing when we swap a jersey. We don't like to swap jerseys because we work very hard for them. The All Blacks are the same. We get two jerseys for each Test, so we can have a dry one for the second half. That second jersey is the one we swap on special occasions. If a Lions player got, say, Bryan Habana's jersey, it would have said: 'Bryan Habana, 47th cap, 20 June 2009, Springboks vs British & Irish Lions, Durban.' It would have been the one he sweated in for 40 minutes.

We sent our logistics manager Charles Wessels to their change room to ask for their original jerseys. They must have felt bad because they eventually sent back the embroidered originals. They had been cheeky, they had taken a chance and we thought: 'Stuff you, you aren't getting away with it.'

I didn't have much to do with Paul O'Connell but I saw a lot more of him than any of the other Lions because we had to attend a sponsor's function after every Test.

I'd heard out of the Lions' camp before they arrived in South Africa that they chose O'Connell over Brian O'Driscoll as captain because Ian McGeechan wanted someone up front that the Bok captain would literally have to look up to, someone who could give off that Martin Johnson presence. All the successful Lions tours that McGeechan was in charge of had a big lock leading from the front.

I found this quite interesting and I started thinking about how I could spice up the interaction between O'Connell and me at the coin toss. I asked our public relations manager Annelee Murray if we could create a special cap for all the guys who were going to play against the Lions – something different, but something to signify that we had played against them (it's always done for guys who reach 50 or 100 caps). I wanted this special cap to be part of my over-the-top plan to create an overly formal effect in order to throw O'Connell a little.

I anticipated that, like every other rugby captain, he would arrive at the coin toss in his warm-up jersey, shorts, long socks and his running shoes. I thought that if this story of them wanting me to look up to him was true, I would counter it by making him feel slightly uncomfortable at the coin toss.

As usual, we arrived at the stadium in Durban in our tracksuits and I showered as I always do before a match, and then changed into my No 1s, not my warm-up kit.

When I got called for the coin toss, I was wearing my No 1s, I had my cap on my head, which said '2009 British

& Irish Lions', and had a rule book in my left hand. I was quite a sight. When Victor Matfield and Jean de Villiers saw me changing into my No 1s, they laughed at me and thought I was crazy.

As I walked out of the change room, I wondered what the heck I was doing. I arrived first, shook Bryce Lawrence's hand and we chatted, as I know the southern-hemisphere referees well after all these years.

I then noticed the Lions media liaison Greg Thomas walking down the tunnel shouting: 'Make way, make way, Paul O'Connell's coming through. The captain's coming, get out of the way.' Thomas hadn't seen me at first but when he did, he literally took a step back in astonishment. Behind him was O'Connell in his T-shirt and shorts.

I knew I had the Lions on the back foot already. I wanted O'Connell to know this was not just another game to us, that it was something very special. I wanted him to realise that I believed this game was more important to me than it was to him, and this was the first way I could show it.

It was a small thing, even a little funny, and I'll never know whether it had an effect or not, but I had a little chuckle to myself when I went back to the change room. I repeated the drill for the second Test, but, ironically, not for the third.

I didn't have much time to change because of my little game with O'Connell and I had to sacrifice half my warm-up but I believe you have always got to keep thinking out the box.

The Test series wasn't conducted in a good spirit, if you compare it to the spirit of a World Cup or the Tri-Nations. There was a lot of niggle and I think it had a lot to do with the hype of the Lions.

They came out here with the premeditated intention of disrupting us. They wanted to get in our faces, irritate us and tease us into doing stupid things to get our focus off the ball, which is something we don't really have to deal with against other teams.

The All Blacks and Wallabies, for instance, know they can beat us if they play well, so they focus on the ball and on tactics, and can't be bothered with the other nonsense. But I think the Lions saw us as a huge threat, especially our physicality. They wanted to get under our skins and force us to react, but the more they whined – on and off the field – the more we laughed at them.

In contrast, during the three 2009 Tri-Nations matches in South Africa, the All Blacks and Wallabies accepted our drinks invitation and, after having smashed each other to pieces, there wasn't an ounce of ill feeling or whining. In rugby, you've got to be able to climb into each other for 80 minutes, and then let it end there, but it didn't happen with the Lions.

The first time I had any interaction with their players – and some of them I know well, such as Lee Mears and Phil Vickery – was after the third Test at the gala function to commemorate the series.

I promise you, if you hadn't seen the games, you would have thought the Lions had won the series, such was the tone of their speakers.

There were a lot of speakers. Deputy Minister of Sport Gert Oosthuizen, Regan and I were the South Africans who spoke, while O'Connell and Lions manager (and ex-Lions wing) Gerald Davies spoke on their behalf.

Davies' speech went on forever and gave the impression that it had been a 3-0 whitewash for the Lions, so you can only imagine how they would have behaved if they had won the series.

They also didn't win any friends by behaving rudely during Oosthuizen's speech. When one of their players got up to go to the toilet or the bar, they would clap him while he walked off and when he returned. They showed total disrespect to the deputy minister. It was awkward and uncomfortable.

Looking back now on my experience of the Lions, it's a pity that my fondest memory dates back to the aftermath of the few minutes I played for the Sharks in 1997 when Jason Leonard brought me his jersey afterwards. Sadly, I don't have a single memory like that from the 2009 tour.

28
KONTIKIS AND INITIATIONS

Please don't get the wrong idea about Bok Kontikis. It's not all about revelry, especially when we've lost. Often there are guys who don't drink and their choice is completely respected, although the night we won the Test series against the Lions, everyone was happy to hold a beer, take a puff of a cigar, savour the achievement and make sure it was forever etched into our memories.

I think a wonderful feature of Bok rugby is the contrasting characters that make up our team. For example, the ages range from 21 to 32. We had a young buck like Fransie Steyn, who's in the prime of his life and discovering who he is, and having a fat *jol* as he goes along, and we've got guys who are religious and shun the nightlife. There are also guys who are very professional and try not to drink at all because their bodies are the tools of their trade. There are guys who love to crack open a beer and relax, like Schalk Burger, who never gets out of hand but needs no second invitation to have a beer or three.

The consumption of alcohol is where the Kontiki could potentially be a bad thing, but the beauty of it is that different views are tolerated. Those who don't drink end up downing a Coke or an Energade. If their 'crime' is particularly bad, or really embarrassing, they might find a little Tabasco or half a yoghurt in their Energade to make it unpalatable.

No one's forced to drink – it's not about that – and if I look back over the years on all the drama that our opponents have had with alcohol and drug abuse – which has resulted in curfews and breathalyser tests – I'm grateful that we have never had that problem.

We've had a few guys who have overstepped the mark. We had an incident with a senior player who lost the plot one day in the week leading up to one of our Tests. He had way too much to drink during the day and arrived in a paralytic state at a team dinner.

We have had our parties, believe me, but always within boundaries. Drinking has never been an obstacle for us; it's never been a distraction. It's really just been a way to relax and build spirit among the guys. I'll give you an example. A guy like Bismarck du Plessis doesn't drink a lot of alcohol, but he loves to party, loves being with the guys, and he'll go out with them till 4am and drink Sprite.

He's not scared of having a down-down. If he gets a fine and he's found guilty, he'll have a beer, but he's not interested in getting pissed, and his view is respected. People just fit in at the Boks. I think it's indicative of where we are as a nation. South Africans have become accepting because of our shaky past. We tolerate differences and embrace all cultures.

The Kontiki also plays host to the initiation ceremony.

When a player gets his first cap, he is initiated at a Kontiki at the first opportunity. Everyone gets called into the team room at the hotel – players, wives, girlfriends and the player's parents – for the blazer presentation and the capping of the player. He's not allowed to wear his Bok blazer until he's been initiated.

Once that's done, the family and friends are excused and the Kontiki gets into full swing. The first thing one of the main guys at the table will say is: 'If there's anyone who doesn't feel comfortable or welcome here, please feel free to leave.' Invariably the new guy gets up to leave and everyone says, 'No, no, no, no.' Then he sits down and everyone says, 'No, no, no, no' and eventually he leaves, before returning again.

It's usually the scrumhalf or the reserve scrumhalf who has to keep order at a Kontiki in terms of keeping the guys quiet, and making sure they stand up when the Kontiki committee walks in. I don't know why it's the scrumhalf – it's just tradition – and with us it has often been the reserve scrumhalf, Ricky Januarie.

He delegates to a greenhorn – like Heinrich Brüssow or Morné Steyn – to pour the drinks, and so on. He's basically the organiser, the facilitator of the Kontiki and the guy responsible for making life as difficult as possible for the new cap, so he often gives them ridiculous instructions.

The whole exercise is to make it a night the new cap will never forget.

Several players prepare stories of past glories or funny episodes, basically Bok anecdotes that will make a lasting impression on the new cap. It's a special thing.

At the climax of the process, the new cap has to stand in front of the Kontiki and accept the code of conduct, which the coach reads in English or Afrikaans. He starts with 'I solemnly pledge', which the new cap echoes, and so on until he has gone through it all.

The reason I bring this up is because when Jake White was Bok coach, he brought back a lot of the old-school traditions, like the blazer with the golden beading, which did wonders for this team's ethos.

At every initiation Jake would stop at one particular line in the Springbok code that says, 'I'll put the interests of the team above my own.' He would repeat this line, which the new player would also repeat, because that really is what teams are about. Jake was uncompromising on this. It is the most important line.

Luke Watson's initiation was inevitably different.

The way Bok rugby has worked, from day one, is that a player is picked by a selection committee or by the coach. Luke is the one exception.

The administrators completely disregarded Jake and were disrespectful when they forced Luke into the squad in 2007. When have you ever heard of that happening in sport?

For us, it was unacceptable, especially because as a team we had put a strong emphasis on tradition and respect for what had gone before. We had worked really hard for our selections, and it was a very special moment when they came.

The bottom line was that Jake was told that he had to pick Luke to start against Samoa at Ellis Park. We were pissed off. In 116 years of Springbok rugby, no one had ever had a free passage into the team.

We went to Jake during the week and told him we didn't feel comfortable giving Luke the same initiation ceremony as everyone else because he hadn't entered into the group in the same way we had.

Jake, to his credit, said: 'I'm not happy about the situation either, far from it, but the fact remains that Luke will become a Springbok on Saturday, and you are not bigger than the game, you don't get to decide who gets initiated or not.'

Those were powerful and honest words. I can assure you that the Luke episode was a major stress for Jake, but he wanted us to treat him in the same way as any other player.

As I said earlier, we didn't have a Kontiki on the night of Luke's debut, as occasionally happens for logistical reasons. It just happened that way and resulted in the conspiracy stories in the media that we had refused to initiate him. But when we got together again at a camp for the Tri-Nations, on the first Saturday evening of our week together, Luke was initiated, exactly like any other Bok who had gone before him.

CAPTAIN IN THE CAULDRON

Luke joined the Sharks after a season at Eastern Province and made a big impression on me. He was the most driven young guy I had met in a long time. He was well-spoken, confident and trained like an absolute animal. He was vibrant and enthusiastic and good at what he did. When the SA U21 squad was announced, and Luke hadn't been included, I was outraged on his behalf and phoned Jake (who was the coach of the side) and asked him how this oke could be ignored, never mind not made captain.

Jake said: 'John, believe me, I have a better openside flank than Luke. Remember this name: Schalk Burger.'

'Who the hell is Schalk Burger?' I asked.

In Luke's second year he became more problematic when he started getting *windgat*. He started irritating the guys with his superior attitude and nobody was too fussed when he signed for Western Province when his second year was up.

He wrote in a newspaper column that he wanted to go to Cape Town to play in a team that was going to win trophies and help him become a Springbok. So he was basically saying that we were *kak*, which didn't go down well. The feeling at the Sharks was: 'What a jerk. Good riddance.'

Luke had been having problems with Kevin Putt, but I can't hold that against him because most of the guys had problems with Putty.

In Cape Town Luke was probably more in the limelight and played really well for WP and the Stormers. Public support was firmly with him – until he went too far in a *Sports Illustrated* article in 2004. He showed his true colours and public sentiment did a 180° turnaround. He completely rubbished Jake in the article, saying he had no integrity. The feeling among the guys was that he was too big for his boots in the way he spoke about the Springbok coach.

I kept that article and compared it to his comments in 2008 about the Bok jersey. In 2004 he raved about how honoured he would be to wear it, yet in 2008 he allegedly wanted to vomit on it!

Luke never held back, he always said exactly what he felt. You can appreciate his honesty but you can also understand why the guys who played for Jake couldn't stand him.

He also had a heck of a lot to say about me as a captain. He had painted me with the same brush as Jake because the two of us were pretty close. He criticised how I played and said that I wasn't the best hooker in the country, that I was Jake's protected game. I certainly didn't lose sleep over those comments, but when he eventually got into the squad, it was hard to pretend they hadn't been made.

During the time that Luke's supporters were asking why he wasn't being selected, it was alleged that Jake had a personal vendetta against him. If I think back, Luke did play some really good rugby at stages – most notably in 2005 – but he was a loose forward in a country blessed with abundant riches in that department. We had established flankers in the side, and every time Luke chirped it took selection even further away from him.

The fact is that as good as Luke is, he's not the kind of flanker who's going to tackle someone 5m back or smash him in the contact situation. He's a very good ball-carrier and has good ball skills, but he was never going to play the robust, physical game that Jake got the Boks playing because of his relatively small stature. Almost every team we play is overshadowed by our size and physicality. That's just the make-up of the Springbok team. It has been and always will be the case.

At Luke's initiation he swore the oath like every other Bok, so when the story broke about him allegedly wanting to vomit on the jersey, my initial reaction was that I hoped it wasn't true, but sadly it was (Luke has never denied it).

The thing is, once you become a Bok, you can no longer speak as you please, you really have to be careful about what you say, and you can't get away with explosive things.

My cellphone didn't stop ringing for a week. Players and former Boks were livid and they wanted blood. The guys couldn't believe the statements he had allegedly made. I hope he regrets saying those things, if he did say them, but I've never spoken to him about it.

My policy with Luke throughout the time he was in the Springbok camp was to treat him like any other player. My job as captain is to put the team above my personal opinions or those of senior players. I've got to make everyone feel part of the Bok team.

I never belittled Luke. I gave him encouragement ahead of his Test debut against Samoa. I spoke to him throughout the warm-up, and I stayed on his shoulder in the opening minutes. I gave him every opportunity that I would give every other Springbok because he had that jersey on. I made it very clear that he wasn't to be mistreated in the team, but he later made things very difficult for us by refusing to participate in team meetings and gatherings.

29

CHASING
THE TREBLE

I can honestly say that we barely gave the 2009 Tri-Nations a minute's thought until it was practically upon us. The Lions series was all-consuming, and all our planning for the previous year or so had been with the Lions in mind.

After the third Test, it was a case of, 'Crikey, we play the All Blacks in less than three weeks, time to refocus.'

So what did the coach do? He sent us on holiday for 10 days and we got together just a week before the first Test against the All Blacks in Bloemfontein.

I'm convinced that break played a pivotal role in our success in the competition. We were physically and mentally frazzled and a total break from rugby was literally what our doctor, Craig Roberts, ordered. I took the family on a road trip around the country and switched off completely.

When we reconvened in Bloemfontein, we were thoroughly revitalised and immediately the talk was that we had a good opportunity to add the Tri-Nations title to our series victory over the Lions and our World Cup crown.

I told the guys we weren't just going to compete, but were going to make sure we won the damn thing, and the whole squad switched on. Our sessions that week were extremely sharp and focused, which had a lot to do with us tightening up our preparation.

While it went well during the Lions series, we still felt that we weren't giving an exact message to the squad in terms of game plans, strategy, preparation and review. Peter de Villiers and his assistants Gary Gold and Dick Muir all had ideas on how we should play, as did the senior players (including Victor and me), but these different messages were confusing the squad. In order to solve this problem we decided that the leadership group and coaches should sit down together on a Sunday morning and thrash out our plan for the week so there was one unambiguous message to take to the players on the Monday.

This streamlining of information was developed out of the Lions series. It's one thing to allow empowerment, and another to consolidate the points of view in a controlled environment, so that you don't confuse youngsters like Frans and Morné Steyn. When they are in certain game situations and they aren't sure what to do, they will revert to the clear instruction that was given to them.

This was the cornerstone of our success. We were so well organised. After we had beaten the All Blacks 28-19, I said: 'Well done, you all brought your A-games but let's remember that this performance was based on how organised we were. We didn't have to spend needless hours on the training field because we were so well prepared. It's not about how much we train but how cleverly.'

We were even better in Durban the following week. We knew the All Blacks would come out frothing at the mouth, as they always do after losing a Test, and we fine-tuned our game even further. We were able to raise our performance mostly because of the confidence a team has when each guy knows exactly what to do.

There was a lot of hype surrounding this Test because I was going to break Will Carling and George Gregan's shared record of 59 Test caps as captain. I wished it could have waited until after the match. I have realised over the years that personal milestones are unwanted distractions in the build-up to big matches. They detract from the team focus.

When I did take to the field in Durban, the applause was unbelievable. I couldn't believe that I had done this 60 times and, make no mistake, I was immensely proud as I waited for the team to join me.

That night Saru presented me with an expensive watch to mark the occasion (they had asked Roxy what I might want and she knows all too well that cars and watches are my big obsessions). Saru didn't have to get me a gift as they had already given us the all-expenses paid holiday to Mauritius when I reached 50 Tests as captain.

The All Blacks performed their traditional 'Ka Mate' haka in Bloemfontein but in Durban they opted for the 'Kapa o Pango' version they introduced in 2005 (it used to culminate in the index finger being drawn across the throat, but that was omitted after an outcry that it was too bloodthirsty). They use the new haka only when they feel they need a special performance, and when we were taking our tracksuits off (we keep them on during the haka and use up a few minutes afterwards to take them off as a ploy to diffuse its impact) I told the guys the All Blacks were clearly in the mood for war.

But that ace they had pulled out didn't work. It was the first time they used it against us and lost. We put so much pressure on them that they couldn't play. We gave them nothing and forced them into trying to run the ball from perilous field positions. We throttled the life out of them and in their desperation they conceded penalties regularly. Morné kicked eight of them and added a try and conversion for all 31 of the points we scored (they got 19).

Our kick-and-chase game rattled their back three and once again we killed them in the lineouts. Victor is a lineout genius but his prowess has rubbed off on the other forwards over the years, and now Juan Smith, Pierre Spies, Bakkies Botha and Danie Rossouw are all good at contesting.

An enjoyable development in the 2009 Tri-Nations was the teams getting together for a beer after the matches. In Bloemfontein, the All Blacks had taken up the same invitation that the Lions had declined. It became the trend. After every Test in the Tri-Nations there were beers in the home team's change room after we had showered.

In Durban, I said to Richie: 'Talk me through a Test in Hamilton' and he smiled and said: 'Talk me through a Test in Bloemfontein'. With hindsight, that was quite apt given the storm that would erupt over us choosing to prepare in Surfers Paradise in Australia for the Hamilton Test.

The accuracy of our game against the Wallabies in Cape Town the following week was not quite as good, but we won 29-17 by manufacturing a lot of pressure through pinpoint kicking and very good chasing, and again Morné brilliantly converted that pressure into points (this time via seven penalties and a drop goal). Our try was scored by Victor after he had followed up a grubber I'd put through following a dummy pass. The pair of us milked that one in the Kontiki, I can assure you. We had shown the backs how it should be done!

There was also a negative from this match – it was the start of the story about my perceived scrumming deficiencies, and boy did it run and run.

We got good results from our scrums but I got burnt two or three times by Wallabies loosehead Benn Robinson, who had also out-scrummed me earlier in the year in the Sharks-Waratahs Super 14 game.

I find him very difficult to deal with. Of all the guys I scrummed against in 2009 – Gethin Jenkins, Adam Jones, Tony Woodcock – I found him the biggest challenge from a technical point of view. He's shorter and smaller than me and has a number of tricks – some of which bend the rules

– and I haven't been at tighthead long enough to learn how to deal with them. I find it easier to scrum against big props as it becomes a straight arm wrestle.

I learnt from that Newlands game and improved in our next match in Perth (which we won 32-25) and also the one in Brisbane (which we lost 21-6), despite the negative criticism. In fact, the Brisbane game was the one where I felt we gave our best scrumming performance.

During the fortnight of the Brisbane and Hamilton Tests, I felt I was back in 2005 when I was criticised for not being the best hooker in South Africa. People wanted my head. I'd just been a hero in the Lions series and was now getting it in the neck. I felt like I'd gone back four years in three days. Fortunately, I got a lot of backing from my team-mates and from people who understand the game.

The truth is that I did battle in some of the scrums, but not all of them. I felt it was unfair that the press made it out to be 10 times worse than it was. We still had a much better launch percentage from scrums than the other Tri-Nations teams – we were 40% better than the Wallabies – and we scored the most tries from scrums.

Also, the scrums weren't the winning or losing factor in any of the Tri-Nations Tests. But I was an easy target and the topic of the captain changing from hooker to prop was an obvious one for debate. The Aussies are good at angling in on a target and the South African media followed suit.

I'd been through it all before and it was another reminder of how fickle the rugby world can be. I felt a bit betrayed by some of the reporting from home that I should have taken Jake White's advice and retired.

Robinson had the upper hand on me in all three Tests. He gets in at an angle and then scrums up, but he gets away with it. He hides his shoulder under the hooker's shoulder, which we did when I was at hooker, and now it's getting done to me! I'm learning every week in a very difficult area with the world watching and waiting for me to fail.

One-on-one Robinson came out on top, but I know I got better in each Test and I will continue to improve the more I play in the position. He's not going to have the same result the next time we play.

On the morning of the Brisbane Test, ex-Wallabies scrum coach Alex Evans said in the *Courier-Mail* that I was a danger to scrum safety, but that kind of criticism was easier to take because it was just manufactured bullshit planted in the paper. It was a silly thing for the Wallabies to do because all it succeeded in doing was to motivate me, and it culminated in my strong performance against Woodcock in Hamilton. By the time we got to New Zealand, I was thoroughly fed up and said to myself: 'Enough is enough, this is what I can do, and this is what I will do.'

The Wallabies deviate from the rules in that they creep before the put-in because they don't want you to have a full whack at them. If I am 6ft 2in and a 5ft 8in guy creeps up and gets in my face, he's going to get the upper hand while it's not in his best interests for me to come at him from the legal gap with my full weight.

When you try and tell referees that the Wallabies are not respecting the mark, they get annoyed because it's an obvious thing but one they forget to police.

One of my big problems with referees in the 2009 Tri-Nations was that the more they saw me get beaten in a one-on-one contest, the more they seemed to think: 'Well, that's to be expected, he's just moved from hooker to prop.'

In general, I feel we got it wrong by taking on the referees on the away leg of the Tri-Nations. We got a little precious, and in hindsight, shouldn't have complained as much as we did. None of the referees tried to cheat us deliberately. The fact is we were ranked No 1 in the world and we would go on to win five out of six Tri-Nations games, so what were we moaning about?

You could say that in Hamilton the penalty at the first kick-off and the first scrum penalty were premeditated by

Nigel Owens and had no substance, but that's the nature of how he referees when he's away from home and it doesn't mean he was out to cheat.

We need to be cognisant, too, that in world rugby the referees are ranked just as the teams are, and in 2009 four of the top five were South Africans, so we never got them. We got the refs from the bottom half of the top 10, so we should have expected them to make mistakes.

We learnt from Brisbane that we need to roll with the punches and accept there will be good and bad calls. The more you work yourself up into believing that referees are against you, the better the chance of it happening.

We got our minds right on this issue before Hamilton, and during the match we didn't get fazed by some curious decisions against us. You can lose it in the blink of an eye overseas and other Springbok teams might well have lost the plot after those first-half penalties.

Before that Test, I'd read everything that had been said about me on the rugby websites and some of the stuff was ridiculous. I couldn't believe that at 31 and with 89 caps I was having to prove myself again.

But I knew I would play well and was desperate to get my first win in New Zealand.

The moment of affirmation for me was when Richie took a scrum from a penalty on our 22 and we scrummed them off their ball. That was the equivalent of running past the media box and giving an up-yours.

I'm going to get better at tighthead prop. There will be somebody who will catch me again but I know I'm getting there. It was only in 2008 that Clermont coach Vern Cotter asked me to help out in a crisis when we lost three tight-heads to injury in a week-and-a-half. Vern asked how I felt about it and I was happy to put my hand up and show my commitment to the club, but I had no idea how I would cope. He started me off in some lower league games and it went well.

Peter picked up on this, and to be fair, what coach in his right mind wouldn't want to find a way to accommodate Bismarck du Plessis in the front row?

People have often asked me how I felt about being side-lined to prop but it wasn't like that. Peter told me that I would remain his first-choice hooker, and if it didn't work out at tighthead, I would revert to hooker. That gave me the confidence to have a full crack.

I also realised that it's a lot more difficult at 31, 32 or 33 to carry on playing as a 123kg hooker at the ever-increasing pace of international rugby.

I'm honest enough with myself to know that I can't do what Bismarck does – I'm not physically capable of it – but I also know that there are no other tightheads out there who can make as many tackles and ball-carries as me, or hit as many rucks.

If Bismarck left South Africa, I'd consider going back to hooker, but as long as he's here, I'm proud to know that he's taken what I taught him and made it even better because he's stronger and fitter.

Bismarck is a bloody good player, he's a thorn in the side of the opposition. His work rate is up there with Schalk Burger's and he steals as much ball as the flanks.

I was open to the move to prop because it would prolong my career and also allow the coach to pick Bismarck. I didn't see it as a slap in the face.

After our three Tri-Nations wins at home we were labelled 'boring' by All Blacks coach Graham Henry and Wallabies coach Robbie Deans, which I thought was silly because they were saying that they didn't know how to deal with us.

Before we left for overseas, we had a meeting about the negativity we'd encounter and I told the guys the worst thing they could do was believe it, that what had worked for us at home – such as the kick and chase – might not be suitable overseas and we might have to find another way to win. We had to believe that we could play any type of game.

In the first tour match, in Perth, we scored four tries and the running game felt as natural to us as kick and chase.

Before kick-off, I was condescendingly asked by Fox sports commentator Greg Clark if we were going to spend the evening kicking and I answered that a lot depended on what the Wallabies threw at us. If they left guys behind for the kick there would be opportunities for us to run; if not, we'd put on the pressure behind their forwards with kicking.

Our team can easily adapt to situations. In 2004, I was too nervous to change our game but now, not only am I comfortable to change and read the game, but I also have Victor, Juan, Fourie and Jean de Villiers (until he left for Ireland) who can do it.

I'll give you an idea of how it works in our team. Richie McCaw takes a scrum from a penalty on our 22, we scrum them and get the turnover penalty. While the other guys are high-fiving, I say we are going to kick for touch, drive from the lineout, box kick, and then drive until we get the penalty. Victor reminds me that penalties aren't coming our way, and I say we need to be patient and if we don't get the penalty, we will have bought time in their half. Fourie says if we don't get the penalty he will box kick accurately enough for Bryan Habana to catch the receiver. So we are three steps ahead of the game before the ball has even gone out. If the ball goes out further downfield than expected, we will change it on the way to the lineout to a wider, more attacking play, or whatever. It's strategy on the move.

Before the Hamilton Test, our video guy Peter Maimane asked me to recommend a song for a motivational video he was putting together. I suggested the vibey Black Eyed Peas song 'I gotta feeling', which was all over the radio at the time and which repeats the line 'Tonight's gonna be a good night'. This video was played at our pre-match meeting and the first clip was of Brad Thorn tipping me over in Wellington in 2008, and my team-mates exploding all around him, with the music pumping. It was brilliant.

On the morning of the game I wrote letters to each member of the 22, explaining what I felt about where the player was in his game and what his country needed from him that day. I've done it before on occasions and slipped the letters under the players' hotel room doors. Before the second Test against the Lions I folded them into the special caps that the guys were given to commemorate the Lions series and which were presented to them on the bus trip to Loftus.

I felt the time was right to repeat the exercise and I arranged for fitness coach Neels Liebel to take them to the change room before the team bus arrived (he gets to the ground earlier to set up our warm-up gear), and they were waiting at each guy's station in the change room.

Obviously the letters have to be tailored to suit the personality of the individuals – nothing overly serious for a young buck like Frans, but something more profound for a deep thinker like Fourie.

I felt we were in control of the match in Hamilton and were never in danger of losing it, despite the All Blacks' comeback at the end, which was what you would expect from them on their own soil.

In the change room after our 32-29 win, I said: 'Guys enjoy this, get rat-faced tonight!' And we did. We trashed the change room (without breaking anything), we ripped each other's shirts to pieces – it was like a school break-up day. Childish, maybe, but great fun!

There were so many moments to commemorate and so many reasons why this team had made history: winning the Tri-Nations title, winning three matches in a row against the All Blacks, winning in New Zealand (a first for Fourie and me), Jean and Frans leaving for Munster and Racing Metro respectively, and Victor's record 20th game against New Zealand.

On a personal note, a positive out of the Brisbane Test the week before was that I was given our team award for the biggest hit – my midfield tackle of Stephen Moore.

For every Test, the substitutes and non-playing squad members choose our Man of the Match and rule on our biggest hit. The former award is a Springbok skin autographed by the match 22 and the latter is a Kershaw hunting knife. Juan is in charge of this and buys the knives and skins with money drawn from our players' fund.

After Hamilton I got the knife and the skin and I was bloody chuffed. It was a big accolade for me after what I'd put up with over the previous fortnight and I was choked up when the presentations were made in the Kontiki.

President Jacob Zuma was waiting for us at OR Tambo International in Jo'burg. It was a much appreciated gesture. His office had contacted us in New Zealand and invited us to go from the airport to his residence, but when we explained that half the squad had connecting flights home, he said no problem, he would come to us, and he ended up waiting an hour for us at the airport.

He wore our blazer and he accepted my No 3 jersey. He spoke about the joy we had brought to all South Africans and how proud the country was of the Springboks. Those words really were the icing on our Tri-Nations cake.

'Teams used to be scared of playing you in South Africa, now they are also scared to play you in their homes,' he said.

I was struck by JZ's sense of humour. We were all in good spirits and full of banter, and when Peter went forward to speak, the guys were yelling 'stand up', teasing the coach about his height.

The president thought this was funny. He reckoned we were comedians as well as pretty good rugby players.

30

PETER'S EMPOWERMENT PLAN

When Fourie du Preez was presented with his special 50th cap during the Kontiki after the Test in Perth in 2009, the guys shouted 'Speech! Speech!' as they do when someone hates speaking in public.

Fourie is extremely shy – he hates speeches and probably had to be cajoled into speaking at his own wedding – but he did make a little speech on this occasion. 'I want to thank everyone for the most enjoyable year I've had in rugby. This is the best environment I've ever experienced in Springbok rugby,' he said.

That was a big statement from Fourie. The 2007 World Cup environment was exceptional, but for him the 2009 season was better. For Peter de Villiers, a coloured man from the Cape, to create an environment that appealed so much to a conservative Afrikaans guy from Pretoria, says a lot about the coach's management style and people skills.

It was also uplifting praise for a coach who's had to fight from day one, when his new employers did him serious harm by attaching a rider to the announcement of Jake White's successor in February 2008. Saru president Regan Hoskins admitted that Peter's appointment was not for 'purely rugby reasons' and those words have clung to Peter ever since. Before he had completed one day of work as coach, there was a readymade explanation for any future failures. 'Ah, well, what do you expect?' people would say. 'He didn't get the job because of his coaching capability.'

Peter has handled that really well. He has taken it like a man. If you knew his background, you would understand that he's a tough bugger. At the height of apartheid, his family were uprooted from their home in the Western Cape and relocated under the hideous Group Areas Act. He and his daughter once suffered the humiliation of being chased by a white security guard out of a park where he had been pushing her on the swings.

Peter has really been through the mill in this country and perhaps it explains some of his celebrated press conference comments such as 'I am what I am and I don't give a damn'. Most of the players had never met him when he took over from Jake and there was understandable scepticism, but the way he's conducted himself and the manner in which he's coached and managed the team from the start has been key to our success.

When Jake left, I thought my time as a Springbok was up. I didn't think another coach would trust me because of the partnership Jake and I had enjoyed for four years. That didn't bother Peter. He told me he wanted me back from France to captain my country. He was completely open, he had no agendas and because he had an open mind to me, I had an open mind to him.

At the start of his tenure his strength was sticking to what was already there while not promising anybody a free ride. This kept the guys on their toes. They were pleased this wasn't a case of a 'new broom sweeps clean' but they also knew that they had to perform.

If you had given this job to 10 South African coaches, nine of them would have said that the Jake era was over, that they were going to do it their way, that they were going to make changes and put their stamp on the team, and that anybody who didn't like it could leave.

I can promise you now, that would have been the end of this team. Most of the players would have gone overseas and we would have been back to the rebuilding days of 2004. There could well have been a lot of painful defeats instead of the staggering success we enjoyed under Peter in 2008 and 2009.

He was aware of the fact that there was already a strong team culture. We worked hard, had a family *gees* (spirit) that had been generated over almost half a decade and obviously had a lot of things in place to have won a World Cup. Peter wasn't envious of this environment or threatened by it. He respected it and changed little. The things he tweaked were very popular. He encouraged guys to prioritise family and home life, he increased the opportunities for partners to come in and be a part of Test weeks.He also emphasised that the guys should speak up about issues they were upset about so they could be sorted out.

Peter's unique in that he's a coach who can be relied upon for being completely open and honest with the players. It's a potentially dangerous approach but one he got right. It didn't work instantly because the guys didn't know how to take him and they didn't know if he was being genuine. That's human nature. But it all fell into place as time went by and the better we have got to know him as a person, the more he's been appreciated and the more effective he's been as a coach.

What kind of coach is he? He's a rare animal who doesn't want to be seen on a pedestal – describing elaborate moves that are going to win us big matches. He will come to the senior players and tell us what he's thinking about for the weekend – that he expects the opposition to do X, Y and Z, so why don't we look at doing P, Q and R. He lets the leaders filter that message into the team, knowing full well that the players react better to each other than to anybody else.

This background approach has generated the unfair criticism that he's not 'hands on' and has no technical ability. It's more a case of him not having an ego that needs to be fed by him standing up front shouting the odds, and a lot of the technical stuff does in fact originate from him. He subtly manages the environment of the team, passing on the messages he wants through the people and players who have the most influence in the team.

The coaches meet on a Sunday and agree on broad themes to take to the Monday morning forum, which is open to anybody in the squad to attend, but usually about eight or nine senior players sit down with the coaches and thrash out a plan for the week. One message then gets taken to the team. I don't know of any other rugby team that has this kind of democracy and consolidation of intellectual capital, and this forum has worked extremely well for us.

When we were losing Tests in 2008, the coach was an idiot according to the public; and by the same token, the success in 2009 was because we have fantastic players. But the truth is that we're all in it together in terms of planning, preparation and strategy.

A coach does have a massive influence over a team. It's easy to get things wrong. It's easy to have a group of talented players and treat them in the wrong way so that they don't perform. That hasn't happened under Peter. So many people have asked me to tell them the real story about Peter, and I can sense they want me to tell them he's useless, because that's the assumption they have made. Peter has said some silly things in press conferences and people judge him on that alone.

Sadly, if you strip a lot of the criticism bare, you'll find it's racist. Unfortunately, the old-school mentality that a black coach can't possibly be better than a white coach still lingers, but the positive from the situation is that the success

Peter has enjoyed can change attitudes. The success of our first black Springbok coach will hopefully take South Africa another big step down the road to full post-apartheid recovery because it's now evident that the Boks can win under a black coach.

What type of person is Peter? He's a relaxed, jovial guy. Perhaps he hasn't been in the position long enough to succumb to the paranoia and pressure that inevitably pulls the Bok coach in seven different directions, and so far he has been calm.

Some of the outlandish stuff he's blurted out at press conferences has given the impression that he's an egotist but in the squad we have found him to be sensitive and caring.

In 2009, the wife of one of our most senior players suffered a sudden serious illness. Peter heard about it and without consulting the player, booked him on a flight home even though it was a Test week. I've mentioned earlier how he did the same thing when I told him my son was sick. In that case, I never volunteered the information. He noticed that I was worried and approached me, he said he could see something was bothering me. He had 30 guys to worry about but could still pick up that I wasn't myself.

What sets Peter apart is his view that rugby is only a part of his life, not his entire life. He has brought that balance into the team and the players have warmed to it. Rugby is a massive part of our lives but we also have to look after the part that is not rugby-related because we are all going to end up out of the game at some point. The things that last are your family and friends.

When we beat the All Blacks in Hamilton to win the 2009 Tri-Nations, I stood up in our change room and congratulated the guys, and then added, 'But let's not get ahead of ourselves. We are the best because we are humble, work hard and are a good example to the people around us, and that example is set by our coach.' The guys ears' pricked up. I said: 'Last year, when it was going badly, he was getting ripped apart in the media but didn't remove himself from the spotlight and today, when it comes to trophies and photos, he's nowhere to be found.'

Peter had remained in the coaching box by himself during the on-field celebrations and presentations. When I asked him why he hadn't come down to the field, he said the players had won the match, not him.

The next day, Schalk Burger, Jean de Villiers and I were having a beer in the hotel bar in Auckland and reflecting on the season. There was a consensus that Peter has been the right man at the right time for this team. We had four very good years under Jake where our rugby was built up out of the rubble of the 2003 World Cup and the strongest foundations were laid. We were given direction, structure and focus, and won a World Cup as a result. Peter has now created an environment where the players are empowered, which has enabled us to move up a level and has led to greater freedom of expression. I don't think I know of too many other coaches who could have done what he did to allow us to progress.

This empowerment also means he trusts us with what's at stake for him too. He basically tells us to take responsibility to get ourselves to the next level but if it goes wrong, he will share the blame.

31

MAKING THE BOKS TICK

Not many people know that Bakkies Botha has a brilliant sense of humour that's at odds with his tough guy image, as irritating Lions scrumhalf Mike Phillips found out.

Phillips was a right pain in the backside, so it was fitting that one of the best put-downs of the Lions series came from an exchange between Bakkies and Phillips in the first Test in Durban.

Bakkies and Pierre Spies had come over the top of a ruck and smashed into Phillips, who screamed up at them: 'You fucking steroid monkeys, what the fuck's wrong with you?'

Bakkies jumped up, grabbed him by the collar and while giving the impression that he was about to knock Phillips's head off, smiled sweetly and cooed: 'My, you've got sexy blue eyes!' The flabbergasted look on Phillips's face suggested that Bakkies' pearl had more of an effect than the anticipated flat hand.

In the second Test at Loftus, they had a similar altercation, and Phillips let rip once more with his foul mouth. Bakkies grabbed him by the collar, wound up his right arm for a sledge-hammer blow and then said softly: 'How about dinner on Tuesday?' Priceless! Again, the words were better than a punch in the solar plexus.

It's the kind of stuff I have been getting from Bakkies since I've known him and it illustrates the rich character of our team.

I've never felt anyone as powerful as Bakkies in the set scrum. People will never know how hard he pushes. I've got to limit the number of scrums we do on a machine during the week because with Bakkies' power behind me, I end up smashing against steel. My spine tells me that I might as well be driving my car into a brick wall, and eventually I've got to say to our forwards coach Gary Gold: 'If I do more than three of these I'm going to be a flipping hobbit!'

Unless you feel that raw power, you will never understand it. We are talking about massive strength allied to the priceless ingredient of total commitment.

It's one thing being that strong, but it's another having the commitment to deliver when nobody in the stands has a clue how much you choose to contribute, and that's what sets Bakkies apart.

Alongside him in the second row, Victor Matfield is the rapier that complements the broadsword.

We first played together at U21 level but mostly locked serious horns in the Currie Cup and Super 12 before getting to know each other as fellow Springboks, and our close friendship was forged when I found myself managing the testy relationship between him and Jake White.

For some reason, Jake perpetually had a problem with Victor and vice versa, and I think it had a lot to do with the fact that Victor was undeniably a Heyneke Meyer man, which was understandable because they had formed a bond at the Bulls.

Their rift reached a head in 2005 when Jake sent Victor home from a Tri-Nations tour. Jake dropped him and told the media he was carrying an injury, but a few days later he played for the Bulls in the Currie Cup …

Jake was always on about Victor not hitting enough rucks and not working hard enough in the tight-loose, but they sorted out their issues in the end. I spent a large portion of the Jake era trying to soften the relationship between the two, and thankfully so, because Victor is invaluable on many fronts. He doesn't have Bakkies' unique physicality, but his mobility and ball skills gave balance to the second row and this was helped because I was a big hooker who thrived in the tight-loose.

And that's where Jake was really good with selection. Even though he and Victor didn't get along at first, he knew that he had workhorses in the likes of Bakkies and me, so Victor could be effective as more of a loose forward than a lock.

I often reminded Jake that Victor was critically important because he helped me so much on the field as a leader.

Victor's a natural leader. He's exceptionally intelligent and has a brilliant rugby brain.

Lineouts are his obvious speciality and he can analyse the opposition's lineout until he knows their lineout better than they do. In some Tests, it's been too easy for Victor, as he can get inside the head of the opposition hooker to the point where we can see that the hooker doesn't want to throw the ball in anymore.

I have grown to rely significantly on Victor's leadership ability. I've never been the kind of captain who wanted to do everything. I never wanted to choose the side, make the calls on the lineouts and scrums and tell the backline what to do. From the word go with Jake, I created a captaincy system where I incorporated four to five guys to assist me all the time.

Victor was always in charge of the defensive lineouts. If there was a ball that was kicked out in our half, I would just run and get the ball while he made the call. It was his baby and it took a lot of the load off me.

Over the years, Victor and I have built up a rapport on how to handle referees.

When we have a problem with a referee, we will consult, and he will come down hard on the referee in his capacity as a respected Super 14 captain and I will then interject and instruct Victor to back off. I will say to the ref: 'Sorry about that, I'll speak to Victor,' and the referee will be pleased that I have such control of my players while subconsciously taking note of Victor's point. Basically, we play good cop, bad cop.

Victor is essentially another captain of the team, as is a guy like Jean de Villiers, who controlled so much of our attack and backline defence.

I'll have key players leading the team in different areas of the game at all times. Victor, Fourie du Preez, Jean and I made many decisions together.

Fourie has a rugby brain second to none that this country – in fact, the world – won't see again for a long time. He has an introspective nature that counter-balanced Jean's gung ho approach.

Fourie is a very interesting character. We first started playing together in 2004 and it took three years before we became close. I trust people until they let me down, but some guys don't trust you until you prove yourself to them, and Fourie is like that. It took him a long time to suss me out and sort of half-accept me, and now we can be as open as we like with each other. He's a quiet, unassuming leader. He doesn't really have a way with people but he's got an amazing ability to point players in the right direction.

Incredibly, Fourie was dropped a few times. As I mentioned earlier, the first time was in 2004 in Jo'burg when Jake was forced to pull him out on the day of a match against the All Blacks because of interference from politicians who were unhappy about the lack of black representation.

Jake, with the best of intentions, suddenly told Fourie that Bolla Conradie would be starting the Test because he wanted to play a more attacking game, but a player as clever as Fourie was never going to buy that, and he distrusted Jake as a result.

During these formative years, I was aware of the differing personalities in our team and it was incredibly satisfying to witness how the chemistry eventually sorted itself out to produce the core of what would be a great Bok team.

In that core, we had our introverts and extroverts.

Take Juan Smith for instance. One of his nicknames is Venter because of his many similarities to André Venter, the legendary former Bok flank. They play the same position, both come from Bloemfontein, have the same rock-solid values and refuse to compromise on their beliefs.

Juan is to our team what the great Ruben Kruger was to the Springboks of the first half of the '90s in that he doesn't get the credit he deserves for his unseen work. Juan has often been the silent partner in loose trios that have had flamboyant players such as Schalk Burger and Joe van Niekerk, but he's been the cornerstone of those trios because of his incessant abrasiveness.

It took a while before Juan and I bonded. Like Fourie, people have to show him they are trustworthy by their actions. My words didn't mean much to him until I backed them up with actions on the field, and now he's one of my most trusted friends. Juan has meant so much to me as a quiet leader.

It has been fascinating to witness Bryan Habana blossom into the world's best wing. Jake brought him in as a youngster and in no time at all he had a seriously big marketing profile. He has a hard time in public, much more so than I do. He's loved by everyone from all walks of life and is mobbed wherever he goes. He's under a lot of pressure but always makes an effort to please people.

Our initial relationship was one of captain and young player but that has grown into close friendship. He's a perfect gentleman and I admire his excellent manners.

What sets Bryan apart and makes him such a great player is the fact that he knows how good he is. He knows he can change games, and whenever I've asked him to produce something special for the team, he's obliged.

The wonderful thing is that these guys who I've played more than 50 Tests with for South Africa have become my blood brothers. I've seen them break up with girlfriends, get married, and suffer tragic losses.

I also have to mention Butch James here. He's one of my best mates and the time we shared in digs and as team-mates was always awesome. His career has been hindered by injury (I often wonder how much more of an impact he would have had on world rugby had it not been for his five knee operations) but every single opponent fears him.

Butchie is big, he plays on the gainline and he smashes anyone who comes into his channel on defence. His other great attribute is one he probably doesn't even know about – when a Sharks or Springbok team was read out, and we heard he was at No 10, everyone felt safer.

But his value didn't end there. Off the field he was always the heart and soul of the team, and had a joke to tell or a prank to play. He's one of those priceless team boys.

As is Schalk, who burst onto the Test scene as a 20-year-old in 2003. He does the work of two or three players, and also adds a lot to the team off the field.

The Boks have been lucky to have had free spirits like Jean, Butch, Schalk and Bryan allied to salt-of-the-earth, loyal campaigners such as Os du Randt, Juan and Fourie.

32

MY GREATEST SUPPORTER

I had two subjects left to write in my matric finals when my mate Shane Chorley convinced me that we needed to relax and have a few beers at our local Spur. He had invited a few people, and as Cupid would have it, my old Standard 4 flame was one of them.

Roxane Rech and I got along brilliantly that night. I drove her home and there was a lot of awkwardness as I deliberated over whether to kiss her goodnight. I decided against it, opting for a cautious approach instead, and invited her for coffee the next night, even though I didn't drink coffee at that time. It was the only thing I could think of!

I had only two days to land this delectable fish because we had to return to school to finish matric. After coffee on the second night I got hold of the number at her hostel and a few days later plucked up the courage to call, although I was worried that I was coming on too strong!

When I called, a Standard 6 pupil on duty answered and I could hear a mad rush in the background as the juniors went to find Roxy. We chatted for ages on the phone, carried on calling each other over the next week, and decided that we would celebrate finishing matric together. Roxy was at Potchefstroom Girls High, and the Potch kids normally drive through Jo'burg, so I suggested to Roxy that she carry on to Pretoria.

I will never forget the day I finished matric and began our summer *jol*. There's nothing quite like that break-up day freedom, especially when you're in love!

Roxy and I were very young, and didn't quite know what we were doing, but we clicked perfectly from the outset and decided to go on holiday together, much to the disgust of one of my best mates because we'd planned a wild holiday down to the coast at Plettenberg Bay, and now I insisted on bringing a bird!

I'd been given my first car and off we all went into the sunset. I still can't believe that both sets of parents approved of this venture, but I like to think that all concerned knew we were not the reckless type and trusted us.

Roxy didn't know too much about me. She didn't know about my school experiences or about my decision to play rugby professionally. In fact, she didn't even know that I played rugby. During this period, I told her that I was going overseas for two weeks and she said 'that's nice'. She probably thought I was a spoilt brat, but I'd been invited to go on tour with the Natal U21 team to Wales.

When I returned from that trip, Roxy was working at Jet in Rustenburg and I rocked up at the store, hugged her, gave her a kiss and said 'howzit!' At that stage, I had no money for phone calls, and I didn't have a cellphone, so we hadn't communicated at all while I was overseas.

She asked where I had gone and I explained that it was a rugby tour. I told her that I had signed a contract with Natal which would see me move to Pietermaritzburg.

Roxy was enrolled at Tukkies to do her BSc – she wanted to get into medicine at that stage – so our relationship could very well have ended right then. But thankfully we decided to give it a bash. She finished the first year of her BSc and decided to change tack completely and switched to a BCom Accounting in order to become a chartered accountant.

Whenever the Sharks played an away match on the high-veld I would stay on for a night in Pretoria to see her and occasionally she would catch an overnight bus from Jo'burg to Durban at 11pm.

The beauty of our long-distance relationship was that we had our own space and time to establish ourselves in our careers. While my rugby career was developing quickly, she was giving accounting a full go. She didn't have a lot of free time and when we made the effort to get together it was really good.

It was almost the perfect scenario for both of us because by the time Roxy moved to Durban after four years of long-distance romance, all she had left to do was her Honours, and by that stage I had become a Springbok. We had both achieved a heck of a lot in those four years. It was tough at the time but beneficial in the long run.

Roxy is extremely ambitious and she was never going to settle for a standard degree. I can vouch for the endless hours she put in and anyone who has done a CA has my respect, because it's so much hard work. She really is a perfectionist when it comes to studying and is hardcore when she has set her sights on a goal.

Roxy came down to Durban in 2000 and found her own place and I was very appreciative that she had moved for me. I'd established myself at the Sharks, so I couldn't really move to the Bulls. She had to be the one to come down to Durban, but I never took it for granted.

That's one of many things I've always appreciated about my wife throughout our relationship – she's always had to plan her life around me because of my career. The reality is that what I do isn't more important than what she does – after all, she's the one with the academic letters after her name.

Roxy finished top of her Honours class at the University of KwaZulu-Natal and was destined to be pretty big in her field. She did her three years of articles at Deloitte and then at 25 was recruited by the Illovo head office.

When we got married in 2004 and had our first child, it was very difficult for Roxy to maintain her business career, so she put it on hold once again while I carried on doing my thing. She has been incredibly understanding that rugby players have a limited career. I've been lucky that I've had one of the longest rugby careers going but it will still only end up being 14 or 15 years (depending on when I retire), and then I'll have to find a new job!

There are so many difficult things about being a rugby player's wife or girlfriend that people will never understand. The attention is always on the player. When you get stopped in the mall, the fan wants a picture with his rugby hero – not of the rugby hero and his wife, who has to step aside. It's the wife who gets ignored at a function where everyone's only interested in talking to the Springbok. The partners are forever in the background, and my wife's not a background person. She's an extremely strong character, which is why the two of us are so attracted to each other. She's ambitious and a no-nonsense type of person, yet she's never complained about having to play a difficult supporting role.

Let me give you an example of the kind of stuff she's had to deal with.

During a five-week Super 12 tour, I'd arranged to take her to the Drakensberg Sun for three days as soon as I got back so that we could spend some quality time together and catch up (that's what our relationship was like for many years – using what time we could steal to catch up as best we could).

On the first morning, as we sat down for breakfast, one of the guests recognised me, came up to our table and said 'Ah, you're John Smit' and I politely said, 'Yes, how's it going?' He pulled up a chair and proceeded to have breakfast with us, leaving his wife on her own.

It's not in my nature to be rude to people even when they're rude to me first, and I felt that it wouldn't be right to ask him to go away.

He ruined our whole first meal and Roxy and I didn't get to say one word to each other. Eventually we cut our breakfast short and I said to him, 'Nice to meet you, cheers.'

Lo and behold, at lunchtime, he imposed himself again! He just parked himself down at our table. This oke wanted to have a *Boots & All* every frigging mealtime.

Before dinner, I asked the restaurant manager to reserve the smallest table he had and to make sure there were only two chairs! However, this guy pitched up again and started dragging a chair across to our table. I decided that enough was enough and said, 'Look sir, if you don't mind, I've been away for five weeks and I haven't seen my girlfriend for eight weeks, including the three weeks before the tour. We've only got three days and we really would like to spend some private time with each other.'

This guy was outraged and yelled, 'Who do you think you are?! You don't have the right to chase people away. We pay money to come and see you play!'

This type of intrusive behaviour is awkward for a player, but it's worse for the wife or girlfriend.

In the real world, you would tell a rude idiot to piss off, but I can't do that. Well, I suppose I could, but it wouldn't be right because of who I am and what I represent, and our partners just have to suck it up too.

Then, as I mentioned earlier, there are the girls who hang around the guys at bars. They want to claim a Springbok head – for want of a better term – and obviously irritate our partners for whom it's a big issue to deal with. It's one thing to tell your partner that you don't care about the 18-year-olds in their short skirts prancing around the shooter bar, but the partners aren't stupid! They continuously have to deal with issues, and wonder what the guys get up to on tour. Our relationships take a lot of work and it's not all rosy.

Thankfully Roxy and I haven't had too many rip-roaring fights or moments where we've felt like calling it quits, but we have had to work bloody hard at our relationship over the years.

We are fortunate in that we are both loyal people. Look, guys love birds, and looking at them, but as I've already said, that wasn't really my thing. I loved going out and having a good time after every single game for the majority of my first three years, but I was never interested in counting notches on my headboard. That's just who I am and it took a few years for my wife to realise that.

There are so many instances where Roxy has had to bite her tongue, and she isn't that kind of person. She doesn't take nonsense in any way or form in her own life. She doesn't suffer fools gladly.

Fortunately, she has known me from day one of my rugby career – from that very first U21 tour – and the bottom line is that every single thing I've achieved in rugby has been with her by my side.

She's known me as a fat primary school kid, Joe Soap the matric student, a Shark, a Springbok and then Bok captain.

Our lives have changed dramatically with each step. She hasn't asked for it but by choosing to stay with me she had to accept those changes, and it hasn't always been easy for her.

Going to the mall on a Sunday to have lunch and watch a movie can be a nightmare. I put on my cap and sunglasses and hope that Roxy doesn't have to deal with something rugby related because our whole lives are dominated by rugby every time we set foot outside our home.

The attention only intensified after our World Cup win and again when I returned from Clermont. We've had to remind each other that we chose for me to play rugby, and having to spend our lunch at the mall signing autographs is part of the deal, and we must accept it.

I keep telling Roxy that there's a light at the end of the tunnel because no matter what I've achieved as a player, I'll soon be forgotten when I retire and the next guy has taken my place.

And it will happen. As celebrities, our stars burn bright and then they burn out. I know this for a fact, and I find it quite amusing. For example, the scary thing is that Gary Teichmann was a hero to me when I was a young player. But ask rugby fans under the age of 20 who he is and chances are they won't know, and he would be cool with that!

I don't know what retirement is going to be like for me, but while a lot of guys struggle to adapt to going from hero to zero, I'm confident I will cope. I've never been full of myself and don't see myself having a mid-life crisis at the age of 33! And I must be honest, I'm looking forward to a bit of 'normal'.

If the young guys in our team go on to be senior players, I'd like to believe I've made them realise that they have a responsibility as Springboks. They can't just say and do what they like because a fan has invaded their personal space or is being obnoxious. You have to turn the other cheek. You will only lose if you say no when a guy stops you in the middle of a restaurant with a fork in your mouth and asks for a photo of you with his son. It's not about whether it's fair or not – it's the territory you enter when you become a Springbok. You can't be quick to enjoy the benefits of having a high profile and being a hero in your country but then have no patience with the responsibility that goes with our status. Being a Springbok also means sacrifice and surrendering much of your privacy to the public.

33

WEDDING BELLS AND NEW ARRIVALS

Most of my mates were forever finding ingenious ways to put off long-term commitments to their girlfriends, but I always knew I was going to marry Roxy and would've done so much sooner if it hadn't been for the relentless travelling in rugby.

We had been dating since 1996 and by the end of 2003 it really was time to take the next step. Planning a romantic proposal was just about the only comfort of the horrendous experience of that year's World Cup. I was rooming with De Wet Barry and apart from my mother, he was the only person who knew I was getting engaged. I had to let him in on the secret because I was spending evenings designing the ring, and would fax my creations to my mother at the school where she worked, for appraisal.

My plan was to take Roxy to Paris and whip the ring out at the top of the Eiffel Tower. You don't get more clichéd than that, but I thought it would be a nice story to tell our kids one day!

I told Roxy we were going to London and Paris for a week so that I could get rugby out of my system and I'm pretty sure she didn't suspect there was a proposal in the offing.

I had arranged for us to stay with my old Sharks team-mate Geoff Appleford in London and for my old Natal U21 mate Trevor 'Bennie' Boynton to fetch us from Heathrow and take us to Geoff's.

Bennie picked us up bright and early from the airport but said that Geoff would only be back from rugby training with London Irish at 5pm. He didn't have keys to the flat, so he recommended we kill time by doing some shopping. Roxy had been looking forward to going shopping in London for ages so she was delighted to hit Oxford Street on day one of our holiday. She hadn't been overseas much at that stage so it was a big thing for her.

It's a huge mission to find parking in London and when we eventually found a spot I went to pay for the ticket. The ring had been in my rucksack since we left Durban. I had been guarding it with my life and had gone to great lengths during airport check-ins to make sure Roxy didn't see the little box and get suspicious.

But I slipped up when I went to get the parking ticket and left the rucksack in the car with Roxy and Bennie, at which point Bennie decided to be clever and said to her: 'I'm sure Barney doesn't want to lug this bag around Oxford Street, so why don't you take out the stuff he's going to need and chuck the bag in the boot?'

She agreed that it was a good idea and started rifling through the bag, saw the box and freaked out.

I didn't know any of this had happened but soon noticed that Roxy was behaving very strangely. After every second shop she had to go to the toilet. She was vomiting and feeling nauseous. I had never seen her like that.

What I thought was going to be a breezy shopping spree turned into a nightmare. She was in and out of the toilet and so nervous she couldn't talk. I was thinking that this wasn't what I'd expected, although the silver lining was that she didn't spend too much money!

We eventually made it to Geoff's place, had a nice dinner and hit the sack. At about 2:30am, Roxy woke me up in a state. She said: 'I think I saw something I shouldn't have seen. I went through your bag and I saw a box. I can't get it out of my mind, what's going on?'

So the whole flipping plan was stuffed! She had been completely thrown because she wasn't expecting it, and her mind had been in overdrive ever since.

Roxy's an ultra-curious animal, so there's no way she could have waited it out, no way!

So at 3am, in Geoff's humble London abode, I went down on my knee and asked her to marry me …

We SMSed everybody we knew later that morning, and when a friend SMSed Bennie about it, he came to us and said: 'I'm your tour guide here in London and I find out via someone in South Africa that you're engaged!'

A week later, I took Roxy to the top of the Eiffel Tower and, looking out over Paris, I explained that this was where it would have happened had Bennie not stuffed it up.

So that's the story of our engagement. Roxy loved the ring – it fitted perfectly – but what a cock-up of a proposal.

I had done my bit and was quite happy to hand the wedding plans over to Roxy, who threw herself into a frenzy of planning, as fiancées tend to do!

Our wedding was held at the Collisheen Estate in Ballito up the KZN north coast on 16 December 2004. It was a big wedding with around 200 guests but I wanted to keep it private.

We didn't want to do the whole *You/Huisgenoot* magazine thing and when I ended up getting a phone call from one of their staff writers, Richard van Rensburg, I politely but firmly told him that we wanted total privacy.

He said he would pay R20 000 to take photos and do an article. I said: 'I really appreciate the offer, but there's not much in my life that's private and I'd like to have a private wedding and keep it between my friends and family.'

He then upped his offer to R40 000 and I said: 'Look, it's not about money, so no thanks.'

He called back an hour later.

'We'll give you R50 000.'

I said: 'Please, I'm really not interested in …'

And before I could finish the sentence he interjected: 'OK, we'll give you R100 000.'

I said to him: '*Boet*, if you offered me a million I wouldn't take it. You can't ask me to put a price on the privacy of my wedding which is something I want very much. You don't have to keep on upping the offer. I'm not playing a game here. We just want to be left alone.'

He said: 'You don't have the right to a private wedding. You're the Springbok captain and it's your duty to allow the world to see your wedding photos.'

I was getting seriously annoyed and said: 'Excuse me?!'

He said: 'Whether you allow me to or not, I'll get those photos, even if I have to have a helicopter above your venue. I know the date, I know where it is, and I'm going to take those photos regardless of whether or not you give me permission, so you might as well take the money.'

What a prick!

I said: 'I don't appreciate being threatened. If you want to go to those lengths, go for it, take the photos. But I'm telling you right now, I'm not going to sell my soul so that you can have a scoop in your magazines. This is a private matter and your magazines are not welcome.'

He said: 'OK, well, we'll see what happens,' and put the phone down.

I refused to let this arsehole win and had to have security guards posted all around the wedding venue to check invitations. It was almost militant.

Thankfully there was no helicopter. I've got a feeling *You/Huisgenoot* had the wrong day. The way they harassed us was a disgrace. I realised I had become public property and it was going to be difficult to have a private life.

But what a great day we had. We hired comedians Aaron McIlroy and his wife Lisa Bobbert to do a show during the down time after the wedding ceremony when the bridal party disappears for photographs and the guests sit around like spare parts and have a few pots. Those two contributed greatly to our wedding's success. The guests didn't even know we were gone and were in stitches when we arrived back.

It was a fantastic night. My best man, Shane Chorley, spoke well. It was great that he was almost my wife's best man, so to speak, because he was in our primary school class and a mutual friend. He was the one who arranged the dinner during matric finals when Roxy and I got reacquainted.

The next day we left for Madagascar. That was the best time of my life. We were exhausted after everything and slept for three days, emerging only for meals, and went fishing together. It was a storybook honeymoon.

The next big event in our lives was Roxy falling pregnant. We had been talking about having kids but I was hesitant because I didn't want to be a part-time father, given that rugby players are on the road all the time.

I said I'd rather wait until I was home more often than not, although we never knew when that was going to be. So I kept on stalling but eventually in early 2006 – in fact on Roxy's birthday (6 January) – I decided to quit procrastinating and put a footnote on the birthday card saying: 'How about some babies?' I gave her a gift and the card and she read all the usual happy birthday stuff and when she got to the note at the bottom she went crazy. That was probably the biggest present I could have ever given her!

But the irony was that on 8 January she took a pregnancy test because she hadn't been feeling well and discovered that she was two weeks pregnant. So here I had been the big hero making the decision to start our family and we already had!

Emma's birth was the most emotional experience of my life. The biggest ordeal was watching my wife go through her caesarean. Roxy had never had an operation before and when they prepared her for the epidural, which is basically anaesthetic by syringe into the spine, she freaked out.

She jumped off the table, saying: 'I can't do this!'

I said: 'My baby, what are you doing?'

'No, I can't do this!'

'But the baby's got to come out.'

Eventually she had the epidural and the gynae started cutting away ...

Waiting for the baby's cry was more terrifying than any pre-Test nerves I have ever had, and when it came, the tears just flowed. I've never cried like that. You just can't contain what's inside you. It was the most incredible moment ever. You count the toes, you count the fingers, you listen for the crying, you listen to every word the doctor's saying, praying you aren't going to hear any alarm in his voice.

From then on I found it twice as difficult to spend days away from home – to miss those special moments like first steps and first words. My little girl needs me to tuck her in, chase the geckos out of her room and lie with her when she's had a bad dream, but when I'm on tour I can't do any of this for my princess. We named her Emma-Joan – Emma being the name we chose and Joan being the name of my grandmother, who embraced Roxy and was an angel on this earth.

My son Tyron was conceived in Clermont but born in Durban on the eve of the 2008 Currie Cup final in the same hospital that Emma was born in. The timing wasn't ideal because the caesar could only be scheduled for 24 October, the day before we hosted the Blue Bulls in Durban. By the time he had been born and settled and Roxy was back in her ward, it was time for me to go to the captain's practice.

That night I looked after Emma at home, visited Roxy and Tyron in the morning, headed to the hotel for our pre-match meal and then won the Currie Cup final.

I finally forced my way out through the crowds at the stadium at about 10pm and then had to sweet-talk my way into the hospital just to say goodnight to my wife because visiting hours had finished at 8pm.

As I made my way to the hospital to visit my first son, I couldn't believe how much the Lord had blessed me. I had an amazing wife, a beautiful princess and now a little boy to teach all the things I had been taught by my father. I had thoughts of fishing rods, pellet guns, remote-controlled cars, etc! This little legend was going to carry my family name into the future.

I knew that every day away from home from then on would be a day away from the three best things in my life. It sounds like I'm bitter about this, but that's not the case. I've never resented rugby for taking me away from my family, it just makes me appreciate the real treasures in life.

I took Roxy and Tyron home on the Monday morning and left on a six-week tour on Tuesday.

That's the furthest I've ever pushed my wife. It was really tough for her, and if I could do it over again I would find a way to do it differently. Six weeks was too long for a mother to cope alone with a newborn baby and a two-year-old.

Roxy has spent our whole relationship pulling the short straw and I have never stopped feeling bad about it.

34

RUGBY 101

I've often thought that rugby veterans should write an advice manual to assist youthful newcomers through the minefield that is professional rugby. There have certainly been enough occasions in my career where I needed to consult a manual! But I learnt the hard way and 13 years down the track, I reckon I'm in a good position to at least map out the warning signs that are there if the new recruit knows what to look out for.

Firstly, let's talk about the many business opportunities that miraculously come our way as rugby players. Don't get me wrong, you have to have an open mind because there are opportunities for a young person to earn good money, but you have to be very careful. There are many sharks out there (excuse the pun) who want to help themselves to your healthy monthly income and use your high profile as a business tool.

I've been involved in good and bad ventures and learnt from both. It's important to be meticulous about who you venture into business with and you need to be very clear on these subjects: What do they want from you? Is it surety on a loan? If so, the first alarm bell should sound off. If they want capital outlay from you and it exceeds what they plan to outlay, then a second bell should ring. What's the core of the business and does it fit in with the type of profile you would like to create, or have already created? For example, don't get involved in a biltong business if you are a vegetarian! Your involvement while playing rugby will mean your association is an endorsement of the business.

I had an opportunity to get involved in a nightclub, which would have been a pretty good business decision due to the people involved. But I took a step back and considered whether it was appropriate for the Springbok captain to own a nightclub, and the answer was no. What would have happened if I was on tour and an under-age person slipped into my club, got drunk and a horrific accident ensued? The headline in the paper would have been 'Springbok captain allows underage drinking'. Some players have had clubs without any drama because it didn't jar with their profile.

I tried my hand at a restaurant with AJ Venter and it was a lot of fun and pretty cool to have our own place to go to for coffee and lunch. But we learnt quickly that the hospitality industry required our full-time attention, which we were unable to give due to our rugby commitments, so Roxy, as a chartered accountant, stepped in and rescued us from a potential disaster! We sold the restaurant to people who knew the business and today it's a success because they are on site and know what they are doing.

I've already discussed my automotive business experience and, there again, I should have listened more carefully to the people close to me who advised me against it, but at 24 I thought I knew better! It was an expensive lesson, even though there were some cool cars along the way.

It's important to make sure the people you get involved with have reputable names in the city you live in, and you need to conduct research and your own investigation.

Contracts, agreements and things like shareholdings need to be signed and in place. *Everything must be in black and white and signed!* For peace of mind, get your father, agent, lawyer or whoever you trust to check the deal out.

The same can be said about endorsements. Carefully select the brands you want to get involved with and don't just grab the first thing that pops up. Decide how you want to align your profile – do you want to be trendy, hip, fashionable and 'with it', or do you want to be family-orientated – a solid role model better associated with more conservative brands – or perhaps place yourself with elite brands and try to create a more hard-to-get image? Decide early where you see yourself going.

A career in rugby in this country is tricky because there are so many talented players, and patience has to be an important ingredient in your challenge. Work hard, train well, be fit, get good advice and follow the lead of players you respected growing up. When you start breaking onto the scene, you are likely to spend time on the bench until you have proven yourself. And even after you have 'made it', there will still be plenty of bench time.

Don't hate the bench, it can be your friend. Don't see it as your final destination, but rather a stop on the road to success. Making your mark as a newcomer is an exciting time, as no one quite knows your game and you can catch people off guard with your particular talents. You feel at the time that you should have been starting long ago! I've been there.

The bottom line is that a team's true spirit is judged by the attitude of the bench and you need to understand that in a team sport like rugby. No matter how good you think you are, the team is always more important. Get caught sulking on a bench and it will say a lot about your character in a team environment. Don't ever be happy or content there, but use it as inspiration to train harder, chase faster and serve the team better, and soon the results will be visible.

When the team gets into a huddle after captain's practice and the reserves are on the outside looking in at the starting XV circle, remember one thing: your attitude must be good whether you are looking in at the circle from the outside or in it. Make no mistake, you will be faced with both scenarios in your career and when you display a difference in attitude – depending on whether you are in or out of the starting XV – your team-mates will see straight through you in a heartbeat.

You must serve the team in the same way, whether you are starting or benching. When you're a substitute, nothing goes further than bringing your direct competition a cold water at half-time, and if you are the one starting, it will go a long way if you ask for advice from the guy on the bench to see if there's anything he's picked up from the opposition or if there's an area he thinks you can exploit better.

To sum up, I believe you can pick 22 superstars randomly and put them together, but a 22 that trusts and believes in each other is far more dangerous and tends to beat talent nine times out of 10.

Respect is vital. Learn from those who are more experienced than you because not only will they teach you what to do but sadly some of them will also teach you what not to do! Be respectful but never be drawn into something you believe is wrong, whether it's being told to cut your wrist with a scalpel before a game and to strap it up in case a blood replacement is needed for you, or having to cover for an older married guy leaving a club on an overseas tour with a dolly who isn't his wife!

Gossip in a team is a killer, so stay away from it. If you have something to say, be sure the people you are referring to are present – a tough one, I know! If conflict is not your thing, just keep quiet (my mother once wisely told me that if I have nothing positive to say I should rather hold my tongue).

Never take short cuts in training. If there's a shuttle to be run, touch the line. If you don't, you are not only lying to your team but worse, you are lying to yourself. Doing every set every time shows your team-mate that in the dying seconds of a game – when you are one point ahead or behind – you can be counted upon. Make sure your team-mates would happily go to war with you.

No matter how much you may disagree with your coach about something, never argue with him in front of the team. Pay him the respect of voicing your opinion in private and then you can judge him on how he reacts.

Be tolerant, as everyone is different. Embrace diversity and let it help create balance in you as a person. Variety is the spice of life!

Always remember where you came from. There are few things worse than becoming successful at the expense of your personality or soul.

Finally, make as many friends in the game as you possibly can. Play as hard as you can against any opponent who comes before you, and afterwards see how many of them you can get to know. Believe me, rugby is awesome but it's a small part of your life in the bigger scheme of things, while friendships can last a lifetime.

I met my best mate Shane Chorley when we were just 11 years old and he's always treated me the same way. We have known each other for the majority of our lives and a bond like that is priceless – to know you can always rely on someone no matter what. He doesn't care whether I'm playing well or whether we're winning, all he cares about is how I am and when we can share our next cold pot and catch up. These may seem like simple qualities but believe me they are rare commodities.

Shane, you are my brother, buddy! I hope everyone out there is blessed with someone like you in their lives.

35

MY SELECTIONS

O K, enough of the deep stuff! I've played rugby with a lot of guys and decided to put three teams together under different banners to remember them by, in case all this scrumming erases my memory one day!

Funniest XV (Criteria: The fun-makers, Kontiki menaces, tour sparkers, and *gees* builders)

15. *Percy Montgomery*
Most people don't know the real Monty, who's good fun off the field and never shy to pull a prank, and his comments often broke the ice. He was renowned for telling big stories at the back of the bus but he's a lot quieter now that he's with the coaching staff at the front! A legend on and off the field.

14. *Jaque Fourie*
Mossie never stops cracking jokes! He's always laughing and

causing mayhem! In Sydney in 2003, he tried surfing for the first time and was a dismal failure. His spectacular wipe-outs kept beachgoers entertained.

13. *Robbie Fleck*
An absolute gem on tour, he took good care of me when I was a youngster in the team from 2000-2001. The ideal man for a good night out but suffers really badly the morning after! I had some memorable nights with Fleckie.

12. *Trevor Halstead*
Here's a guy who thundered his way through most defences with sheer brute strength and clever running lines, but he provided another dynamic to a team when it came to the humour department. He always had a chirp on the bus when someone was making an announcement and regularly put smiles on faces.

11. *Jean de Villiers*
I know I've moved him to the wing where he played for us in 2004 but I needed to find space for this guy! He and Butch James together in a team was like having a non-stop *Laurel & Hardy* show. Jean's funniest moment was in 2007 when he was about to run out for our warm-up before our game against Wales and needed to pass some wind, but there was a follow through from a dodgy dinner the previous night so he did an about turn and rushed back to clean up the mess! On his return to the field he ran to Butch and said: 'Butchie, I literally just shat myself!' They were both in hysterics!

10. *Butch James*
Here's someone I have a number of stories about. He too is the heartbeat of a team and made our tours that much more fun. Like Deon Carstens (see No 1), he wasn't too partial to wearing clothes and wasn't shy to add his bodily fluids to some of Deon's down-downs.

9. *Craig Davidson*

This guy can bring laughter to a team at any time. He's always the life of the party and renowned for laughing at his own jokes! Famous for singing the last song at weddings, 'I'm leaving on a jet plane', and for his disgusting rugby war cry, 'Eat, bite!' As competitive as you could ever find, Davo will stop at nothing to win and makes a simple game of squash feel like a World Cup final with his incessant chirping.

8. *Braam Immelman*

Braam spent a few seasons with the Sharks before choosing a career in Italy. He and Deon are good mates and that says a lot for his funny side. He became renowned for introducing himself overseas not as *Super*man, not *Spider*man, not *Bat*man but the incredible *Immel*man! His mark can still be found on Mr Carstens' rear end (see No 1).

7. *Schalk Burger*

He doesn't seem the type to make this XV, but Schalla is the most laid-back dude ever! He has a moment for everyone and his main goal in life is to have a good time, even though he's a Terminator on the field! This guy is great for a team off the field and not too bad on it either!

6. *Shane Chorley*

Shane didn't play representative rugby but according to him he could easily have made it had he not chosen a career in scuba diving! I seriously don't think I have ever met anyone more mentally tough than this guy. Shane is my best mate, he was my best man at my wedding and I have known him since we were 11 years old. We played together at Fields Primary and I honestly believe he can build spirit like no other. The Duracell bunny has nothing on this beast! We've shared many funny moments but my favourite is the one I shared at his wedding about him taking a slash on the chips section of the late night shop we were in while I was ordering us some graze! He said he couldn't find the toilet! Understandable.

5. *Pieter 'Spud' Myburgh*
Spuddy was one of the guys contracted with me to the Sharks from the 1996 Craven Week and shared digs with Jaco van der Westhuyzen, Shaun Sowerby and me for a few years. He's named Spud after the character from *Trainspotting*. Spuddy was very happy to have left the Vaal Triangle for the bright lights of Durban and fancied himself as a bit of a raver. I once walked in on the lanky lock raving/dancing/ having a fit in my room with my hi-fi playing the fastest and loudest music I've ever heard. All arms and legs at 100 miles an hour, it was quite possibly the funniest thing I've ever seen.

4. *Bakkies Botha*
Stu Dickinson had warned Bakkies three times during a Test at Kings Park for overly robust play and when he over-stepped the mark once more, after about 25 minutes, the ref called me over for a chat. 'John, this man has been in trouble since the first minute, he has been hovering on the edge of illegal play all day and is now very close to getting a yellow card if he transgresses one more time!' As I was about to offer a few diplomatic words to calm the situation, Bakkies chirped from behind me in his best English, 'Excuse me sir, but you must know ... I like living on the edge!' Dickinson actually smiled and Bakkies probably avoided a card through that ice-breaker.

3. *Adrian Garvey*
One of the first guys I ever played with professionally and a great bloke on and off the field. He would make the Funniest XV on one story alone. During take-off after a Currie Cup game in Kimberley, the plane's right wing burst into flames and an emergency landing ensued. On the way down, Garvs

started singing at the front of the chartered plane: 'He's got the whole world, in His hands; He's got the whole world, in His hands!'

2. *Pieter Dixon*
Dixie has the most elastic rubber arm I've ever seen, and thankfully so, because his presence makes any pub, party, practice or round of golf all the more enjoyable. I won't go into detail but for those who know him, let us never forget the sideways rounder at Bourbon Street!

1. *Deon Carstens*
Deon has been my room-mate for many seasons and lights up a room with his energy, and wonderful abuse of the English language. He's famed for his habit of stripping naked in public in his younger years. At a Sharks team-building camp, he arrived naked at our camp fire only to be branded with red-hot braai tongs by Braam, his housemate. I love this man and any team would.

Toughest XV (Criteria: Guys you least want to play against!)

15. *James Small*
For 80 minutes, James was a psycho who genuinely hated his opponents.

14. *Dean Hall*
The white Lomu, enough said.

13. *De Wet Barry*
In New Zealand they called him the human wrecking ball, and for good reason.

12. *Pieter Müller*
The Hitman was the toughest tackler I ever saw. He caused a lot of pain.

11. *Frikkie Welsh*
Has one of the shortest fuses in rugby. I've seen him run from the stands to join a fight on the field.

10. *Butch James*
How he didn't break his neck from the way he flung himself at opponents remains a mystery.

9. *Robert du Preez*
A martial arts expert and an aggressive nature made for a lethal combination.

8. *Trevor Boynton*
My Natal U21 mate took to the field with the express goal of getting his retaliation in first.

7. *André Venter*
Hard, hard, hard. He had no concept of pain and commanded respect from his team-mates without having to say a word.

6. *Corné Krige*
Loved the fight even more than he loved the game. A strong body but even stronger mind.

5. *Johan Ackermann*
A mobile railway sleeper – they don't come harder.

4. *Bakkies Botha*
The best enforcer in world rugby. Say no more.

3. *Willie Meyer*
Tough, immensely strong and took no shit.

2. *Lukas van Biljon*
The original bull in a china shop. His knees, elbows and head always found targets.

1. *Robbie Kempson*
A quiet piano-playing gentleman off the field but quite the maniac on it.

Best XV (Criteria: Players I've played with)

15. *Percy Montgomery*
When Monty resumed his Springbok career after returning from Wales, he soon developed a regal, inspirational air at the back that reminded me of the Rolls-Royce himself, André Joubert.

14. *Napolioni Nalaga*
The Clermont Auvergne and Fiji winger is lethal even by Pacific Islands standards. If we could get the ball to him, a try was invariably scored.

13. *Jaque Fourie*
Tall and gangly, Jaque is deceptively fast and strong. He's confident and aggressive. I would hate to mark him.

12. *Jean de Villiers*
A brilliant attacking centre who has superb organisational skills. His love of a party completes the all-round package!

11. *Bryan Habana*
Thirty-five tries in 54 Tests by the age of 26 illustrates why he's my go-to man when we need something special.

10. *Henry Honiball*
A hunting knife is presented to our best tackler in each Test. If Lem (Blade) was in our squad, he would have a shed full of them by now.

9. *Fourie du Preez*
If there's a better rugby brain in the world, I haven't come

across it. Joost van der Westhuizen, a very different type of player, is my next in line.

8. *Gary Teichmann*
I hero-worshipped Teich as a teenager and when I made it into the Sharks squad I discovered he was everything I believed him to be. Shaun Sowerby is another great No 8 and it's a tragedy that he was chased to France.

7. *André Venter*
It's been said he was the fittest Springbok forward anybody could remember. In Afrikaans, you would call him a *Meneer* (Mister). Corné Krige came close here – he would have been exceptional had he played in a better Bok team.

6. *Schalk Burger*
The Incredible Schalk epitomises what a Springbok forward should be: uncompromisingly tough and utterly fearless.

5. *Victor Matfield*
Probably the best lineout forward the world has ever seen, although Mark Andrews wasn't far behind him.

4. *Bakkies Botha*
Bakkies is everything his legendary status makes him out to be, and more. Choosing between him and Mark was a thankless task.

3. *CJ van der Linde*
Immensely strong and a frustrated centre to boot! One of rugby's great sights is a prop who can throw a dummy and run 50m with the ball.

2. *Bismarck du Plessis*
Bismarck is a physical freak, a dedicated professional and has the heart and aggression of a lion. I honestly believe he's

going to grow into one of the greatest front-row forwards the world has seen.

1. *Os du Randt*
A colossus in every respect. A one-off.

36

MY BUCKET LIST

I guess retirement can't be that far off when I occasionally find myself day-dreaming about my 'bucket list' – as in the things Jack Nicholson wanted to do before he 'kicked the bucket' in that excellent movie.

While I certainly don't plan on departing this mortal coil any time soon, the frantic nature of my rugby career has left me yearning to do a number of special things that have been impossible over the past 13 years. Nearly all of them involve major payback to my wife and children.

I would love to take my family and vanish for a few months to a Mediterranean village. I can picture a quaint, lazy town on the Italian coast where we could escape from it all. I can see myself in an undemanding little job, maybe making pizzas or working in a restaurant for a few months just to let the whole family experience that wonderfully laid-back and healthy Mediterranean lifestyle.

It will have to be quite soon after I finish playing, while my kids are still young enough not to go to school. That's the only time Roxy and I will have them completely to ourselves

– a few precious months of pure bonding. This is a dream, I know, but it's on the list!

High up on the list is a road trip from Cape to Cairo. I love cars, I love Africa and I love exploring.

Closer to home, I want to learn how to cook properly. It makes sense given my appetite and love of food! I enjoy cooking, but my repertoire is seriously limited. I think it would be pretty cool to be able to create special dishes in the kitchen and treat my wife and guests to gourmet food.

The Oktoberfest in Munich has always fascinated me and the first October that I'm not playing Currie Cup rugby I'm going to be chugging back some serious German lager!

Cars have been a huge passion of mine since I was a youngster. My Dad's a car enthusiast and every year when he had to choose a new company car, he and I would have great fun going through car magazines, examining the options in his price range and weighing up the different attributes of particular vehicles. That sparked an obsession with cars that has never waned and I can see myself swapping the engine room of the Springbok team for long afternoons under the engines of vehicles I'm restoring.

The first really cool car that I bought was a Jeep Cherokee, in 1999 – my last year of U21 rugby. I loved that car and reckoned I was quite the hero blasting around Durban in it.

I've always had an affinity for American muscle cars and I've been so grateful that rugby has given me the resources to follow through on that passion.

In 2002 I bought my first muscle car, a black 1965 Mustang which I restored to its original form. I didn't have the time to personally work on it but I oversaw the project. Post-rugby, I will definitely try and restore a vehicle on my own. Lovingly tinkering away on a beautiful old car is my idea of the perfect hobby.

I can see myself as an old man working away in the garage in my blue overalls with Roxy shouting at me to get clean and come in for lunch.

My dream car? If I won the lotto, I'd probably buy myself a Lamborghini Murciélago or a 1967 Ford Shelby GT 500. Man, that would be a tough choice. There are so many amazing cars out there.

As I said earlier, I would love to combine my passion for cars with a family road trip across this great continent.

I know a lot of folk would think that's crazy but I'm an extreme Afro-optimist. I'm not naive – we certainly have our problems in South Africa – but if you just take a step back and look from the outside in, you will see we have made good progress as a nation since 1994. You would be a fool to say that we haven't moved forward.

One of my favourite sayings in life is attributed to Trevor Manuel, the former finance minister and current head of the National Planning Commission, and was told to me by Peter de Villiers: 'If you spend your life looking back into the past, that's the direction you'll move. In South Africa, the only people who are struggling to adapt to the way that South Africa's going are the people who continually look backwards.'

I believe in that sentiment wholeheartedly. Look, it's easy for me to say 'forget the past and go forward', because I wasn't oppressed but, equally, I can tell you right now I wasn't part of a generation that oppressed anyone. It's up to us to make sure we continually look forward.

After rugby I would like to get more involved in my church. My parents are Anglican and my mother taught at a Catholic private school, so I was taken to Sunday school at a young age. I was baptised and started taking communion at 14. Roxy and I have been going to the same Anglican church in Durban North, St Margarets, since 2000. Our minister, Steve Harrison, married us and christened our children. Whenever Roxy and I are both in town, which is seldom with rugby always being on the weekend, we go to church on a Sunday and I enjoy listening to him. Steve is a spiritually gifted man.

The thing I will probably enjoy most about retirement is putting my feet up on a Saturday afternoon and watching the Springboks in action with a cold beer in my hand. I was a passionate Springbok fan before I became a Bok and I'm looking forward to that going full circle!

This may be the end of my book but it's certainly not my last rugby chapter. I believe there are many more exciting chapters to come in my life, just as there are for you. And the beauty of life is never being sure how it will unfold! Things don't always go exactly as planned, but that's when you learn.

I remember telling my team after the 2009 Tri-Nations loss in Brisbane to not be disillusioned by defeat but rather continually defiant of it. You make a conscious decision to be optimistic and when you don't, you automatically revert to pessimism. Call it human nature, call it what you like, but being positive is your decision.

I hope this isn't the last you hear from me and I thank you for allowing me to live my dream by supporting me – whether it's cursing me for a crooked throw or shouting your lungs out when we win a Test.

CAPTAIN IN THE CAULDRON

SMIT'S FIRST-CLASS APPEARANCES (at 12/09/2009)

KEY

C = Captain	R = Replacement

SPRINGBOK TESTS

DATE	OPPONENTS	POSITION	T	C	P	D	PTS	SCORE*
10/06/2000	Canada	Hooker (R)						51-18
08/07/2000	Australia	Hooker (R)						23-44
22/07/2000	New Zealand	Prop (R)						12-25
29/07/2000	Australia	Hooker (R)						6-26
19/08/2000	New Zealand	Prop (R)						46-40
26/08/2000	Australia	Hooker (R)						18-19
12/11/2000	Argentina	Hooker						37-33
19/11/2000	Ireland	Hooker						28-18
26/11/2000	Wales	Hooker						23-13
02/12/2000	England	Hooker						17-25
16/06/2001	France	Hooker						23-32
23/06/2001	France	Hooker						20-15
30/06/2001	Italy	Hooker						60-14
21/07/2001	New Zealand	Hooker (R)						3-12
28/07/2001	Australia	Hooker (R)						20-15
18/08/2001	Australia	Hooker (R)						14-14
25/08/2001	New Zealand	Hooker (R)						15-26
10/11/2001	France	Hooker (R)						10-20
17/11/2001	Italy	Hooker	1				5	54-26
24/11/2001	England	Hooker						9-29
01/12/2001	USA	Hooker (R)						43-20
11/10/2003	Uruguay	Hooker (R)						72-6
18/10/2003	England	Hooker (R)						6-25
24/10/2003	Georgia	Hooker (C)						46-19
01/11/2003	Samoa	Hooker						60-10
08/11/2003	New Zealand	Hooker						9-29
12/06/2004	Ireland	Hooker (C)						31-17
19/06/2004	Ireland	Hooker (C)						26-17
26/06/2004	Wales	Hooker (C)	1				5	53-18
17/07/2004	Pacific Islanders	Hooker (C)						38-24
24/07/2004	New Zealand	Hooker (C)						21-23
31/07/2004	Australia	Hooker (C)						26-30

DATE	OPPONENTS	POSITION	T	C	P	D	PTS	SCORE*
14/08/2004	New Zealand	Hooker (C)						40-26
21/08/2004	Australia	Hooker (C)						23-19
06/11/2004	Wales	Hooker (C)						38-36
13/11/2004	Ireland	Hooker (C)						12-17
20/11/2004	England	Hooker (C)						16-32
27/11/2004	Scotland	Hooker (C)						45-10
04/12/2004	Argentina	Hooker (C)						39-7
11/06/2005	Uruguay	Hooker (C)						134-3
18/06/2005	France	Hooker (C)						30-30
25/06/2005	France	Hooker (C)						27-13
09/07/2005	Australia	Hooker (C)						12-30
23/07/2005	Australia	Hooker (C)						33-20
30/07/2005	Australia	Hooker (C)						22-16
06/08/2005	New Zealand	Hooker (C)						22-16
20/08/2005	Australia	Hooker (C)						22-19
27/08/2005	New Zealand	Hooker (C)						27-31
05/11/2005	Argentina	Hooker (C)						34-23
19/11/2005	Wales	Hooker (C)						33-6
26/11/2005	France	Hooker (C)						20-26
10/06/2006	Scotland	Hooker (C)						36-16
17/06/2006	Scotland	Hooker (C)						29-15
24/06/2006	France	Hooker (C)						26-36
15/07/2006	Australia	Hooker (C)						0-49
22/07/2006	New Zealand	Hooker (C)						17-35
05/08/2006	Australia	Hooker (C)						18-20
26/08/2006	New Zealand	Hooker (C)						26-45
02/09/2006	New Zealand	Hooker (C)						21-20
09/09/2006	Australia	Hooker (C)						24-16
11/11/2006	Ireland	Hooker (C)						15-32
18/11/2006	England	Hooker (C)						21-23
25/11/2006	England	Hooker (C)						25-14
26/05/2007	England	Hooker (C)						58-10
02/06/2007	England	Hooker (C)						55-22
09/06/2007	Samoa	Hooker (C)	1				5	35-8
16/06/2007	Australia	Hooker (C)						22-19
09/09/2007	Samoa	Hooker (C)						59-7
14/09/2007	England	Hooker (C)						36-0

CAPTAIN IN THE CAULDRON

SPRINGBOK TESTS *(continued)*

DATE	OPPONENTS	POSITION	T	C	P	D	PTS	SCORE*
22/09/2007	Tonga	Hooker (R)						30-25
30/09/2007	USA	Hooker (C)						64-15
07/10/2007	Fiji	Hooker (C)	1				5	37-20
14/10/2007	Argentina	Hooker (C)						37-13
20/10/2007	England	Hooker (C)						15-6
24/11/2007	Wales	Hooker (C)						34-12
07/06/2008	Wales	Hooker (C)						43-17
14/06/2008	Wales	Hooker (C)						37-21
05/07/2008	New Zealand	Hooker (C)						8-19
08/11/2008	Wales	Prop (C)						20-15
15/11/2008	Scotland	Prop (C)						14-10
22/11/2008	England	Hooker (C)						42-6
20/06/2009	Lions	Prop (C)	1				5	26-21
27/06/2009	Lions	Prop (C)						28-25
04/07/2009	Lions	Prop (C)						9-28
25/07/2009	New Zealand	Prop (C)						28-19
01/08/2009	New Zealand	Prop (C)						31-19
08/08/2009	Australia	Prop (C)						29-17
29/08/2009	Australia	Prop (C)						32-25
05/09/2009	Australia	Prop (C)						6-21
12/09/2009	New Zealand	Prop (C)						32-29
90 matches			**5**	**0**	**0**	**0**	**25**	
Record			P: 90; W: 59; D:2; L: 29; Win%: 66					

South Africa score first

SPRINGBOK TOUR MATCHES

DATE	OPPONENTS	POSITION	T	C	P	D	PTS	SCORE*
09/12/2000	Barbarians	Hooker						41-31
1 match			**0**	**0**	**0**	**0**	**0**	
Record			P: 1; W: 1; Win%: 100					

South Africa score first

BARBARIANS

DATE	OPPONENTS	POSITION	T	C	P	D	PTS	SCORE*
03/12/2008	Australia	Hooker (C)						11-18
1 match			**0**	**0**	**0**	**0**	**0**	
Record			P: 1; L: 1; Win%: 0					

Barbarians score first

CAPTAIN IN THE CAULDRON

SOUTH AFRICA 'A'

DATE	OPPONENTS	POSITION	T	C	P	D	PTS	SCORE*
25/06/2003	Argentina	Hooker (R)						30-30
1 match			0	0	0	0	0	
Record		P: 1; D: 1; Win%: 0						

*South Africa 'A' score first

SOUTHERN HEMISPHERE XV

DATE	OPPONENTS	POSITION	T	C	P	D	PTS	SCORE*
05/03/2005	N Hemisphere XV	Hooker						54-19
1 match			0	0	0	0	0	
Record		P: 1; W: 1; Win%: 100						

*Southern Hemisphere XV score first

SHARKS (SUPER RUGBY)

DATE	OPPONENTS	POSITION	T	C	P	D	PTS	SCORE*
27/02/1999	Waratahs	Prop						13-13
05/03/1999	Brumbies	Prop						21-16
13/03/1999	Cats	Prop (R)						36-20
26/03/1999	Highlanders	Hooker (R)						32-8
03/04/1999	Hurricanes	Prop						18-34
10/04/1999	Stormers	Prop						19-35
17/04/1999	Bulls	Prop (R)						29-0
24/04/1999	Blues	Prop						12-6
30/04/1999	Chiefs	Prop (R)						19-32
08/05/1999	Crusaders	Prop						29-34
14/05/1999	Reds	Prop						13-34
25/02/2000	Hurricanes	Prop (R)						23-40
03/03/2000	Highlanders	Prop (R)						20-27
10/03/2000	Brumbies	Prop (R)						10-51
18/03/2000	Waratahs	Prop (R)						26-19
01/04/2000	Bulls	Prop (R)						14-14
08/04/2000	Cats	Prop (R)						27-28
15/04/2000	Crusaders	Hooker						24-32
22/04/2000	Reds	Prop (R)						13-24
30/04/2000	Blues	Hooker						19-30
06/05/2000	Chiefs	Hooker						31-44
13/05/2000	Stormers	Prop (R)						28-32
23/02/2001	Bulls	Hooker	1				5	30-17
03/03/2001	Brumbies	Hooker						17-16

CAPTAIN IN THE CAULDRON

DATE	OPPONENTS	POSITION	T	C	P	D	PTS	SCORE*
10/03/2001	Highlanders	Hooker						30-29
17/03/2001	Hurricanes	Hooker (C)						39-21
24/03/2001	Waratahs	Hooker						42-17
30/03/2001	Cats	Hooker						25-26
07/04/2001	Blues	Hooker	1				5	41-27
14/04/2001	Chiefs	Hooker						24-8
22/04/2001	Reds	Hooker (R)						27-32
28/04/2001	Crusaders	Hooker						24-34
12/05/2001	Stormers	Hooker						23-19
19/05/2001	Cats (semi-final)	Hooker						30-12
26/05/2001	Brumbies (final)	Hooker						6-36
02/03/2002	Highlanders	Hooker						5-45
08/03/2002	Brumbies	Hooker (C)						8-38
15/03/2002	Hurricanes	Hooker (C)						17-40
23/03/2002	Waratahs	Hooker (C)						8-42
06/04/2002	Blues	Hooker (C)						20-13
13/04/2002	Chiefs	Hooker (C)						21-18
20/04/2002	Crusaders	Hooker (C)						34-37
28/02/2004	Waratahs	Hooker (R)						14-48
06/03/2004	Brumbies	Hooker						20-23
12/03/2004	Highlanders	Hooker						36-35
19/03/2004	Hurricanes	Hooker						21-20
03/04/2004	Cats	Hooker						42-28
10/04/2004	Crusaders	Hooker						29-25
16/04/2004	Chiefs	Hooker	1				5	27-34
24/04/2004	Reds	Hooker						5-6
30/04/2004	Blues	Hooker						26-37
08/05/2004	Stormers	Hooker	1				5	24-31
25/02/2005	Stormers	Hooker (R)						12-26
11/03/2005	Hurricanes	Hooker (C)						23-29
19/03/2005	Highlanders	Hooker (C)						7-43
26/03/2005	Brumbies	Hooker (C)						36-24
16/04/2005	Blues	Hooker (C)						13-36
23/04/2005	Reds	Hooker (C)						25-30
29/04/2005	Crusaders	Hooker (C)						34-77
07/05/2005	Bulls	Hooker (C)						17-23
14/05/2005	Cats	Hooker (C)						20-20
11/03/2006	Brumbies	Hooker (R)						30-35

SHARKS (SUPER RUGBY) *(continued)*								
DATE	**OPPONENTS**	**POSITION**	**T**	**C**	**P**	**D**	**PTS**	**SCORE***
18/03/2006	Highlanders	Hooker (C)						26-11
24/03/2006	Hurricanes	Hooker (C)						17-23
01/04/2006	Reds	Hooker (C)						36-28
15/04/2006	Cats	Hooker (C)						36-8
22/04/2006	Blues	Hooker (C)						32-15
29/04/2006	Bulls	Hooker (C)						27-34
06/05/2006	Stormers	Hooker (C)						24-17
12/05/2006	Force	Prop (C)						41-25
03/02/2007	Bulls	Hooker (C)						17-3
09/02/2007	Waratahs	Hooker (C)						22-9
17/02/2007	Highlanders	Hooker (R)						23-16
03/03/2007	Crusaders	Hooker (C)						27-26
10/03/2007	Cheetahs	Hooker (C)						30-14
17/03/2007	Hurricanes	Hooker (R)						27-14
24/03/2007	Brumbies	Hooker (C)						10-21
30/03/2007	Force	Hooker (C)						12-22
07/04/2007	Reds	Hooker (C)						59-16
14/04/2007	Blues	Hooker (C)						32-25
21/04/2007	Chiefs	Hooker (C)						27-35
28/04/2007	Lions	Hooker (C)						33-3
05/05/2007	Stormers	Hooker (C)						36-10
12/05/2007	Blues (semi-final)	Hooker (C)						34-18
19/05/2007	Bulls (final)	Hooker (C)						19-20
14/02/2009	Stormers	Hooker	1				5	20-15
21/02/2009	Lions	Hooker						25-10
28/02/2009	Chiefs	Hooker (R)						22-15
07/03/2009	Blues	Prop (R)						35-31
14/03/2009	Reds	Prop						13-25
21/03/2009	Force	Hooker						22-10
28/03/2009	Brumbies	Prop (R)						35-14
04/04/2009	Hurricanes	Prop						33-17
11/04/2009	Cheetahs	Hooker						6-31
18/04/2009	Crusaders	Prop (R)						10-13
02/05/2009	Highlanders	Prop						23-15
09/05/2009	Waratahs	Prop (R)						12-16
16/05/2009	Bulls	Prop						26-27
98 matches			5	0	0	0	25	
Record			P: 98; W: 47; D: 3; L: 48; Win%: 55					

CAPTAIN IN THE CAULDRON

DATE	OPPONENTS	POSITION	T	C	P	D	PTS	SCORE*
08/06/1997	W Province	Prop (R)						34-22
25/07/1998	Elephants	Prop (R)						43-24
01/08/1998	Griquas	Prop (R)						17-23
08/08/1998	Lions	Prop						10-11
21/08/1998	Eagles	Prop						15-14
28/08/1998	Falcons	Prop						40-29
05/09/1998	Griffons	Prop						57-3
04/06/1999	Falcons	Prop						17-12
11/06/1999	Leopards	Prop						54-15
18/06/1999	Griquas	Prop (R)	1				5	23-29
09/07/1999	Cheetahs	Prop						30-22
11/09/1999	Lions (final)	Prop						9-32
04/08/2000	Cavaliers	Prop (R)						18-13
01/09/2000	Falcons	Prop (R)						43-22
09/09/2000	Lions	Prop (R)	1				5	35-42
16/09/2000	Cheetahs	Prop (R)						44-12
23/09/2000	Eagles	Hooker (R)						49-13
30/09/2000	W Province	Hooker (R)						28-19
06/10/2000	Pumas	Hooker						60-27
14/10/2000	Griquas	Hooker						35-33
21/10/2000	Cheetahs	Prop (R)						29-15
28/10/2000	W Province	Hooker (R)						15-25
05/08/2001	Griffons	Hooker	1				5	47-31
01/09/2001	Elephants	Hooker	1				5	58-7
08/09/2001	Falcons	Hooker (R)						25-30
15/09/2001	Cheetahs	Hooker						28-36
22/09/2001	Blue Bulls	Hooker						24-17
28/09/2001	Griquas	Hooker						65-17
06/10/2001	Pumas	Hooker						37-11
13/10/2001	W Province	Hooker						36-13
20/10/2001	Lions	Hooker	1				5	16-9
27/10/2001	W Province	Hooker	1				5	24-29
24/08/2002	Leopards	Hooker	1				5	52-10
31/08/2002	Blue Bulls	Hooker						17-17
07/09/2002	Pumas	Hooker						69-26
14/09/2002	Lions	Hooker	1				5	37-46
21/09/2002	W Province	Hooker						36-29

SHARKS (CURRIE CUP) *(continued)*

DATE	OPPONENTS	POSITION	T	C	P	D	PTS	SCORE*
27/09/2002	Cheetahs	Hooker						33-6
12/10/2002	Griquas	Hooker (R)						78-7
19/10/2002	Blue Bulls	Hooker						19-22
25/07/2003	Eagles	Hooker (R)						45-13
02/08/2003	Griquas	Hooker	1				5	47-32
09/08/2003	Pumas	Hooker (C)						44-20
16/08/2003	W Province	Hooker (C)	1				5	39-34
28/08/2004	Blue Bulls	Hooker (C)						27-41
11/09/2004	Pumas	Hooker (C)						54-14
02/10/2004	W Province	Hooker (C)						26-32
09/10/2004	Eagles	Hooker (C)						63-33
10/09/2005	W Province	Hooker						19-47
17/09/2005	Griquas	Hooker	1				5	29-10
24/09/2005	Leopards	Hooker (R)	1				5	65-43
01/10/2005	W Province	Hooker						21-45
27/09/2008	Lions	Hooker (R)						34-20
04/10/2008	Griquas	Hooker (C)	1				5	66-12
11/10/2008	Lions (semi-final)	Hooker (R)						29-14
25/10/2008	Blue Bulls (final)	Hooker (R)						14-9
56 matches			**13**	**0**	**0**	**0**	**65**	
Record		P: 56; W: 40; D: 1; L: 15; Win %: 71						

Sharks score first

SHARKS (INTERNATIONAL MATCHES)

DATE	OPPONENTS	POSITION	T	C	P	D	PTS	SCORE*
14/06/1997	Lions	Prop (R)						12-42
19/06/1998	Wales	Prop						30-23
2 matches			**0**	**0**	**0**	**0**	**0**	
Record		P: 2; W: 1; L: 1; Win %: 50						

Sharks score first

CLERMONT AUVERGNE

DATE	OPPONENTS	POSITION	T	C	P	D	PTS	SCORE*
11/11/2007	Llanelli Scarlets	Hooker (R)						48-21
18/11/2007	Munster	Hooker						13-36
01/12/2007	Bourgoin-Jallieu	Prop (R)						20-14
15/12/2007	London Wasps	Hooker						24-25

CAPTAIN IN THE CAULDRON

DATE	OPPONENTS	POSITION	T	C	P	D	PTS	SCORE*
21/12/2007	Toulouse	Prop (R)						21-17
23/02/2008	Montauban	Hooker						40-13
01/03/2008	Bayonne	Hooker						27-3
08/03/2008	Dax	Hooker						40-22
16/03/2008	Stade Français	Hooker (R)						50-12
22/03/2008	Montpellier	Hooker						56-14
12/04/2008	Bourgoin-Jallieu	Hooker (R)						36-7
19/04/2008	Toulouse	Hooker						23-11
26/04/2008	Auch	Prop						36-15
02/05/2008	Castres	Hooker						28-35
09/05/2008	Biarritz	Prop (R)						16-11
17/05/2008	Perpignan	Prop (R)						29-15
23/05/2008	Brive	Hooker	1				5	38-7
21/06/2008	Perpignan	Prop (R)						21-7
28/06/2008	Toulouse	Hooker (R)						20-26
19 matches			**1**	**0**	**0**	**0**	**5**	
Record					**P: 19; W: 15; L: 4; Win%: 79**			

Clermont Auvergne score first

SMIT'S SPRINGBOK RECORDS (at 12/09/2009)

Most capped Springbok hooker (77)

Most capped Springbok forward (90)

Most Tests as Springbok captain (64*)

Most consecutive number of Tests for the Springboks (46)

Most consecutive number of Tests for the Springboks as captain (41)

Also a world record

INDEX